SNAP ME PERFECT!

The Darrell Porter Story

By
DARRELL PORTER
With
WILLIAM DEERFIELD

THOMAS NELSON PUBLISHERS

Nashville • *Camden* • *New York*

Published in Nashville, Tennessee, by Thomas Nelson, Inc., and distributed in Canada by Lawson Falle, Ltd., Cambridge, Ontario.

Printed in the United States of America.

Second printing

Scripture quotations are from the King James Version of the Bible.

To protect the privacy of certain people, a number of names in this book have been changed.

Library of Congress Cataloging in Publication Data
Porter, Darrell, 1952-
  Snap me Perfect!
  1. Porter, Darrell, 1952-   . 2. Baseball players—United States—Biography. I. Deerfield, William.
II. Title.
GV865.P67A37   1984   796.357'092'4 [B] 84-3414
ISBN 0-8407-5367-5

I still have days when I don't think I can make it....sometimes I wish the Lord would snap me perfect in an instant, but I'm learning patience. I know I can only do it with God; there's no other way for me.

Darrell Porter

Contents

Acknowledgments

The authors wish to thank all those who helped in the research and preparation of this book. We would like to thank the entire Porter family, particularly Mr. and Mrs. Ray Porter, and their children, Mrs. Pat Watson and Mr. Eddie Porter, for the many hours they gave in being interviewed.

We would also like to thank Ms. Teri Brown for agreeing to be interviewed and depicted in this book; as well as Darrell Porter's agent, Mr. Bill Katzbeck, and his business manager, Mr. Frank Knisley.

We would particularly like to thank Mr. Eddie Porter for making available to us his extensive file of press clippings on his brother's career.

We would also like to thank Mr. Doug Tucker of the Associated Press and also Mr. Jeffrey Japinga of *Guideposts* magazine, who read over and corrected the descriptions of the baseball games and Mr. Larry Weeden of Thomas Nelson, Inc., our editor, who worked so patiently with us on the revisions of the manuscript.

The authors wish to acknowledge the editors and writers of *Sports Illustrated, The Sporting News,* and the sports departments of *The New York Times, The New York Post,* and the newspapers of Oklahoma City, Milwaukee, Kansas City, and St. Louis, for the source material used in reconstructing the baseball games described in this book.

Co-author William Deerfield wishes to thank Mr. Van Varner,

the editor of *Guideposts* magazine, and Mr. Jack Haring, managing editor, for their kind cooperation and encouragement during the writing of this book.

Prologue

THE MEADOWS, MARCH 1980

I'm so sick of my attitude toward myself and other people. Ever since I started taking drugs I've been a cold-hearted person who doesn't give a flip about anything, except the way I feel. I've drifted away from my family and friends. I used to be able to feel what other people felt. But now I don't even care. I want to care, but it's no use. I really don't. I love my mother. I want her to know how much I love her, because I'm not sure I ever told her. . . . I want to be able to love again. I want back what drugs have taken away from me. . . . Before I got into drugs, I could make friends easily. Now I only feel comfortable when I take drugs, and that's only part of the time. I hate my attitude. I want to regain my compassion for other people. I want that peaceful feeling I used to get when I prayed. I used to pray for my family and other people. Now I only pray for myself. . . . I want my relationship back with my brothers and sister. I want to feel love like I had for my wife. I just want to love people again. . . . I hate drugs, and I hate what they've done to me. I can't cope with anything anymore. I just don't give a s——. I hate myself so much!

I want to feel like I'm being listened to when I pray.
I want to feel wanted and needed by other people.
I want to feel comfortable when people compliment me.
I want to feel comfortable with myself and with my family.
I want to love a woman like I used to.
I'm tired of not really giving a flip. I just want all this to stop.

Book 1

*The Road to "Glory"…
and Beyond*

1

The Return

"Ladies and gentlemen, we are making our final approach to Kansas City International Airport," the stewardess was saying in her silky voice. "Please fasten your seat belts and extinguish all smoking materials."

I glanced out the window. The flat, green and brown patchwork that had been Missouri at thirty-three thousand feet had now become Monopoly-sized farmhouses, barns, and trees, as the jet dropped lower and lower.

They say that taking off and landing are the most dangerous parts of air travel, and I've always been conscious of that. But the case of nerves I was having now had more to do with what awaited me on the ground, inside the terminal—and at Royals Stadium.

The TWA jet touched down and bumped along the runway, its engines roaring in reverse to slow it down. Nothing could slow down the rush of events, of time, of the unavoidable confrontation that was upon me.

"You all right, Darrell?" John Schuerholz, vice-president of the Kansas City Royals, was yelling in my ear above the noise of the engines.

"I'm just fine, John," I lied with a smile. Well, not exactly lied. I mean, although I was nervous, scared even, I was proud of what I was about to do. It was something I *had* to do, no matter how

15

hard, how painful. I sent up a quick prayer for courage. I was praying a lot lately.

Inside the terminal a group of reporters immediately surrounded John, Herk Robinson (another team VP), and me, following us to the baggage-claim area. "How does it feel to be back?" somebody yelled.

"Just fine!" I yelled back, without looking.

"Darrell," a reporter said at my elbow, "your dad said you were at the treatment center for alcohol. Was that the *only* reason?"

As we walked toward the baggage claim area, I shot him a glance. No sense being angry or annoyed; he was only doing his job. "Look, I'm happy to be back, but I'm pretty nervous. Please. I'll see you guys at the ballpark after the game."

Undeterred, the reporters followed us. As we waited for our luggage to appear on the carousel, they kept badgering me with questions, most of which I tried to ignore. Then they tried Schuerholz. "Were you with Darrell at the hospital?"

"Yes, I was," John replied coolly. He was immediately surrounded by the pack, hungry for any scrap of information. "I spent a week there with Darrell. I took part in the counseling sessions, as a friend."

"A *friend*?" one of the journalists asked, an edge of cynicism in his voice.

Ignoring him, John snapped, "Darrell's going to make a statement after the game tonight, if you'll all just be patient!"

"What's he going to say?"

John fixed the man with a long-suffering look and replied, "We want to allow Darrell to say what *he* wants, from his heart. It's important for *him* to say it. And none of us club officials can speak for him."

"Is that Darrell Porter?" a motherly-looking woman asked in a stage whisper. Then eyeing the army of reporters, she said, "Well ... *I'm* not going to bother him for an autograph. But I sure think what he's done is a fine thing!" I smiled at her. The reporters were taking down her words as studiously as they had taken mine and John's. I picked up my golf bag from the carousel.

"Get to play some golf out there, D.P.?" someone asked.

"Heck no!" I replied. "They sure laughed when I brought my

clubs into that place. One guy said, 'Buddy, the only club you're going to get to use is the foam-rubber one.' And I didn't know what he meant at the time, but I sure found out! But no way did I have time for golf! Guess I thought The Meadows was going to be some kind of country club!"

Everybody laughed. It somewhat broke the tension.

We hefted our bags and walked to Herk's car for the trip to the stadium. The press was right on our heels. I didn't want to hold a conference there in the parking lot, but I felt bad about leaving them standing there. "I'm really nervous," I repeated, just to say something.

"You look great. You in shape to play?" someone asked.

"Thanks, but I don't think I'd be ready to step in there tonight. See you guys later."

The car door slammed, and we pulled away. A cool blast from the air conditioner washed over me as I settled back. I had gotten over the first hurdle, but the worst lay just ahead.

At the stadium, I watched the last few innings of the game. The Royals were playing Baltimore that night, and we were ahead. I felt strange sitting there in the team suite, watching the team play. All at once I felt like an outsider, just another fan. It was as if I had never played professional baseball at all, as if I had never been catcher for the Royals. It was just a momentary fantasy, but it was scary, as if the past ten years of my life hadn't happened. But they had happened, and I was at Royals Stadium in Kansas City watching my teammates from the sidelines, waiting.

We—or I should say the team—whipped the Birds 7–0. I felt glad and sad at the same time—sad because I wasn't part of it when I should have been. As soon as the game ended, I was hustled into the clubhouse.

Mass confusion. Half-dressed players mingled with newspaper reporters and Royals brass. Showers hissed. The crowd parted for a TV camera crew.

I blinked as a floodlight hit my eyes, and suddenly the locker room was full of moving shadows, surrounding me, converging on me. It was like a bad dream.

"If everyone will be quiet," John Schuerholz began. The bedlam ceased. "Now, you've all been wondering why Darrell left spring training so abruptly on March 15. Most of you know he was at a treatment center, The Meadows, in Wickenburg, Arizona. This afternoon he was released with a clean bill of health, and he has a few words to say to you." Turning to me, he said, "Darrell?"

I stepped forward, unfolding a written statement that John and Herk had helped me prepare. As I held the paper, my hand was shaking a little. "I am very happy to be back," I began, thankful that my voice was fairly steady. "Six weeks ago God gave me the strength, courage, and determination to face up to my personal problems and to seek professional help. I went to Joe Burke and advised him I was a drug addict and an alcoholic."

I had hoped it wouldn't happen, but maybe it was inevitable: my voice broke. Tears stung my eyes, blurring the page. I had said it: *I had told the whole world I was a drug addict and a drunk.*

I plunged on: "My whole life has been affected. I have hurt my family, my friends, the great baseball fans of the Royals, and my teammates, and I almost destroyed myself."

Again my voice cracked as I struggled with a pent-up need to cry. Joe Burke, the Royals' general manager, gently touched my shoulder and reached for the paper. Shaking my head vigorously, I said, "No, Joe, I'll read it myself!

"For the past six weeks, the doctors, the counselors, and the staff at The Meadows have made me realize the most important thing we have on our side is our life and good health. With their help I have a greater understanding and appreciation of myself and of my responsibilities. I have been successfully treated, and I graduated this afternoon." I looked up and managed a small smile.

"I will always be grateful and thankful to those who prayed for me, sent letters of encouragement, and supported me. From this day forward, I will be facing the greatest challenge of my life. I am confident with the help of God—"

Then it hit me again. Maybe it was mentioning God—the God on whom I had turned my back so long ago. I began to sob audibly. A few agonized seconds passed in slow motion as I pulled myself together.

"I am confident, with the help of God and your support and understanding, I will be successful. I will be in uniform tomorrow to complete my spring training."

I paused a moment and then looked up and added, "I hope that this statement has answered questions about my personal problems, and I sincerely ask, for the present, that your questions to me be about baseball."

I stood there for a few seconds, folding the paper, feeling drained. But I also felt *cleansed*. Then the room was in an uproar. Jerry Terrell, my road roommate, was pumping my hand. Cameras were flashing in my face, and my teammates were welcoming me back. One of them, Pete LaCock, was giving me a crushing bear hug. "Welcome home, buddy!" he said in my ear. Tears were in my eyes again. I was back in the clubhouse with my teammates. I was back in baseball.

How did my painful journey to that press conference begin? It had started out simply enough with a beer, just a single beer in a little bar in Appleton, Wisconsin, back in 1970. I was away from home for the first time, with the Milwaukee Brewers Class A team.

But before the beer there was something else—fear of letting down my family and friends back home in Oklahoma City. I had to show them I could do it. What was it Dad used to say? "Darrell, you'd better be good at sports, 'cause you ain't worth a flip at anything else." I *had* to succeed—I was afraid not to.

At The Meadows they said my relationship with Dad was part of my problem. They had practically ordered him to come out there. I had confronted him, shouted at him. We had both cried. I told him I loved him. And Dad told me he loved me. It was the first time he had ever said that. I just bawled like a baby.

They say that every demanding parent was himself a childhood victim. Not that Dad ever abused me *physically*. Shoot, I can remember only two times when he hit me. But just the sound of his voice struck terror in my heart. I feared what he *could* do, and that was enough. Maybe that fear was worse than being beaten; I don't know.

I do believe that the legacy of my Dad's harshness toward me, my brothers, and my sister, was the legacy he had received in his own childhood. The sins of the parents are indeed visited on the children to the third and fourth generations. Unless the cycle is broken. At The Meadows the cycle had been broken, and now he and I had a chance to start over.

What I mean to say is that the horror of my descent into alcohol and drugs didn't really begin with that bottle of beer in Appleton, or even with my fear of failure. It actually began years before I was born. It began with the blighted childhood of my father, Ray Porter.

2

The Orphans

GRACEMONT, OKLAHOMA, 1924

When we were kids, we knew almost nothing about Dad's background, except that he had been an orphan and had a brother, now dead. Maybe he would have talked more about his childhood if he had had a real family, with roots and traditions and happy times. But harshness and cruelty were all Dad ever knew as a child, so perhaps he wanted to blot it from his mind.

Had I known about my father's tragic childhood, would it have helped me understand his harsh attitude toward us? I doubt it; I was a child myself, though in later years, after Dad told us the story of his childhood, I was able to forgive him from my heart, and it helped begin the healing of our entire family.

Dad was born in 1924 in Gracemont, Oklahoma, "a little bitty old place," as he describes it. His mother died bearing him. He believes his father had been killed in an accident in the oil fields.

Gracemont is basically an Indian town, and Dad suspects there is Indian blood flowing in our veins because of his dark coloring and strong nose (both of which I inherited). But knowing one's family tree is a luxury reserved for those who have families.

Dad's earliest memory is of huddling with other kids to keep warm—like pups. He was at an orphanage with his older brother, Calvin. His other memories of that place were of bad food and whippings, which were standard for the time and administered frequently.

One day in 1927 a farm couple named Porter visited the orphanage. The orphans were lined up. After a brief consultation with his wife, Mr. Porter said, "We like the little feller with the dark hair."

"Looks mighty like our darlin' dead boy," his wife added.

Today, replacing a dead child with a look-alike would probably be interpreted as slightly bizarre and would result in the prospective parents being turned down. But not in 1927.

There was only one problem, and it wasn't with the Porters. "His older brother's here, too," the director told the couple. "We don't separate kin. You'll have to take them both. This one's Raymond. He's three. Calvin is six."

The Porters didn't want the older boy, but they took him anyway—kind of a "package deal." In later years aunts and uncles of the family told the boys that the main reason they were adopted at all, aside from Dad's resemblance to their dead baby, was that the Porters needed help to work their farm "real bad."

The boys could have figured that out for themselves. The Porters' farm was in western Oklahoma, unpleasant country with rolling, sandy hills. Their place was a chicken farm with five thousand leghorns. As soon as the boys were able they had to gather eggs—some thirty dozen a day. They also hoed the cotton and corn and the vegetable garden, made butter in an old-fashioned churn, and fed the livestock. On Saturdays they did the housework. They worked from morning till night like two little slaves.

The Porters already had one living son who was almost fifteen years older than Dad. He was just finishing high school at the time of the adoption. According to Dad, his adoptive brother was treated like a prince, and to his recollection never did a lick of work around the place.

The Porters were religious people, and they raised the boys to practice the Ten Commandments and to believe in God and the Bible. But the way they applied their beliefs was harsh. The thing Dad remembers most about the Christianity of his adoptive parents and their friends and neighbors was its hypocrisy.

On Sundays Grandpa Porter would hitch up the team and take the family to church. If either boy dared wiggle or fuss during the long sermon, he would be slapped or pinched, and that would be merely a foretaste of the licking that would be administered when they got home.

In the wake of the Wall Street crash in 1929, hard times set in. Grandpa Porter struggled along for awhile, but something terrible happened. He had just sold a hundred purebred hogs. He didn't have the money in the bank, but on a Monday he made a verbal agreement with the buyer. The man was due to pick the herd up on Saturday.

On Tuesday, those hogs came down with blackleg, a deadly disease. By Saturday, every last one of them was dead. Grandpa Porter was wiped out. The bank foreclosed.

Those were the years when Oklahomans ("Okies," they called them) were losing their farms by the thousands and trekking west. Instead of succumbing to the false lure of California and nonexistent jobs, however, the Porters went east—to Arkansas, where they worked a small farm.

Times continued to be tough, but the family managed to be self-sustaining by growing all its own food. Wood was the only cash crop. The boys, Dad and Uncle Cal, would cut a wagonload and haul it into town, where they sold it for a dollar. When they were a few years older and stronger, they learned to fell trees—their only "power tools" being their strong arms. Then, with hewing axes, they would fashion railroad ties, which they hauled to a siding nine miles away to sell for a dollar each.

One day in 1935, Mr. and Mrs. Porter hitched up the team and drove into town. Before leaving, they told the boys to hoe the big vegetable garden, with instructions that the job was to be finished when they got back.

The brothers worked for a spell, but then, as boys will, they began fooling around and forgot all about the hoeing. They only remembered the unfinished work when they heard the wagon wheels coming up the road.

Grandpa Porter was enraged. "Worthless, ungrateful kids!" he shouted. "You'll never amount to nothin'!" Turning to my uncle, he bellowed, "Cal! Git over here you lazy good-for-nothin'! You're gonna git a lesson you ain't *never* gonna forget!"

Then he tied my Uncle Cal to a tree and beat him with a snake whip until he passed out. Dad was spared—he only got whipped with a strap.

The next day, Dad and Uncle Cal ran away, but a few days later they were caught in town and returned to the farm. They knew they were in for it. Uncle Cal was the mouthpiece; he always did the talking for the two of them, and he was a good liar.

This time he made up a fantastic story about how he and Ray had been kidnapped by "gangsters" who thought the Porter family had money. He was so convincing that he had Grandpa Porter believing it—until his adoptive brother did some checking.

"Those brats is little liars," he reported to his father. "I been to town and talked with some fellers they been hangin' with. They just run away is all. Kidnapped my foot!"

Both boys were beaten again. Three days later, Uncle Cal ran away for good.

After that, life was pure hell for Dad, who caught double the work and double the abuse. Grandpa Porter ran him into the ground.

In 1939 Dad's adoptive mother died, and the family returned to Oklahoma to work his grandmother's farm. There Dad attended a little country grammar school with about thirty kids during the winter months.

When he was fourteen, he switched to a city school, Weatherford High, in Weatherford, Oklahoma. It was there he discovered organized sports and his own athletic ability. Dad was convinced there wasn't a city dude who could beat a good old country boy at anything, and he set out to prove it, to them and to his father— who never stopped telling Dad he wasn't worth a darn.

Dad took to football like a pro and became a star halfback. Although he was little, he was tough and fast. In his freshman and sophomore years he also became an all-state wrestling champion. But baseball was his favorite sport. He played shortstop and second base and had a dream of becoming a professional baseball player. He even had a tryout, but his throwing arm wasn't the greatest.

Years later, Dad would look at me and my three brothers, all of us three-sport athletes, and say with pride, "It's in the genes." (Mom was also an athlete who played championship women's softball and basketball, so if it *was* genes, the Porter boys got *double* their share!)

Anyway, who knows how far Dad could have gone had his life been different, had he had concerned, loving parents and the opportunities and encouragement? But the summer he was seventeen, his playing days and his dreams came to a brutally abrupt end.

It was a routine summer day and a routine job. Dad was harvesting the corn crop with Grandpa Porter. Two stubborn old mules with the unlikely names of Tom and Jerry were pulling the wagon. The only way Dad could get the animals to move was to chuck dirt clods at them on the sly. One of the clods accidentally hit old Tom in the ear. Now mules have very sensitive ears, and the mule let out a wild bellow, bringing Grandpa Porter on the run.

"Boy, you just don't hit mules in the ear! You never do learn nothin', do you? You gonna git it *real* good!"

"It was a accident, Dad. Honest! Don't—!"

The older man had picked up a pitchfork and was coming toward him, his face distorted with rage. Dad was sure Grandpa Porter had gone crazy and intended to stab him. He wasn't about to wait to find out. Grabbing his own pitchfork from the wagon, he faced his dad.

"You *dare* raise a fork to your own daddy?" Grandpa Porter bellowed.

"I don't want to hurt you, Dad, but don't you come a step closer, hear!" my father cried, sweat suddenly popping out on his forehead.

Grandpa Porter lunged. Dad parried the thrust, knocking the fork from his father's hands. He stood there, his own fork poised, glaring at him. Then with a cry, he drove his fork into the ground and turned and ran back to the farmhouse. He grabbed a clean pair of jeans and took off through the fields, vowing never to come back, just like Cal.

Dad hitchhiked all the way to Kansas, where his mother's people, Aunt Mable and Uncle Glenn Taynn, took him in. The Taynns were good people who had always been as warm and loving to him and Cal as the Porters had been cold and mean. "Don't you worry none, Raymond," Aunt Mable soothed. "You got a home here just as long as you please!"

25

The way Dad tells it, he came out of Oklahoma "with cow manure between my toes and grass coming out of my ears." But a series of jobs, including a stint as a bellhop at a Wichita hotel and as a door-to-door magazine salesman, polished him up as fancy as a city slicker.

Dad married in 1940, but a few weeks before Christmas in 1941, the Japanese attacked Pearl Harbor and World War II was on. Dad joined the Marines and saw action in the Pacific. He only saw his wife and little daughter twice during the war years.

Except for a bit of shrapnel in his tail, he survived the war—but the marriage didn't. From that marriage came two daughters, my half-sisters, Barbara Ann and Joy.

In 1947 Dad returned to Grandpa Porter's home in Weatherford, Oklahoma, where he had a brief reunion with Uncle Cal. Just before he was to leave for California with his brother, Dad met Mom at a square dance in Clinton, Oklahoma.

Mom was one half of a set of pretty blonde sisters, the Conley twins, who resembled 1940s movie queen Alice Faye. Mom was Twila Mae, and her twin was Gwyla Faye (twin sisters with twin names).

The twins were just nineteen and shared a small apartment in town. Mom came from a family of ten children. Their mother was dead, and their father was ailing and had all he could do to keep the younger Conleys fed. So the girls had struck out on their own.

"He looks like Clark Gable!" Mom sighed after first meeting Dad.

"I don't trust them good-lookin' ones!" Gwyla Faye warned. "Could be a gangster or a con man. He didn't get that fancy suit parkin' cars!"

But Mom was smitten by the dark-haired stranger with the smooth ways and the expensive suit. He swept her off her feet.

At the wedding, the bride had to slip her handsome bridegroom five dollars to pay the preacher.

The young couple moved around for a few years, wherever the work was: Dayton, Ohio; Joplin, Missouri; Bonner Springs, Kansas; and Yakima, Washington. Along the way, two children were born—a girl, Patricia, in 1948, and later a boy, Jim.

In the spring of 1950, Dad accepted a job with United Transport at Joplin, Missouri, hauling new cars long-distance. In Joplin, Mom and Dad bought a small six-room house. The extra rooms were going to come in handy, because two years later Mom bore another boy at Freeman Hospital in Joplin. The baby weighed in at six pounds, two ounces, with a shock of black hair and dark coloring like his dad's. In fact, folks were to say the baby was the spitting image of Ray Porter. They decided to name the little fellow Darrell—Darrell Ray Porter. The date was January 17, 1952.

3

A Quiet Little Boy

Mom says I was a "good baby," which, I suppose, means I didn't fuss or cry much. My sister Pat, who was four when I was born, describes me as a "quiet, dark-haired little boy who had something about him that made you want to mother him." Maybe that sympathetic description has to do with the fact that she was my big sister, and big sisters tend to regard their baby brothers as play dolls.

I don't remember those early years in Joplin. I'm told that when I was two or thereabouts, I knocked my front tooth out while carrying an old tin pail that was almost as big as I was. So I was gap-toothed for a few years until my permanent teeth grew in.

When I was three, my kid brother Eddie was born; two years later Denny came along. So there were five of us Porter kids: four boys—Jimmy, Darrell, Eddie, and Denny—and a girl, Pat.

In 1958, when I was six, Dad was on a prolonged layoff from United Transport and moved the family to Bonner Springs, Kansas, and then to Yakima, Washington, where there was the promise of work. The family remained in Yakima six months. When United Transport called him back to work, they informed him that he would be working out of Kansas City. All this moving was unsettling on the family, so Dad and Mom moved back to Oklahoma where their roots were and where Mom had kinfolks. They rented a tiny two-room house on 52nd Street in Oklahoma City, in a neighborhood called Capitol Hill.

It was a working-class neighborhood of very modest homes,

much like rural working-class areas all across America, with over-grown yards and rusting junked cars. In our part of town, daddies carried lunch pails and meant shut up when they said shut up.

It didn't matter to us kids that our folks didn't have money or live in a fancy section of town. In the early sixties, before Okla-homa City caught up with the times, you could stand on the porch and see open fields to the east and south. You could fill your lungs with good "country" air. Heck, by the time I was a teen-ager, my brothers and our friends were familiar with the best fishing spots and rabbit runs in the area, all within a few miles of our back yard.

There were no black people in our part of town. Racial preju-dice, I'm sad to admit, was a part of our world. Though Mom and Dad taught us that we were all the same, what we heard on the streets and in the school yard was poisonous.

One of the most valuable things I've gained from baseball has been contact with men like Hal McRae, Frank White, George Hen-drick, Amos Otis, Ozzie Smith, and Willie McGee. They have shown me by their actions that we are all indeed the same. It's what's in a man's heart that's important.

But growing up in Oklahoma City in the fifties and sixties, we only *heard* about black people—negatively—in our working-class neighborhood.

In that little bitty house we lived in on 52nd Street, all of us chil-dren slept in one room. Now, summers are hot in Oklahoma, and my earliest memory is of the heat. It was always hot in our little bedroom. I slept next to the wall, and I remember hanging my head off the bed to catch the cool draft that would come up from the floor between the wall and the bed.

Though the house was small, we had a big back yard that seemed to run on forever. It had a rundown fence and an aban-doned chicken coop. On second thought, it may not have been abandoned, because one of my early memories was of seeing Mom wring a chicken's neck when relatives were coming to dinner.

I was horrified; that chicken just jumped all over the place. It was my first encounter with death, and I felt real bad about it. But I didn't cry. Even at that early age I was learning to keep my feel-ings to myself. Dad was already impressing on us that men didn't show their feelings; they *never* cried. Only babies cried. I did cry sometimes, as all kids do—but only when I was alone.

I wasn't interested in sports at all as a young boy. But my older brother, Jimmy, was. As the oldest, he was Dad's pride and joy. When Jimmy was four, Dad had him out in the yard, throwing a baseball—and he expected Jim to do as well as a kid twice his age. Dad was determined he was going to excel in sports, to have the chances he never had.

In school, the only sport I played was dodge ball. I forget the rules, but I remember the other team would throw a big rubber ball at you. If it hit you, you were out.

I was a pretty agile kid with good reflexes, and I did well at this simple game. I had a strong desire to be successful even then. If I got hit with the ball, it would tear me up inside. From listening to Dad lecture Jim, I was already picking up a terrible fear of failure.

Jim's whole life was dedicated to pleasing Dad in his school work and sports. It was Jim, not me, who in Dad's dreams was going to be the professional athlete in the family. And Jim didn't disappoint Dad. When I came home with bad grades on my report card and Dad was displeased, I thought it was because Jimmy always got A's. I loved my older brother, but I also envied his success and the attention Dad paid him.

Jimmy inherited Dad's gift for mechanics, and the two of them worked side by side for hours on large model airplanes they controlled with wires. I never did get the hang of anything mechanical.

"Left loosens, right tightens!" If Dad screamed those words once at me, he screamed them a thousand times as I nervously fumbled with a wrench or screwdriver.

Left loosens, right tightens. The harder I tried, the more fumble-fingered I got and the louder Dad would yell.

I think it was significant that Jim was the only one of us kids who wasn't a bed wetter. Pat and I were the worst offenders; we had a chronic problem. Dad may have doted on Jimmy, but his attentions to us were fierce because of our bed wetting.

Finally, Mom stepped in and took us to the doctor. We had no physical problem, but the doctor suggested no liquids after supper. Things improved considerably after that.

Dad was a drinker. Even as far back as Joplin, Mom had threatened to leave him if he didn't lay off the sauce. Being on the road most of the time, away from his family, didn't help. There was always a bar where a lonely trucker could find solace in the bottom of a glass. And when he was home, struggling to feed and clothe us (not to mention living in a tiny house with five active children) didn't help things any.

Thanksgiving, Christmas, and Easter were fun times for us. Though Dad and Mom struggled to make ends meet, they always managed to have toys under the tree and a turkey on the table. But invariably, when Dad had a holiday drink it would lead to another, and another. "You *always* spoil our holidays!" Mom would cry, wiping her eyes with her apron, after Dad crashed into the Christmas tree or dropped the gravy bowl all over the nice white tablecloth.

I remember one Christmas night when Dad fell down the back stairs. "Just leave him there, kids!" Mom announced, closing the door. "Serves him right!" In the morning I crept to the back door very early and looked outside, but Dad wasn't there. Mom had let him in after the rest of us were asleep.

"I swear, I'm never going to marry anybody who drinks!" Pat would announce on these occasions.

"I ain't gonna take a drink, neither!" I'd chime in. My mom just hated drinking and smoking and swearing and stuff like that. And I *loved* my mom!

Mom was just wonderful. She was a pretty, blondish woman, rather plump without being fat. She always wore an apron and was either cooking or cleaning or mending clothes. How I hated to see her upset or crying when Dad was "that way."

In 1959, Dad bought a house just a block away from our old house. He and Mom still live in it today—a nice, bigger house with a living room, a kitchen, and three bedrooms—a palace compared to the old house. Southeast High School, which employed my mom first as a cook and later as the cafeteria manager, was just two blocks away from the new house.

Even though our living conditions had improved with the new, larger house, things were getting worse in other ways, particularly between Pat and Dad. Dad's drinking might have had something to do with it, along with the added financial strain of the new mortgage. But there were other reasons, not all of them Dad's fault. Pat was also getting more independent as she grew older, and Dad's desire to maintain his authority over her led to some memorable, violent spankings.

Dad only hit me twice that I can remember. The first time was when I was thirteen or so. I don't recall the circumstances exactly, but I think we were supposed to be home at a certain time and stayed out too long playing. When we got home, Dad was waiting for all three of us—me, Eddie, and Denny.

"Now you're gonna get your punishment," he told us. "Each of you gets three swats across the butt. Now, who's going first?" We all looked at each other like soldiers facing the firing squad.

Denny was first. Dad told him to bend over. Denny stood there, hands on his knees, his lower lip trembling even before the first blow.

Thwockum! Dad's belt sang across Denny's rear end. Denny began to bawl. *Thwockum! Thwockum!* Denny was running around the room clutching his smarting behind.

I felt sorry for Denny, and I was really scared, but for some reason, I began to giggle. I couldn't help myself. Then Eddie started to cry even before he got his. I giggled even more.

Eddie took his three swats as brave as he could, and then Dad said, "All right, Mr. Wise Guy, let's see if you're laughing when I get done with you. Get over here!" He was really annoyed—frustrated—that the whipping wasn't having the desired effect on me.

Down came the belt: *Whomp!* (Whomps are harder than thwockums.) I felt it all right, but for some reason it didn't hurt. I tried suppressing a laugh and nearly choked to death. Dad heard me. It made him madder.

Whomp! Even harder than the first. I snickered again, thinking, *Shoot! This guy can't even hurt me!*

By now Dad was fit to be tied, so he backed up three steps and came charging. Just as he began to swing, he slipped on the rug—and missed! I got only a glancing blow on the lower back. Recovering his dignity as best he could, he sent us to our room for the rest of the afternoon. But somehow I felt it was my victory.

The second time Dad lit into me was over Eddie. One day I had him down on the floor of our room, tickling him so mercilessly that he was in tears. "Da—Daaaarrruulll...turn...meeee...loose....Pleeeeese!" he pleaded.

"Little crybaby! Look at the baby cry!" I taunted him, kneeling on his chest and tickling him some more as his legs flailed helplessly.

Suddenly I was pulled backward. Then my father was stiff-arming me in the chest. The blow knocked me halfway across the room. I fell against a chair, knocking it over. Then I was on the floor myself. I sat there, too stunned even to cry. Dad had hit me like a man!

He stood there glaring at me, while Eddie scrambled to his feet, tucking in his shirttails. "Don't you *ever* let me catch you picking on your little brother again!"

"We were only playin'!" I protested feebly.

Ignoring me, Dad turned to Eddie and said, "If Darrell ever so much as touches you again, you just get a ball bat and pop him one good. Okay?"

Eddie sniffed and shook his head yes, eyeing me warily. The corners of my lower lip pulled down; I fought the tears, not letting them come. But I would never forget that Dad had hit me like a man.

Mom would never interfere when Dad punished us. He was king in his own house and nobody interfered. So Mom would just stand there and cry. And, much as she loved us, we could never go to her for comfort after a session with Dad. That would have been to undermine his authority.

There was something more subtly damaging in our family relationships than scoldings and occasional spankings, however. It was the almost total absence of (for want of a better word) intimacy. There was no hugging, kissing, or physical contact of any kind in our family. In retrospect I can't blame my parents; this attitude too was the legacy they had received. There was precious little warmth or hugging in Mom's family and certainly none in Dad's. Dad was raised believing that to touch a woman in any way was a sexual overture. And, of course, men never touched except to shake hands.

We knew, in an intellectual way, our parents loved us, but growing up I wanted to be hugged or kissed, particularly by Mom, whom I dearly loved. But it never happened. I missed out on affection and grew up craving it with a vague, undefined longing.

It's not uncommon for an only child to invent a playmate. But how can I—who had three brothers and a big sister—account for the fact that I had a phantom little sister? I can only guess she was created by my need for someone to dote on me, to give me the special love and understanding I felt I never had.

This "little sister" of my imagination thought her big brother was the neatest person in the world, and nothing anybody could ever do would cause her to doubt me or drive her from my side. And when I met and fell in love with my first wife, Teri, she seemed to embody all the beauty and charm—the love—of this ideal imaginary sister of my boyhood.

As for Dad being a tough disciplinarian—I don't want to give the impression that he was unloving. I believe Dad loved us, but, as I've indicated, he was unable to show it. And he was carrying all that garbage from his own childhood buried inside. The only model he ever had of parental authority was one of harshness. Many years later he told someone that he actually believed he was being liberal with us as far as discipline went. And he was, when you think of the cruelty he experienced as a boy.

If anything, Dad was inconsistent. He could be mean and he could be kind, from one instant to the next. Dad did many loving things for us while we were growing up. For instance, every Sunday we would have three chickens for dinner, and Dad always took the worst parts for himself. He would leave the breasts, thighs, and drumsticks for us kids, while he took the necks and backs. "Dad, why don't you take a *nice* piece?" I asked him once, as he speared the tail-end piece with his fork.

"Don't you children know the parson's nose is one of the *best* parts of the bird?" he said with a wink, adding, "I always like the part that went over the fence last." We all giggled. But it just killed me that Dad never got to eat a decent piece of meat in all those years we were growing up in his house.

And which of us could ever forget the neat presents Dad would bring us when he returned from a long road trip? He always had something super. The best was a beautiful red go-cart with a real motor. I still get warm feelings remembering it.

As you might guess, Eddie, being the next youngest, was the one I usually picked on. Beating on Eddie made me feel as if I had some sort of power and control over things, I guess.

Not that I didn't love Eddie; I did. Every night when I said my prayers, he was the first on my list, after Mom. Still, that never stopped me from teasing and jumping on him.

In spite of the fact that Jimmy was "Dad's boy," he and I were close. Together we formed the "52nd Street Gang." We hunted, fished, and played sports. It gave us a sense of identity and boyish camaraderie.

4

A Baseball Career Begins

The summer I was nine I tried out for Little League. Dad never pushed me into it. Looking back, I think I did it simply because all the kids in my age group were trying out.

The day before the tryouts Dad asked me what position I wanted to play. "I don't know," I replied.

"Why don't you try being catcher?"

"Maybe," I said, looking at the rug. Shoot, I didn't know what position I should play. I hadn't thought about it.

"Well, Darrell," Dad said, "it's easy to progress in the game as catcher, because catchers are hard to find. And if you're a good catcher, you can go all the way to the major leagues."

"You really think so, Dad? The major leagues?" I could hardly believe it was *me* Dad was talking to. But if Dad said it was a possibility, why then it must be so.

"And hey, Darrell," Dad was saying with growing enthusiasm, "catching is where the excitement is. Why, you're involved in *everything* when you're the catcher. Every pitch that's thrown in the game is gonna come right over that plate."

Mixed with my nervousness about the tryouts was another feeling—happiness. For the first time Dad was taking a real interest in me, just like he did in Jimmy.

The next day when Tommy, my friend from next door, asked me what position I was going to try for, I casually replied, "Catcher.

You know, that's where all the action is. Every pitch in the game comes over that plate."

Tommy looked at me with something akin to respect, so I added with even more authority: "If you're a good catcher, you can go on to the majors." To hear me talk, you would have thought the Yankees were about to sign me.

To my surprise I made the team. And as catcher. Something wonderful happened the moment I started playing baseball. I was like the poor boy who suddenly becomes a prince.

Our coach in Pee Wee Ones was Mr. Cheetwood, who had several sons in Little League. He took a liking to me and was a super guy. Mr. Cheetwood thought I had the makings of a first-class pitcher, so a little way into my first season I was put on the mound.

At first I was disappointed to be a pitcher after all the good things Dad had told me about catching, things I had been finding out first hand. But now Dad told me, "Shoot, Darrell. Being pitcher's good, too. Everything good about catching applies to pitching as well, maybe more so. Heck, the game can't even start till the pitcher throws the ball."

Without knowing why, I threw right-handed and batted lefty. I did almost everything else strictly right-handed. Dad, who had an expert knowledge of baseball from his days as a player and umpire, spotted this at once. "Keep doing it that way," he suggested. "That's the quickest way for you to get to the big leagues. Almost every team in the major leagues likes a player who hits lefty and throws righty." He was still thinking about my being a catcher, still filling my nine-year-old head with dreams of the major leagues.

I have a lot of seasons of professional baseball behind me, and lots of good memories. But will I ever forget that first year of Little League in Pee Wee Ones? Our team, the Davis Mustangs, went all the way to the championships. We played the Shields Grade School team.

I don't remember what the final score was. What I do remember is that I was the pitcher—and we won the game! When it was over, Mr. Cheetwood slung me up onto his shoulders and carried me all over the field. What a thrill! Then we all went to the Dairy Queen for a victory celebration.

Mom and Dad were in the stands watching that day. They came

to all my games and really supported me. Mom was jumping for joy.

Dad's willingness to work with me, shaping and developing my natural talent, steadily improved my game. The following year, when I was in Pee Wee Twos, we won our second championship.

If Dad was proud of me, he never let on. His whole message to me, by his actions as well as his words, was: "Be humble. Remember, you can improve and be better." Instilling modesty in me was one thing, but Dad established a pattern those first seasons of Little League that he was to maintain for years, one that bruised my spirit and hung over my head all the way to the majors—and beyond. It was something worse than the occasional outbursts and criticism: *Dad never praised me.*

I could strike out nine men in a game and have two home runs, yet he would tell me about one error I had made. "So you got a couple of homers. Fine. Let's forget about them and work on the error." I learned the lesson well and soon became my own worst critic.

Dad's intentions were good, but because of his constant carping on what I did wrong and what I should do to correct it, the easy, joyful confidence I had felt at first began to fade. It was gradually replaced by a feeling of unrelenting pressure. Pressure to succeed. Pressure to do better. Pressure to be good. No, not good—*perfect.* I was ten years old and had to be perfect.

Baseball is a game, and games should be enjoyed. Baseball should be fun, especially for kids. And if it isn't fun, something's wrong, because then the whole purpose is defeated. I think Little League is great, and we ought to make it available to kids. It's where I fell in love with baseball.

Some of the people handling these kids, however, fail to realize that there are many kids who are slow developers. Because they're not good right off the bat doesn't mean they don't have the potential. But if they don't produce *now*, in *this* game, the spirit gets crushed out of them by adults who may be overzealous for a winning team.

I don't want to give the false impression that my dad was a fanatical Little League father. Although my dad, by his own admission, was living his dreams of sports success through his sons, he never pushed any of us into sports. He never browbeat me about my playing. But though the pressures were more subtle, the effects were the same.

To this day, if I make an error in a game, I suffer over it. But, thanks to my Christian faith, I don't suffer as horribly as I used to. Of course, a ballplayer *should* feel bad when he makes an error. A healthy sorrow over failure is entirely legitimate and helps a person resolve to do better. Dad still reminds me that when *he* makes a mistake on his job, he feels bad because it costs his company money. And he's getting paid not to make errors. The same is true in sports. But it's a matter of degree. Too much pressure, too much self-criticism, ties you up in knots and makes things worse. And this is the kind of guilt, the kind of pressure I played under and unconsciously put on myself for years.

Paradoxically, Dad's constant goading drove me to succeed. To this day he believes that though I had loads of natural ability, I would have squandered it, played around with it, frittered it away. And I never would have gotten anywhere.

I suspect he's right. I never did take naturally to work—no more than Dad did when Grandpa Porter set him to hoeing the vegetable garden that time. I remember Dad used to give me a job to do around the house, and I'd get it half done and then go off to play basketball or baseball. That's when he'd wither me with a glance and say, "Darrell, you'd better make it in sports, 'cause you ain't worth a flip at anything else." Sure, it was humiliating and hurtful to have my own father tell me this. But there was some truth in it, too.

Later Dad was to say that he wanted his children to be something—to have the chances he and Mom never had, which is what all good parents want for their kids. Dad knew it was a hard world and that to accomplish anything you had to work as hard as you could. So he *demanded* that we bust our butts at whatever we did. Maybe I owe my success to that.

If only Dad had mixed his criticism with some praise, however, even a little, I might have been an even better ballplayer. Who knows? But we have to deal with life as it is, as it turns out, not as we would like it to be.

Dad began to coach my teams in Midget B and Midget A Little

League. A buddy of mine was also a talented ballplayer. He and I became Dad's pitching and catching staff. Dad rotated us: one game I'd pitch and my friend would catch, the next we'd switch. Under Dad's guidance we were soon an unbeatable combination. We defeated every team in the area.

Dad provided my brothers and me with everything we needed for sports. He installed a basketball hoop in our front yard that's still there. I reckon the Porter boys sank a million baskets in that old hoop. Mom never could grow any grass or flowers in that front yard like the other, fussier mothers. How could she when the whole neighborhood played there? No matter, to her it was a small sacrifice—or so she said. Our sports were more important to both Mom and Dad. Dad—God bless him—even had the driveway widened to give us more space for our half-court basketball games.

Our sports meant so much to Dad that he eventually quit his job with United Transport so that he could be at home, coaching us. He became parts and service manager for one of the car dealerships in Oklahoma City, a job he holds to this day.

Years later, looking back on it, Dad told a reporter: "Oh, it was a *glorious* little neighborhood for kids, the best in Oklahoma City. And it was a glorious time. I was reliving my own life through those neighborhood kids. I was getting to put a program together that I wished I could have lived, but didn't get a chance to."

My baseball game improved steadily. When I got to junior high school I moved on to prep ball. Of course, in Little League, everything had been scaled down on the field. So the first day of prep ball I discovered to my dismay that the pitcher's mound had been moved back—way back. From here on out we would be playing on a regulation-sized diamond. Home plate looked like it was in North Dakota. I could no longer reach it with a pitch.

I was embarrassed—mortified. Already I was such a perfectionist that I couldn't cope with this development. I probably could have made the adjustment, but I was afraid to take the risk. What if I couldn't? I asked the coach if I could catch instead. He agreed. That ended my budding career as a pitcher.

It was when I began to concentrate exclusively on catching that I really blossomed. Even in those days I hustled my butt off behind home plate. I was a *fiery* catcher. And for some reason I never had trouble throwing to second base. Dad had been right about catching. At last I had found my place in baseball.

5

The Porters of Southeast High

Southeast High School. It was big and kind of scary for a shy, fourteen-year-old freshman. But I was one leg up on the other frosh—my big brother was Jimmy Porter, a popular athlete.

"Hey, are you Jim Porter's brother? Well, howdy! This here is Jim Porter's kid brother!"

From day one I basked in Jimmy's reflected glory. But even as a freshman I began to attract attention on my own—with baseball. The first I heard of it was after a game in which I picked a man off third base. Somebody told me a scout from the Yankees was in the stands and said appreciatively, "Oh, look at *that* young guy!"

Baseball scouts were always buzzing around. It kept us on our toes. Already I had an almost inordinate desire to succeed—no, more than that: I needed to be admired, loved. I needed to hear I was the best person and the best baseball player in the world. It wasn't conceit, but a genuine desire for excellence and a hunger for love. I didn't know then that you can't be loved by masses of people. The favor of the crowd can quickly turn to disapproval. What did I know at fourteen? I craved the attention; I thrived on it.

When I was a sophomore, I went out for football. Jim was the quarterback. I made the first team as a defensive back.

I had played baseball for six years, and I lived for it. But now I discovered that nothing but nothing can compare to the excitement of football. Football attracts the big crowds. There are pep rallies and cheerleaders and brass bands!

What's more, there was an exciting intensity and more than a hint of fear in the rough and tumble of the game. Football was a novelty. Baseball was, by comparison, quiet, loose, and kind of old hat.

That year, 1967, Southeast was having one of its best seasons ever. We finally came to a big game with Harding High School, I believe it was, a larger, more affluent school on the north side of Oklahoma City.

Our hometeam stands were nearly cracking under the weight of a sellout crowd of students and parents. It was quite a game, as I remember. With eight seconds left on the clock, we were stalled at Harding's six yard line, trailing by five points, and it was fourth down. Coach called a time out. It was an obvious passing situation.

I was wondering what was going to happen when the coach turned and scanned the bench. He was motioning someone... ME! I couldn't believe it. I was really nervous as I trotted out onto the field.

But Jim was the quarterback. Coach was putting me in the game, in place of my brother! Jim trotted off the field. I felt like a traitor. I wouldn't have blamed him for cutting me dead, but instead he gave me a playful slap on the fanny as he passed. "You can do it, D.P.!" he said, grinning.

I was petrified. While I tried to hide my fear, I entered the huddle and called the play. I was supposed to sprint to my left and hit the tight end in the end zone with a pass. This was a heck of a time to find out how good a passer I was. I didn't *need* this.

In a voice cracking with tension, I called the signals at the line of scrimmage. An almost unnatural hush had fallen over the stadium, making my voice sound weak, swallowed up by that vast silence.

It was only for a moment. Then the center was snapping the ball into my hands, and I started running to the left, as planned, looking for the receiver. In the noise and confusion that suddenly engulfed me, I couldn't be sure exactly what was happening. Then the receiver I was looking for flashed briefly across my line of vision, surrounded by enemy jerseys. No time to think. Cocking my arm, I fired the ball—*right into the hands of a Harding linebacker!*

43

He caught it on a dead run toward our end zone. It was a nightmare. I seemed to be mired down in blockers and couldn't get untangled quickly enough to stop him. He was racing down the sidelines, moving past me. I turned to see him run an astounding ninety-eight yards for a touchdown!

A massive groan arose from the Southeast stands, drowning out the cheers of the Harding fans. The game was over, and my world lay in pieces. I had muffed the play. I stared at the turf, numb with shame. If I could have picked it up, I'd have crawled under it and pulled it over my head.

I never could stand defeat or making errors. I always suffered horribly. But that time was the worst! I had just lost an entire game for the team—or so I thought. I dressed quickly. I half heard the comments of my teammates, barely felt the pats on my back meant to console me. I couldn't get out of the locker room fast enough. I just wanted to get away.

For more than an hour I wandered aimlessly around our neighborhood, crying to myself, kicking mounds of dead leaves. I even thought of running away. It was the worst day of my life!

Finally, a carload of my teammates spotted me just a block from my house. They pulled up alongside me. They were drinking beer, and a couple of them acted as if they were pretty well along toward a big drunk. I got in. I often went out with the guys after a game, but I never drank. That made me what you might call the "designated driver," as I would see that they got home safely when they were too sloshed to get behind the wheel.

The next day, Jim, my buddy Joe Smart, and I were out throwing a football around. Nobody said anything about the game or my horrible blunder. But they were thinking it, I was sure.

Suddenly Jim tossed the ball to me and said casually, "D.P., you're gonna be the starting quarterback next year. You've gotta be ready!"

Starting quarterback—just like that! I had failed. But somehow it didn't matter. Jim still had faith in me. That had been one of Jim's last games at Southeast; he'd be graduating in June. I had ruined the whole thing for him. If they had left him in the game, we might have won. But he was telling me that it was all right. I stood there for a moment, the ball cradled in my arm, looking at him. I thought of a time, just a few weeks earlier, when I had accused Jim of not being tough enough in football. I told him I could hit harder. The truth was I had been envying his success a little, and I wanted to be better than he was. I recalled an incident the previous spring, when I jumped all over him for making an error in a baseball game. And here he was, in effect passing the quarterback's mantle on to me, his kid brother, generously, freely.

I felt like crying. Instead I said quietly, "I will be ready, Jim."

The following fall, my junior year, I *was* ready. Coach Jerry Haines had his eye on me. So it looked as though a Porter would succeed a Porter as starting quarterback for the Spartans.

I did—just how well I realized when my name began to appear with regularity in the newspapers. At times I wanted to crow and say, "Hey, I'm great! I'm a three-sport letterman! I'm a star!" But I never did. Mom and Dad had taught us to be humble about our accomplishments. Besides, most of the time I couldn't believe I was really all that good. I kept my feelings to myself, and I let other people praise me. Still, after a couple of touchdowns on a Friday night, I could hardly wait for the newspapers on Saturday morning—maybe with my name in banner headlines on the sports pages. They gave me the reassurance I needed.

During my junior year I really came into my own as an athlete. I discovered I *was* a good passer; it was my strong suit, whereas Jim had been a more rough-and-tumble-type player. After a pretty good season in football as starting quarterback, I was all-state catcher in baseball, hitting .560. I was voted Southeast's Most Valuable Player in football, baseball, and basketball. (In basketball I was a guard.)

Now my kid brother Eddie was coming up through the ranks. They were referring to him as "D.P.'s little brother"—even though he was over six feet tall and was carving out his own career in baseball, basketball, and football, like his two brothers before him.

It was about this time they began facetiously calling Southeast, "Porter High."

Jimmy was in college on a baseball scholarship. His days as a football player were over. I suppose from his perspective, his kid brother, who he once thought might almost come up to his dazzling record as an athlete, was in fact doing just that. Outwardly at least he took the whole thing with good grace.

As for my attitude toward Jim: I always wanted to surpass him in scholastic sports. Things came to a head one Saturday while Dad was at work and Mom was out shopping. Four or five of us were playing basketball in the driveway. Jim was guarding me, but I was scoring basket after basket. He just couldn't stop me. Before long we were fighting—the first time I had ever really hit one of my brothers. It ended as quickly as it had started, and we never fought again.

6

Growing Up

Like most high schools, Southeast had its share of cliques. To be in the best clique (in other words, the most exclusive and snobbish) you had to have money, a nice car, or athletic ability.

We Porters definitely didn't have money. And though I dearly loved the old white 1957 Plymouth Dad bought me for my seventeenth birthday, the tires were balder than your granddad's head. And we certainly weren't the fashion plates of Southeast High. Our clothes, in fact, were a source of embarrassment to us. I hated wearing Jimmy's hand-me-downs. After I outgrew them, they went to poor Eddie. Denny was lucky—by the time they got to him they were worn out, so he got new clothes.

It wasn't only that the clothes were second-hand. Jim was shorter than I was; that meant his pants were, too. I felt pretty self-conscious in those used high-waters, while the other guys were dressed in nice, new jeans. I was forever tugging and pulling at those old pants to make them a bit longer, but it never did any good.

I was fairly lazy. Except for a brief stint as a shoeshine boy when I was eleven or so, I didn't work. I loved playing sports too much for that. But those hand-me-downs finally drove me to it. The summer I was seventeen, Joe Smart and I took jobs on a construction site. We got the dirty jobs nobody else wanted—the ones that required crawling under muddy foundations on our backs to adjust something or other.

It was hard work, but I earned enough money to buy a decent wardrobe. I didn't have to feel ashamed in front of my friends anymore.

My clothes situation, however, was of small consequence to the people who ran the top clique at school. They would have taken me if I had dressed in potato sacks. The only thing was that I didn't want to join. They were the kind of people who enjoyed excluding other kids. Deep in my heart I rebelled against that kind of cruelty. Mom and Dad had taught us to be fair to everyone. I'd go out of my way to give a friendly hello to the most unpopular girl in the school or to the skinny bookworm who didn't know a jump shot from a forward pass. Trying to be nice was a lot more fun than putting people down. So I refused to join that clique. And I'm sure I was resented for it.

I always loved girls—ever since grade school. But I was painfully shy around them. And the prettier they were, the more shy and bumbling I was.

From the seventh grade on, though, I always had a "steady." My first was Nancy (not her real name). There was another girl I liked much better, but I felt she was too far above me, so I dated Nancy. I *had* to have a steady girl.

I used to go to dances, although I never did get the hang of fast dancing, even in high school, and I was really bad at slow dancing. I couldn't understand it. Here I was, an agile guy with lots of grace and rhythm on the basketball court or football field. But on the dance floor? Forget it! My feet would suddenly feel as if I had lead weights attached to them. I felt awkward, stupid. I finally figured it out: it's all mental. I thought everyone was watching me. So I shuffled around to the back corner of the room so nobody would see me. Ever have a 190-pound klutz step on your feet? But the girls would simply smile and say, "Oh, that's all right, Darrell! It didn't hurt, really! You're doin' just fine, much better'n last week!" And it would only make me feel more miserable and clumsy.

Shy as I was, I took advantage of the dances just to be near the girls. But I never fell in love and never had a crush, all through school. Well, that's not exactly true. There were a couple of pretty teachers.

First, there was Miss Howard, a pretty, dark-haired teacher I had in the sixth grade. I think I had a crush on her, because she treated me well. I was her pet. That was the first time anybody had ever treated me as if I was something special.

Much as I liked Miss Howard, I never was that good at my studies, though I did fair work. Recess was the thing I lived for, being out in the air and sunshine, running with the gang.

I was that way throughout school. I can't remember one single subject I really enjoyed or really succeeded in. I did just enough to get by. I didn't want to bring home any D's though, or I'd hear it from Dad. Besides, I knew I had to have passing grades to get a football scholarship. (By the time I was a sophomore, I was already thinking along those lines.)

Sometimes I felt dumb, especially in English. Ironically, it was my sophomore English teacher—I'll call her Mrs. Turner—on whom I got my biggest crush. She was a real knockout, a very pretty blonde woman with blue eyes and a terrific figure. She was married or divorced, but I didn't give a hoot about it. I was dazzled by the thought of her.

In the classroom, things were depressingly different from my daydreams. The lovely Mrs. Turner wouldn't give me the time of day! In fact, she seemed to take a perverse delight in putting me down. She would scrawl big, almost violent-looking red words all over my essays: "WRONG! WRONG! WRONG! That's WRONG!" She really knew how to hurt a guy. Why can't teachers emphasize the positive, what you get right instead of what you get wrong?

I was a popular guy and an athlete, so you would think I had it made as far as girls were concerned. Wrong! I'm sure there were pretty girls who would have loved to go out with the starting quarterback. But I was afraid to approach them. I played it safe and never asked them out. I stuck with my steady.

Until I was sixteen, I had experienced only one instance of sexual discovery. It happened when I was—would you believe it?—four or five. (I guess I was the youngest Romeo in town.) I asked the little girl down the street if she wanted to come into the chicken coop to play doctor.

When I reached puberty, it was, of course, inevitable that I would once more venture into forbidden territory. Bible-belt religion, with its hell-fire prohibitions against premarital sex, might have scared me away from experimenting, had it been drummed into me (though I think obedience through fear is a bad thing). But Mom and Dad, although they believed in God and in doing right, were relaxed about Christianity; maybe not in their beliefs (we were Southern Baptists), but in the practice of them.

Mom was the one in our family who most clearly reflected what God was like to me—loving, patient, and kind. Dad had gone through a spate of religiosity when he was younger, but I suppose his drinking dampened his ardor—if you can't live it, it isn't right to preach it. But whenever he attended church, Dad carried his Bible with him.

We attended the Wilmont Baptist Church in Oklahoma City, but not on a regular basis. Mom attended more than Dad, and if he didn't go, we kids weren't required to. Dad always said he felt it would be hypocritical for him to sit home reading the want ads and enjoying a clear conscience because his kids were at Sunday school. I have to give him credit for that.

There were always Bibles in our home, though they were hardly worn with use. And I remember a picture of Jesus hanging on the cross. Grace at meals was only for holidays—Christmas and Thanksgiving. But as far back as when I was eight or nine, I remember praying nightly to God. I would ask Him to protect our family from harm, and I sincerely believed He would. I felt I had a good contact with God.

In spite of the relaxed religiosity of the Porters, Mom and Dad raised us to believe in God and to be kind to everyone, and, as I've already indicated, to be humble. Dad overdid the humble bit, in my opinion. That was why he never praised us. I think he actually had a fear of pride and self-love that had been drummed into him by his adoptive parents to an unhealthy degree. And he passed it on to us, though to a lesser extent. I know I never did buy that kind of fire-and-brimstone religion he had been raised on.

During my junior year, when I was seventeen, a revival at Wilmont Baptist was announced. I was curious. Though we had ceremonies of baptism by immersion at our church (and they were elaborate affairs) and the preacher gave regular altar calls, I had never been to a real, honest-to-goodness revival before.

Of course, I knew all about people being saved. I knew I wasn't, because I had never made my "decision for Christ." In our Southern Baptist belief, it isn't enough to come from a Christian home with Christian parents. At some point after the age of accountability, each person is expected to ask Christ into his or her life by a conscious decision. Then the individual is baptized by immersion.

For some reason, the fact that I wasn't saved didn't bother me. Actually I had never thought much about it. It was something that happened to other people. I wanted to go to the revival, though, because I'd grown up hearing about how exciting they were.

I didn't want to go alone; yet I didn't want to ask Joe Smart or any of my athletic friends. They would think it was funny. So I asked a neighborhood friend, James Pilkington, if he wanted to go with me. "Sure, why not?" he said.

The opening night of the revival was warm. It seemed strange going into the church at night, with all the lights blazing. The windows were open, and an occasional moth or June bug would come fluttering or buzzing into the lighted sanctuary. A sea of paper fans was fluttering in the tightly packed hall. A lot of young people were there doing some cautious flirting. It would hardly be fitting to be too bold with glances at an important religious function like this one. The girls, all pretty and perspired, had assumed very proper postures and looks for the occasion. Whispers went around that the evangelist was dynamic—as well as young and good-looking, according to those same girls.

I don't remember the subject of the sermon, though it *was* dynamic and not anything about God "getting" us for our sins. I do remember I took the whole thing seriously. Toward the end, I recall that the evangelist read a passage from chapter 53 of the book of Isaiah. He told us it was a prophecy about Jesus Christ, who would not be born for hundreds of years after the prophecy was made. Yet it fit Him exactly. I thought that was amazing.

For the first time in my life, something I heard from the pulpit grabbed me where I lived. *Jesus Christ, the man-God who lived almost two thousand years ago, had suffered, bled, and died for me—Darrell Ray Porter!* And here I was, just a no-good, ungrateful sinner, who hardly ever thought about Him, much less how He had been humiliated, beaten, and crucified for me!

People were softly weeping all around me. I was crying too. I could feel James Pilkington staring at me, but I didn't care. I was bawling!

When that young evangelist gave the invitation to come forward, I walked to the front of the church with the others, tears streaming down my face. And I gave my life over to Jesus. Then I began to cry again, but they were tears of joy. People were smiling at me, nodding their heads in approval. They knew what I was feeling, and it was all right to be crying. Oh, I felt happy and clean somehow, as if I was beginning life all over, without a problem in the world! I felt light and easy within myself. So this was what it meant to be born again! Hallelujah! I had been saved!

After the service, I discussed the joyous, wonderful thing that had happened to me with my family and with James. The family was happy for me. So was James. In fact, the very next night he went forward and surrendered his life to Christ, too!

Today, looking back, I can honestly say my conversion experience was genuine, in spite of my later failure to live up to my profession of faith. Of course, when it happened I thought the euphoria and the good resolves would last forever. I had put on the whole armor of God. But I failed to reckon with the lure of the world, the flesh, and the devil.

I had no one to instruct me in the basics of my newfound faith. I continued my regular nightly prayers, but I could barely understand the outdated English of the King James Bible. I had been told I was supposed to "get into the Word." I struggled with the "thees" and "thous" and the "inasmuchas's" for a while, then gave up. It was just too hard. Consequently, with nothing to back it up or to establish it firmly in my life, the glow of the mountain-top spiritual experience began to fade after only a few weeks.

My adolescent sexual urges began to reassert themselves. It bothered me; I felt I was letting Christ down, going back on my promises to Him. But I couldn't seem to help it. The truth was I didn't want to help it.

The one area in which I think my conversion made a difference was at school. There were kids who resented my success in sports and the growing attention I was receiving in the press. I asked the

Lord to help me deal with this problem, to help me handle it, and He did.

My reputation as an athlete was growing daily. No longer was I referred to as "Jim Porter's kid brother."

In the fall of my senior year at Southeast, hardly a week went by that I wasn't being praised in the sports pages.

SPARTANS' PORTER TRAPS BEARS read a typical headline in *The Daily Oklahoman* in October 1969. The story described me as a "do-it-all" quarterback. Typically, Dad was cool about the stories. I longed for him to give me one little word of praise. Strangers were doing it, but my dad never did.

Nevertheless, 1969 was my best year. I could do nothing wrong, or very little. My favorite game was the 26–13 drubbing we gave our chief rival, U. S. Grant High School. In that game I connected on sixteen of twenty-six passes for 286 yards and three touch-downs! It felt good whipping the tar out of those boys from U. S. Grant!

I must report the year wasn't one of total, unrelieved triumph. The following spring, for example, I struck out four times in one baseball game—in front of a bunch of big league scouts! I felt really terrible, not only because of my tendency toward self-criti-cism, but also because I was afraid I had blown my chances of ever being signed to a professional contract.

I needn't have worried. They were looking at my overall per-formance. I had a .415 batting average that year and made all-state catcher the second year in a row. But I could only see the present failure, that one bad day.

7

Hard Choices

Throughout my senior year a steady pressure slowly built up around and within me—pressure to make a decision. Was I going to accept a scholarship to play college football? Or was I going to opt for a career in professional baseball?

There was a snag. A big one. Football is everything to folks in Oklahoma, and college football means only one thing: the Oklahoma University Sooners. Naturally, everybody assumed that I would accept a football scholarship to OU. The snag was I didn't really want to play for OU. Heresy! (Of course I didn't *tell* anybody.)

I visited a lot of schools that year—SMU, Arkansas, Kansas State, Colorado. It wasn't that I was disloyal, but Oklahoma was a team that did a lot of running. (They loved the wishbone formation.) I was a pretty fair runner, but my strong suit was passing. Secretly I wanted to go to Colorado, because they were a passing team.

As the months slipped by, Dad talked more and more about the scholarship to Oklahoma. I would timidly interject, "But, Dad, they throw the ball more at Colorado."

"I know they do, Darrell," Dad would reply, putting me off, "but let's keep this thing going down here."

If I was going to play football at all, it better be with OU, or I'd be ostracized—and maybe tarred, feathered, and hanged!

Colorado sent former Oklahoma football star Eddie Crowder,

who had become Colorado's athletic director. What a coup if Crowder could get an Oklahoma boy away from OU! I was on the verge of signing.

Then OU got out its big guns—or its big gun—in the person of Steve Owens. Owens, the starting fullback for the Detroit Lions and a former OU player, was dispatched to our lowly house on 52nd Street to visit with me and my family. He took me and my girlfriend to a fancy restaurant for dinner. Steve Owens was a Heisman Trophy winner and a monstrously big star in Oklahoma. I mean, they say a cat can look at a king, but to dine with one in a restaurant? I was totally blown away with the thrill of it all. I was breaking bread with a living legend!

It was nearly signing time. The pressure got worse and worse. Thirty-seven schools were after me to sign. At first it had been fun—all the attention, being flown to this school and that, having scouts and celebrity players wine and dine me and my folks. (Dad said he was getting fat from all the filet mignon.) But finally, the pressure got so bad that I hated to pick up the phone. It was upsetting our entire family.

The weekend before the Big Eight signing day, Dad and I went fishing. We just had to get away for a few days.

In spite of the pressures, Dad kept reminding me that the final choice was mine and mine alone—I didn't have to worry about what he wanted. Well, it was good in theory.

We hedged our bets. The Milwaukee Brewers were putting out feelers for me. We began getting calls from all over the country from sports agents, all eager to handle my career in professional baseball, if that was the way I decided to go. "Mr. Porter," one man told Dad, "I can get a $100,000 signing bonus for Darrell." A week later another agent insisted he could get $150,000.

When Dad expressed surprise that a high school athlete could command that kind of money, the man said, "Your son is one of the finest athletes to come out of Oklahoma in recent years. Believe me, he'll get it." We appreciated the free advice, but we decided Dad could handle my career just fine. Why not?

Tuesday, February 12, 1970, was the Big Eight Conference signing day. I gave in and signed a letter of intent to play for Oklahoma. I kept quiet about my preference for Colorado, at least in the papers. "I've always wanted to go to Oklahoma," I told a reporter the night before the signing. "I've been a fan of theirs since I was a kid." Well, it *was* true. Besides, now that I was going to sign with OU, I persuaded myself I had really wanted to do it all along.

As for baseball, Dad's idea was to use the letter of intent as bargaining leverage in my talks with the big league teams. If they thought I might get away from them by playing college football, I would be a lot more attractive to them, and they would up the ante. Then, too, if by some chance they didn't come through with a lucrative deal, I could opt for the football scholarship.

As it turned out, I was the first-round draft choice of the Brewers, and the fourth man picked in the country.

In June, just before graduation, the Brewers called and said they were sending one of their scouts, Bob Mavis, to Oklahoma City to talk about a contract. A real contract with a professional team! I was walking on air.

Well, Dad and I were thinking: since I was number one draft choice, I'd easily get that $100,000 bonus. Maybe even $150,000. Hadn't the agents said I was worth that much? Shoot, we figured I must be.

We were all nervous when Bob Mavis came to the house. Jimmy, Eddie, Pat, Denny—everybody was sitting in the living room when he came in—everybody except Mom. She was getting the coffee.

"Darrell, we want you real bad in the Brewers organization," Mavis said right away, sounding sincere. "We think you've got the stuff to make it to the big leagues. You've got the stuff to be a big league catcher."

It was wonderful and scary, listening to a scout from the Milwaukee Brewers praise me, to think I was so highly valued by professional baseball people. Suddenly I felt like laughing! I was so happy! The thing that most young guys only dream about—playing professional baseball—was about to come true for me, a poor boy from a working-class family! I was going to have it all, just as I always dreamed I would! I was going to be playing the game I had loved since I was nine years old. And—almost unbelievably—I would be getting paid big, big money for it, too!

"And so, Darrell," Mavis was saying, "we'd like to make you a firm offer." Dad was grinning in anticipation; I was grinning, already counting those megabucks.

"We're willing to offer you a bonus of $15,000!"

Whaaaa?

Shock. A stunned silence. Dad and I looked at each other in utter disbelief at how small the figure was.

"Now, I've got the papers right here," Mavis was saying in an easy way, as if he had the whole deal sewed up and in the bag.

"Just hold on there a minute, fella!" Dad said in a not-too-kind tone. "No way are we going to sign for any $15,000! Darrell's worth a heck of a lot more'n that!" As he said it, Dad was shifting back and forth on the edge of the sofa as if he had ants in his pants, he was so burned.

Mavis stopped dead. His face went blank. He glanced first at Dad, then at me. I pretended to study the pattern in the rug. Arguing about money was so—so embarrassing. It was as if we were accusing the man of trying to cheat me. I didn't want to think that, but....

"Mr. Porter. Ray. May I call you Ray?" Mavis asked with the slightest trace of impatience mixed with a fine condescension. "Ray, we're giving Darrell the opportunity of a lifetime. Most young guys would give their eyeteeth—"

"You know and I know that my son is not 'most young guys,' but the best danged athlete to come out of these parts in many a year!" Dad interrupted. "Your own organization made him its number one draft choice. Now he's *got* to be worth more than $15,000. That's chicken feed, Mr. Mavis! Why, thirty-seven colleges have offered him football scholarships. Thirty-seven! And I hope to tell you if you don't come up with a better figure, my boy might just accept one of those scholarships!" And with that, Dad sat back and crossed his arms.

"Well," Mavis said thoughtfully, "perhaps we can go to $20,000, or maybe even as high as $25,000—though I'm not sure we can." He cocked his head to gauge Dad's reaction. Dad was shaking his head no.

"Okay," Mavis said, clapping his hands on both knees in a gesture of finality. "I'm not authorized to go any higher. I'll have to check with our office in Milwaukee. May I use your phone?"

While he made the call, we had a hurried conference. I was really shaken and disappointed—and afraid that if we pushed too hard, we'd lose it all. So was Jimmy.

"These fellows always do this," Dad insisted, without sounding too confident about it. "Trust me. They're gonna come through. But you can't weaken. You gotta call their bluff!"

When Mavis got off the phone, he said the Brewers were sending their head scout, Bobby Mattick, down to negotiate. He gathered his things together and thanked us for our time. I thought I was going to have a fit when he walked out the door. Dad told me to be patient. "All big deals have to be negotiated," he said, "so this is nothing unusual. We'll get what we want. You'll see!"

"I hope so, Dad," Jimmy said dubiously. I couldn't say a word. I was speechless.

Two days later head scout Bobby Mattick drove up to our house in a big shiny car, with Bob Mavis in tow. Mattick, resplendent in a three-piece suit and expensive watch, was a little more brusque than Mavis had been. Friendly, but intimidating. It wasn't so much what he said, but his every gesture, his body language, sent the message loud and clear: *Hey, buddy! You're just a little high school player who's too big for his britches. We're the big leagues, sonny! Don't you forget it!*

Spreading his papers out on the coffee table, Mattick said, "Darrell, as you know, the Milwaukee Brewers is a new organization. We are *not* the New York Yankees. We simply can't afford to give a new, untried player—even one as talented as yourself—big, big bucks. All we can offer you—a very generous figure we think—is $35,000." He waited for our reaction.

Dad and I had already determined we were not going to accept anything less than $100,000. "Mr. Mattick," I began, "my dad and I—uh—we just don't think that's enough. We think I'm worth more'n $35,000." I swallowed hard. *Why, $35,000 seemed like a million to me*. But Dad had said to hold out for more. In spite of my anti-perspirant, beads of sweat were slowly sliding down my sides.

"Darrell, may I remind you that although you are a very talented athlete, you are still an amateur. You've got a lot to learn. You are not in the big leagues yet, and, though I hate to say it, you may not be at this rate." Mattick's tone was disapproving, designed to make me feel guilty for wanting more.

I did feel guilty. I felt *awful!*

"Look, Mr. Mattick," Dad said patiently, "Darrell's got a college education waiting for him worth at least $40,000. Why should we settle for $35,000?"

Mattick sighed heavily and rubbed his forehead. "We could go as high as $50,000," he said uncertainly, as if wondering whether I was worth it, "but really, that would be it."

"All right," Dad replied quickly. "We think he's worth $100,000, but we'd be willing to compromise. Say, $70,000 with an incentive clause. But that's *our* bottom line." (Dad later told me he was hoping, with the incentives, to get an equivalent of $8,000, bringing the total package up to almost $80,000.)

Mattick gave Mavis a sour look and then began scooping up his papers. Suddenly he stopped, and without looking up he said crisply, "We'll give you $65,000. And that's *our* final offer!" With that, he closed his attaché case with a snap that sounded final. Then he just stood there waiting.

"Dad?" I said. Dad seemed to pale a little. Slowly he shook his head no.

"You know, once I walk through that door," Mattick said, "I won't be back."

I looked at Dad. Jimmy looked at Dad. Dad stared off into space.

"Well, young fellow," Mattick said, extending his hand, "I guess you'll be playing football for OU this fall after all! Lots of luck to you, son. Sorry we couldn't do business!"

When the door slammed, I gave Dad a stricken look. It was one of the truly horrible moments of my life. I thought I was about to die. Jim ran to the window and watched the car pull away. Then he banged his head against the wall. "Dad, you blew it!" he sighed. "You really blew it!"

Dad was rigid as a statue. "They'll be back," he said calmly, but without conviction. "They'll be back."

"No, no they won't!" Jimmy said angrily. "Dad, that guy was sincere. He won't be back!"

Ignoring Jim, Dad looked at me and said, "Darrell, I wouldn't steer you wrong. I'm telling you, they'll be back."

How I wanted to believe him! But I was angry, too, though I could never dare show it in front of Dad. I was also confused and disappointed. No, not disappointed. *Crushed!*

I couldn't say a word. It was too awful. We all sat there in a state of numbed disbelief. After a while, Denny went to the window. A minute later he yelled, "Here comes the car again! They're coming back!"

"Oh, wow!" I cried, jumping up and clapping Dad on the shoulder. "Dad, you were right all the time! See, Jim, Dad *was* right!"

"Shhhh!" Dad said, with a small smile. "Now everybody calm down! Let me do the talkin'."

Mattick and Mavis walked back in with blank faces. Opening his attaché case, Mattick began methodically removing his papers once more. "Darrell," he said, "we'll give you the $70,000 . . . plus an additional $7,500 in incentives."

He looked at me; I looked at Dad, who was gently shaking his head yes. Dad's eyes looked positively merry.

"Okay, Mr. Mattick," I said, "where do I sign?"

Mattick grinned for the first time and replied, "Just let me fill in the proper amounts here."

As he leaned over the coffee table, pen in hand, I gave Dad a big smile. He winked, as if to say, "I told you to trust your old man." But I could have sworn there was a film of sweat on Dad's forehead.

8

Down in the Minors

I was going to play professional baseball. What my dad only dreamed about had come true for me, his second son. I had a signed contract and check for $35,000 to prove it. (The second half of the bonus would be paid in January of 1971, for tax purposes.)

Everybody—Mom, Dad, Jimmy, Pat, Eddie, and Denny—was thrilled to pieces over my contract with the Brewers.

I was scared. Along with the contract and the money came an awesome responsibility. They don't give you the glittering prizes for nothing. They would want me to produce, and produce *big*—at least $70,000 worth. Could I do it? *What if I don't make it?* I thought. My life would be ruined.

I couldn't discuss my feelings with Mom or Dad or anybody. I was all alone with my uncertainty, my fear. I had proved I was a top athlete, so this was the next logical step. *This was what I was supposed to do*, no ifs, ands, or buts about it.

On the surface, I was excited and proud and full of expectation and hope for a bright future. But underneath—underneath, along with the fear, I felt a little like a wind-up toy. Somebody had given the key a few turns and pointed me in the right direction, and I was expected to automatically walk that way. It wasn't only the uncertainty of the new career, the new life that lay before me, that was frightening. It was also the feeling that I had absolutely no control over what was happening to me.

But I pushed these fears down and put on a good face. It helped that there were things I had to do before I left home.

The first thing I did was to buy six or seven suits, plus shoes, shirts, ties—the works. I was going to the pros all decked out. I was no hayseed. In high school we had worn ties when we went on road trips, so what would they expect of me in professional baseball?

Next, I went out with my dad and bought a brand-new 1970 Chevy SS-396. All white with a black top.

The Milwaukee management called and said they wanted to fly me to Baltimore for a few days to work out with the major league team. The Brewers were in Baltimore for a series of games with the Orioles. (Ordinarily, a new player would then be sent to rookie league, but they told me they were going to send me directly into Class A ball in Clinton, Iowa. It was their way of telling me they thought I had excellent prospects for becoming a star.)

Going to Baltimore only scared me more. I couldn't believe it: *me*, working out with the Brewers' major league team. And right off the bat!

"Now, Darrell, don't you worry about anything," Mom said as I kissed her good-by at Will Rogers Airport. "It's only for a few days and then you'll be coming home before taking off for Clinton. Remember, we're only a phone call away!"

"You're gonna do just fine, son!" Dad said, shaking my hand.

"I'll try my best, Dad. I sure will try!" I replied, a lump in my throat.

Baltimore was another world. The minute I stepped off the plane, a well-groomed young guy met me at the gate. "Mr. Porter? I'm Tony Siegel of the Milwaukee Brewers. How are you? I'm here to take you to your hotel and then to the ballpark. Did you have a pleasant flight?"

He opened doors for me and had someone carry my bags. A shiny limousine took us to a major hotel, with thick carpets in the lobby that was half the size of Capitol Hill Stadium. In my room there were two big beds with velvet spreads. Air conditioning purred quietly in the background. One whole wall was glass, revealing a spectacular view of the city.

I felt as if I were floating or dreaming. I was just a down-home

boy from Oklahoma City who got D's in English and shared a bedroom with his three brothers. I felt odd being treated practically
like the king of England.

They had me on a tight schedule. After I checked into the hotel,
they drove me to the ballpark. Hordes of fans were waiting around
for the Orioles to arrive, and security was tight. But we breezed
past the guards.

When I walked into the visitors' clubhouse I was shocked out of
my gourd. Here were all these major league players, sitting around
in full uniform drinking coffee and *smoking cigarettes!*

I couldn't believe it. Athletes just didn't *do* that—smoke. It was a
dirty, nasty habit that ruined a ballplayer's body. That had been
drummed into us all through school. Yet these big leaguers were
hanging out and puffing away!

They showed me my locker, which caused me to do a double
take. There, neatly pressed, hung a brand new Brewers uniform,
with the number fifteen. My number. My name was over the
locker. It was really, *really* true: I was a professional baseball
player. Neither the contract, nor the money, nor anything else had
been able to persuade me of the truth of that until now. But seeing
my name, PORTER, in big block letters over my locker finally
convinced me that it was really true.

What a thrill putting on that Brewers uniform! It was a dream
come true. The other players drifted over a few at a time and
shook my hand and introduced themselves. There were no
"names" among them, because Milwaukee was a new team. None
of them were familiar to me.

Then I was walking out onto a major league field for the first
time. And, man-oh-man, what a thrill that was! I had seen major
league games on television before, but now *I* was down on the field
with the players, looking up at the fans in the stands!

It was early evening. The June sun was just beginning to decline,
casting an orange glow over the scene, like a beautiful technicolor
movie. Everything around me seemed new and shiny, sleekly professional and flawless, from the brilliant green grass to the uniforms, the equipment, and the freshly painted dugout. And why
not? This was the major leagues, the big time! And I was part of it
all.

The other players, all much older than I was, had a loose, easy way about them that bespoke total professionalism and self-confidence. They were catching balls or taking batting practice. The familiar crack of balls striking bats filled me with a sudden, urgent eagerness to be playing ball.

First they wanted to see me throw. So I began throwing, and I was throwing really well, loosening up, feeling the adrenalin flowing. I was zinging the ball, I was so excited—some P's that were a foot and a half off the ground, right over second base—THONK!

Nobody was saying anything, but I suspected they were impressed. Out of the corner of my eye, I saw a smile on manager Dave Bristol's face.

Then it was my turn to take batting practice. On the second pitch, I connected and sent the ball out of the park. Same with the third. Everybody was getting quieter and quieter. Finally, nobody was talking at all. There was just the cracking sound of my bat hitting balls. Now I was sure they were impressed. *I* was impressed! Every other pitch, it seemed I was hitting one into the stands or nearly over the wall. I must have done it ten or twelve times.

After the workout, without fanfare I went back into the clubhouse and changed. Then I watched the game. I don't remember whether Milwaukee won or lost that night. But I do remember visiting the clubhouse again after the game. This time I nearly fell over with shock: players in all stages of dress and undress were sitting around, and not only were they smoking, but they were even *drinking beer!*

You have to imagine the effect this sight had on a naive, all-American boy from Oklahoma City. The illusions I had always cherished about clean-living jocks were shattered in that clubhouse for good.

But at the time, I pushed my feelings of surprise and disillusionment aside. After all, this wasn't high school baseball, and these were men, not boys. They were pros, not amateurs. And if they did it, it couldn't be too bad. Not that *I'd* ever do such a thing as drink beer, or even smoke. But what they did was their business, and what I did was mine. And I had done well my first time out.

The next day, I flew back to Oklahoma City in triumph. My baseball career was off to a great start. The family was all ears as I told them what had happened, step by step, from the moment I got off the plane at Baltimore. I tried to describe how I hit those ten or twelve homers as modestly as I could (if such a thing is possible), so I wouldn't sound as though I was tooting my own horn. Dad wouldn't have gone for that. No way. They were all proud and happy for me.

A few days later it was time for me to leave again, this time for Clinton, Iowa. The plan was for Jim to drive up with me in my new car, and then he would take a plane back.

I didn't want to go. For the first time in my life I would be away from home for an extended period—almost three months. The thought gave me a sick, scared feeling in my gut, as if I wanted to hide under the covers and never come out. But that would never do. I was no longer a kid. I was eighteen—almost a grown man. And I was a professional athlete. Of course I would go. *It was what everybody expected*. Again, though, my overwhelming thought was, *Can I do it?*

There was another sad round of good-bys, only this time it was worse. It was awful, especially saying good-by to Mom. How I wanted to make the moment last somehow. But I couldn't. I could have cried buckets. Instead I smiled a smile that was maybe a bit too bright and forced, while everybody was shouting "Drive carefully" and "Call us when you get there" and "Good luck."

Then Jim and I were heading north out of Oklahoma, with the radio blaring rock and that neat SS-396 flying along the highway at about one hundred miles an hour. No need to think about sad stuff for the eight or ten hours it would take to get there. I had lots of money in my pocket and a full tank of gas. I'd just ignore that nagging little voice that kept saying somewhere in the back of my brain, *I don't wanna do this. I don't wanna leave home.*

I was really glad to have Jim along. God bless him; he was really happy for me. Whatever sense of pain or loss he might have been feeling because I was the one with the pro contract, he never showed it one bit. And at the time I was so caught up in the excitement of the new life and career that lay before me, I hardly gave a second thought to what he might be feeling.

My first hint of misgiving about my new life came as we drove into Clinton. It wasn't the major leagues by a long shot. It wasn't even Oklahoma City. It was just a little bitty one-horse town.

We asked directions to the stadium, home of the Clinton Pilots. Little town, little stadium. And rundown—I mean *crummy*. I was depressed.

The "office" where I registered was a little cramped room with unpainted walls and a tiny, cheap-looking desk. The middle-aged woman who sat behind it didn't even look up as she took my name and other particulars. All the time I was thinking of the young man with the suit opening doors for me and the limo at the Baltimore airport.

The locker room was small and airless and hot, without a trace of air conditioning. The narrow lockers, jammed side by side, fairly exploded with players' clothes, mashed together and bulging off hooks. The room had the dirty-clothes smell of a second-hand store, mixed with locker-room sweat.

The shower room had four fixtures, two of which were broken. The tiles were covered with mildew, and the floor was slippery and filthy. I was beginning to feel sick.

"*This* is the major leagues?" I said to Jim in a soft voice, so that none of the guys drifting in and out of the clubhouse could hear.

"No, it's the *minors*, D.P.," Jim gently corrected, adding with a kind of helpless smile, "it *is* pretty bad. Think you can stand it?"

"Guess I'll have to," I replied, eyeing a torn girlie magazine and a dirty jockstrap in the bottom of the locker they had assigned me. I had an urge to run out of there, jump into my car, and take off for home. But I didn't.

We wandered out to the tacky little office again. "Uh, where do the players live, ma'am?" I asked tentatively.

She looked up with a trace of annoyance. "Each player is responsible for finding and renting his own place."

The other players, it turned out, had already been there a month and had taken all the best apartments in that little town. There wasn't much left. We spent the afternoon looking.

I didn't want to rent a suite in the Clinton Hilton (not that they had one). I wasn't one for fancy places. But I had hoped to find something better than what I eventually had to settle for.

It was an old, run-down house that looked haunted. The only thing to recommend it was that it was next door to a nice house where a couple of my teammates lived, and they seemed to be friendly guys.

The landlord put me in the upstairs apartment, even though the downstairs was vacant, too. Maybe it was because there was no lock on the door and being on the second floor gave an illusion of safety. It was awful, almost as awful as the Pilots' locker room, and a lot more spooky.

There was a living room, a kitchen, a bathroom, and a tiny bedroom, all with old wallpaper on which you couldn't see the faded pattern for the water stains.

And it smelled unclean. I hated sitting on the overstuffed chairs in the living room. They didn't feel like the chairs at home. And I couldn't picture myself actually lying down and sleeping on the narrow little cot that passed for a bed, with its ghost-gray sheets. "This is the pits!" Jim sighed. "Maybe you can move in with somebody else in a day or two."

"Yeah, soon as I get to know 'em a little better," I replied without conviction. I felt as if I was in the middle of a bad dream.

The worst thing about the place was the attic. A flight of rickety stairs led up to a blank, black hole with no door on it. Standing at the bottom of those narrow steps, looking up at that sinister gaping hole, I felt the flesh creeping up the back of my neck.

"Jim, this is pretty scary!" I said almost in a whisper.

"Well, best thing to do is check it out!" he said cheerily, thumping up the staircase a little too noisily—no doubt to give the rats and ghosts a chance to disappear.

There was just a bunch of forlorn old furniture and boxes and plenty of dust up there, but still the downstairs seemed almost cheery by comparison to that old attic.

We went out for dinner, and then it was time for Jim to go. I felt so down. "Hey, D.P.!" Jim said, playfully rapping my arm. "Buck up, buddy! Things are going to be okay. You'll see! It's only for a couple of months, and then you'll be home again. It'll go real fast!"

I tried to smile. It almost killed me, because my heart was nearly broken. Here I was, a thousand miles from home, the home and family I loved so dearly. And now my only link with all that, my brother Jim, was about to take off and leave me alone. It seemed more than I could bear.

I didn't say much. I couldn't. If I had, I'd have started bawling like a baby!

We drove out to the airport, and he bought his ticket home. At his gate, he shook my hand. "You take care, D.P.," Jim said, looking intently into my face. I was so choked up I couldn't talk. I couldn't look him in the eye. Instead I shook my head and turned away from my brother's gaze.

Then he was striding toward the plane. That's when I lost it. I began crying right there with people milling all around me. I hurried back to the car.

I sat in my shiny new car with the white body and the black roof, and at that moment it didn't mean a thing to me, nothing more than a pile of junk. I sat there and watched the plane taxi down the runway and take off. I watched it climb into the sky, becoming smaller and smaller, until it became a spot, then a dot. And the farther away it got, the harder I cried.

9

My First Beer

I drove back to Clinton and that awful house. I crawled into that narrow cot with its gray sheets and cried again. I felt totally abandoned. What was I doing in this strange place? In my heart I knew I had the answer: They were all counting on me—Dad, my coaches, my friends, my brothers. I just couldn't let them down. I'd rather have been skinned alive than disappoint them. It was unthinkable, even worse than this misery I was going through. For the first time in a long time, I failed to say my nightly prayers just when I needed them most. I drifted into a fitful sleep.

The next morning, the sun was shining brightly, and things didn't seem quite so frightening, though I still felt lonely and isolated. I dressed and drove over to the stadium. The Pilots were going on a road trip that day.

Now would come the acid test, the trial by fire. I would be playing my first professional game.

I had dressed carefully for the occasion in one of my snappy new summer suits and a tie. When I drove up to the stadium, the others were already on the bus, a ramshackle 1948 job (naturally). I hurried on in my suit. My new suit.

I darn near died! Everybody else was wearing a tee shirt and old blue jeans. I turned beet red inside that spiffy new suit. Then I began to sweat bullets. There were muffled snickers and a few snide "Howdy, Darrell"'s. I wanted to disappear. I walked to the back of that old bus as quickly as I could, feeling the eyes of all my team mates on me. As I walked I shucked my nice new coat and practically tore off my tie. I slunk down in a back seat. After a few minutes I began to feel a little better.

I must admit I was intimidated by my teammates. I was eighteen and most of them looked over twenty-two. I later found out one or two were twenty-six—practically old men. They all had at least one season of rookie ball behind them—and I had thought I was so hot for skipping it and getting right into Class A ball. Now I was regretting it.

We stopped at a greasy spoon for breakfast, then on to Cedar Rapids. We were playing a St. Louis Cardinals Class A farm team.

At the game I hit a home run to center field on the first pitch thrown to me. As I rounded the bases, I was thinking, *Golleee! I'm not gonna be around here long at this rate! I'm not so bad after all! I can handle these guys!*

I think we won the game.

On the second day, the first time up I hit another homer! I was feeling great. I think we won that game too.

From that point, it was downhill all the way.

After that second game, the talent caught onto me. In baseball, every player has strengths and weaknesses. In those first two games the Cards pitchers didn't know my strengths, so they didn't know how to pitch to me, which was probably why I hit those two home runs.

After they had confronted me a couple of times, they knew how to work me. Those first games they had pitched me fastballs. I didn't see a lot of fastballs after that. What I did see was a lot of curve balls and change-ups. I found myself swinging three times before the pitch ever got to the plate. The ball seemed to be moving in slow motion!

I had rarely seen change-ups in high school ball. I had seldom seen really good breaking balls. I was baffled! I never knew there was anything like this in baseball!

The other thing was that in high school, I was used to playing two or three times a week. Now, I was playing every day. All of a sudden, baseball wasn't just a game. It was hard, hard work. After a few weeks, I began to get really tired.

My batting average was an anemic .190. That was difficult for me to take, because in high school I had always been able to hit. And, as I've said, the other players were older and more experienced than I was. They ran rings around me. They were eating my lunch, and I couldn't do a thing about it.

I grew increasingly angry, frustrated, and bitter. I had no idea that somebody could make a ball do things like that, or of the techniques of good catching—like blocking balls, stuff like that. Evidently I had been succeeding all those years on raw talent. Now I knew that wasn't enough. It was a hard way to find out, let me tell you. There's also a mental side to baseball I hadn't been aware of. I found out baseball is a game of failures. A hitter can fail seven times out of ten and still be considered very successful. I grew increasingly tired and frustrated, and as a result my playing got worse and worse.

The manager never said a thing to me. For all practical purposes he was ignoring me. After I had been there about a month, he was suddenly fired, and a new man, Karl Keel, was sent in.

As soon as Keel arrived, he made me report early each day for a workout—throwing balls, blocking balls, hitting. Every day he had me out there, working out in 95 degree temperatures and about 100 percent humidity.

I'd get a little break when he'd buy me a hamburger. Then I'd take regular batting practice with the team, and *then* I'd play a full ball game!

I really wanted to improve, but I hadn't thought it would take so much hard work. Shoot, why was I the only player who had to do it? Shows how immature I was. I was green and eighteen years old. What did I know? In high school, I never thought about baseball. I just did it. It was easy and fun then.

The irony was that after weeks of extra workouts, my game hadn't improved a lick. So many times I wanted to chuck it all, quit, and go home. I've heard that about 95 percent of minor league players never make it to the majors. But I didn't worry about it. I would have been relieved if they had released me that first season. But they didn't; they just worked me to death.

I called home as often as I could. When they'd ask me how things were, I'd simply say, "All right, I guess." And inside I'd be all torn up, wanting to tell them how bad things really were, that I wanted to come home. But I didn't. There was no way I could tell them I was down in the dumps. When I'd hang up, invariably I'd shed a few tears.

I was actually making a few friends. If they weren't really close buddies, it was because they were older. Two guys who lived in a nice house nearby began asking me to come over and watch a little TV. They had a comfortable apartment, and it was good to get away from the "haunted house" for a little bit.

Their names were Charlie and Dan. They knew I was having trouble, so they kind of took me under their wing. We spent whole nights watching TV and talking.

Charlie and Dan always had six-packs of beer in the refrigerator, and they would offer me a can. But I always said, "No thanks." In spite of what I had seen in the visitors' clubhouse at Baltimore the previous spring, I still thought it was really bad for an athlete to drink. I didn't want any part of it; what they did was their affair.

One night, after a particularly bad game in Appleton, Wisconsin, Charlie and Dan said, "Hey, D.P., why don't you come relax with us a little, have a few beers?"

I hesitated. "Aw, come on!" Charlie insisted. "You plannin' to sit in your room all night like a bump on a log, watchin' old movies on the boob tube?"

It did sound ridiculous, so I went with them. They took me to a bar, a little place called The Shack that had only a tiny bar and four or five tables. I remember we had to go downstairs, like going into a cellar.

It was dark in there, and kind of strange and scary. Scary, because I was afraid of drinking and bars. In fact, I had never been in a bar before. Part of me knew it was wrong even before they pushed the door open.

Charlie and Dan ordered beers. "And one for my man here!" Dan said, clapping me on the shoulder. Well, why not? I was tired and frustrated, and I needed the companionship.

I remember that once in high school they tried to get me to drink a beer at a party. I took one sip and hated it. (Everybody had thought *that* was hilarious!)

So the taste wasn't totally unfamiliar. Now, as I took a sip, I remembered—it was bitter and awful. But I took a few more swigs and it tasted a little less bad. Charlie and Dan were tickled to death that they had finally gotten me to try a beer.

Anyway, before I had that first bottle finished, Dan announced, "Men, we're not budging from here until this whole table is covered with empty bottles!" And he dramatically passed his hand over the table, indicating he meant the entire table top.

By now I had a pleasant buzz. Anybody could have persuaded me to do anything and I'd have been game. A part of me was scared by his challenge, but another part said, *Why not*? There was something delightfully wicked and macho about the suggestion. Just like a movie, where they drink one another "under the table." So that's what we proceeded to do—drink one another under the table.

Well, actually I had only about four bottles that first night, but it was more than enough for a greenhorn. All at once life seemed wonderful again. Everybody—I mean *everybody*—was my friend. Especially my good buddies, Charlie and Dan. My rotten .190 batting average didn't seem so bad either.

Another effect was that suddenly I wasn't shy anymore. It seemed like a miracle. All my life I had been afraid of pretty girls. Now, I found myself ambling up to one of those tiny tables, where two girls sat perched on two tiny chairs. I actually asked one of them to dance. The girl looked at her friend and giggled a bit, then got up and walked ahead of me to the postage-stamp-sized dance floor. Just like that! It was easy!

As I held her close, I was mentally kicking myself for not having been bolder up until now. And, amazingly, I wasn't lumbering around like a robot, stepping on her toes. Shoot, I was gliding around that little dance floor like old Fred Astaire! I thought happily, *Hey, this beer brings out the real me! I'll have to try it again!*

And I did. Not that I became a raging alcoholic, but a couple nights a week, I might have a few bottles with my buddies. It helped me to relax; it took the edge off things after a hard, discouraging day. I couldn't figure out why anybody would be down on drinking.

That dismal first season finally (mercifully) came to an end, and I returned home. Oh, boy, was I one happy guy the day I said good-by to Clinton, Iowa. I was so glad to see the family again. I

73

was as honest as I could be about my less-than-brilliant first season.

Three weeks after arriving home, I left for Tempe, Arizona, to play winter ball. I wasn't looking forward to it. I had had enough baseball for one season. But the Brewers practically insisted that I go.

10

Pot and Other Pleasures

Winter ball in Tempe might have been better called "fall ball," because it lasted only a month or so, ending just before Thanksgiving. I was pleasantly surprised that my stats improved a bit. I put it down to the fact that things were more relaxed, less pressured. The games we played were for practice; they weren't "for real," so I played better. Also, I was getting used to being away from home, and the professional baseball environment wasn't new or strange anymore. The minute I got to Tempe, I had a reunion with Charlie and Dan, who had also gone to winter ball.

I moved into an apartment complex near Arizona State University. The new place was nice, a lot better than that old house in Clinton. Just talking about that "haunted house" gave us some good laughs.

A few weeks after I arrived, we were watching TV one night. Then Charlie told Dan in a conspiratorial tone that he had some "great Colombian gold." I didn't know what he was talking about. He disappeared into the bedroom and came back a few minutes later carrying some stuff. He sat down on the floor Indian-style, with a small plastic bag filled with something that looked like oregano. I had never seen it before, but I knew right away it was grass. Then he took cigarette papers, licked the end of one, sprinkled some of the pot in it, and rolled a lumpy "joint." The ends looked pinched, and he lightly moistened them in his mouth.

Of course I had heard of marijuana; everyone had, but none of the kids at Southeast High ever smoked it, at least none that I knew. They were into beer-drinking. We always thought of pot as evil stuff. Seeing Charlie roll that joint really turned me off and made me wonder what kind of guy he was behind his friendly exterior.

He lit the joint and took a long drag (he called it a "toke"). He held his breath and passed the joint to Dan, who also took a "hit." Dan held his breath, too, and then passed the cigarette to me.

"No, I don't want any!" I protested. "I've never done that before. I've never even smoked regular cigarettes."

"This ain't like cigarettes. It's good for you!" Charlie laughed.

"If he don't want it, he don't want it!" Dan said, taking another toke. "Stuff's too good to waste anyway." Then he cocked his head and pushed the joint toward me. "Wanna try it anyway, D.P.?" Though his voice was casual, there was more than a hint of challenge in it.

I hesitated—the same way I had when they introduced me to beer. But this was a lot more serious. At least beer was legal! I'd never done anything illegal before. And in 1970 the penalties for possession were really harsh. I think you could get five years in some states just for having a joint *on* you. I didn't want to get a record, maybe go to jail. Nothing was worth that!

Still, I hated being a party-pooper. I looked at the lumpy white joint between Dan's fingers, the smoke curling and eddying.

"Come on, D.P.!" he chided. "Don't be a total pain in the a——!" (I *knew* that's what he had been thinking.)

Reaching out, I carefully took the joint. They both leaned forward, suddenly very interested. Charlie's expression was positively gleeful; Dan's was mildly approving.

"Now, take a slow drag and hold it in for as long as you can, so you can get the full benefit," Dan instructed me.

I put the joint between my lips and breathed in, but not too deeply. I held my breath and passed the joint to Charlie, like an expert. When I thought I couldn't hold my breath any longer, I exhaled. A pale steam of moist smoke emerged.

"That's it!" Charlie said. "Now, next time draw in a little more! Wait. Here, let me roll another one!"

We smoked six joints that night, or maybe eight. Those guys acted as though they were in seventh heaven, but I was wondering what all the fuss was about. It didn't do a thing to me or for me. They couldn't believe it. "Don't worry about it, D.P.," Charlie said when I told him. "Sometimes you don't feel nothin' the first time, or even the first two times. Give it a while."

The apartment complex I lived in was filled mostly with single students from the nearby university. It was a swinging place with a swinging name: Sin City.

One night my friends and I were sitting outside our building, partying. I had had a few beers, but instead of being relaxed, I was still restless. The night was warm, and I wanted to do something, but I didn't know what. I knew I *didn't* want to waste such a beautiful night getting soused with my teammates. Besides we had a game the next day.

A girl was coming along the walk. It was hard to see her features in the soft darkness, but I could make out blondish hair. Not too pretty, but not that bad looking either, at least in the dark. She slowed a little as she approached us.

"Hi," she said in a soft voice that didn't sound at all unfriendly.

"Well, hi, yourself!" I replied. "Whatcha doin'?"

"Oh, nothing much . . . just hanging out. Can I have a beer?"

From the way she was looking me up and down I could tell she was interested in more than a beer. I gave her a beer. A short while later, she was up in my apartment, and I had my first experience of complete sexual intimacy.

I was a grown man and single, full of energy and a hunger to experience all the pleasures life has to offer a young man. What was I supposed to do in my off hours? Read a book?

After Tempe, I returned home for the Thanksgiving and Christmas holidays. By now I figured I could have a few beers with my brothers and my buddy Joe Smart, as long as we didn't do it at home.

In March, I reported to spring training at the Brewers' major league camp in Tempe. Now the pressure was back, but not as bad as it had been in Clinton. The Brewers' training camp was much like a minor league complex, nothing fancy like Dodgertown in Florida. Still, it was the best training facility in Arizona, and we played out of Diablo Stadium, the closest thing to a major league ballpark in the area.

I did fairly well that spring. I was the last guy to be cut from the major league roster.

I remember one incident that is still etched in my memory. I was only there a week or so when the Brewers got whipped in an exhibition game. After the game, another minor-leaguer, Jerry Bell, and I took batting practice for about an hour before we hit the showers. We were both southern boys, so while we lathered up we sang country-western songs: "It's cryin' time again...." Oh, we were having a grand time; just two good ol' boys, trying to outsing one another.

All of a sudden Dave Bristol, the manager, came flying into the shower room, fit to be tied. "Don't you *ever* let me catch you singin', whistlin', laughin', or smilin' after we lose a game!" he bellowed. "I don't care if it's the next day. If I do catch you, I'll ship you rookies right back to the boonies!" Then he turned and stomped out of the clubhouse.

We stood there, stunned. The only sound was the hissing of the showers. We got dressed quietly and slipped out of the clubhouse.

It was my first real encounter with Dave Bristol, a man who was to have a profound effect on my career in baseball.

On St. Patrick's Day we played a long exhibition game (almost three hours) against the San Francisco Giants. In the top of the sixth they put me in to pinch-hit. There was one man on base, and I was nervous as all get-out. The Giants' formidable star Gaylord Perry was pitching.

Perry fed me two fastballs. I connected on the second one. The crowd of almost fifteen hundred was on its feet as the ball flew out of the park at the 365-foot mark—a two-run homer! It was the crucial hit of the game, resulting in a 10-3 win for us.

The next day the papers were full of news about the Brewers' "current phenom." I told the reporters that I credited my improved performance to winter ball. I concluded my remarks by saying, "Being here in spring training gives you a kind of incentive."

I was tickled pink when a few days later, Brewers general manager Frank Lane confirmed my hopes by telling sports reporters, "If Porter doesn't make it to the major leagues, then we might as well junk our minor league system."

So what if they were going to send me back to Double A or even Class A again? The fact remained that management had its eye on me, determined to give me as much exposure as possible, which made my future look bright. And then to read statements like Lane's, well, it was all extremely flattering. I didn't mind being the last guy cut.

There was some talk about bumping me up to Triple A with the Evansville, Indiana, team. But in the end I was sent back to Class A ball in the Midwest League with a new team—the Danville (Illinois) Warriors.

11

The Danville Warrior

It was a great experience to return to Class A. I can only compare it to the feeling you have returning to high school in your senior year, after having been a lowly underclassman. You've got it made in the shade; you know what it's all about, and you're comfortable with yourself and your surroundings.

And Danville was a neat town. The Warriors were a popular team with Danvillites. We were real stars to the locals. Our team averaged bigger crowds than any other team in the Midwest League. We always got big play on the sports pages of the local papers. Just being on the team made folks admire us.

We had a nice little apartment, and I met many nice people. Not that there weren't nice people in Clinton; there may have been, but I had been in a kind of shell that first year, hiding away. Now it was, "Look out world, here I come!"

There were a few guys on the Warriors that I had played with in Clinton but most of them were fresh out of rookie league. So returning to Class A ball, I felt like one of the top guys.

We played our season opener on April 25, 1971, against the Quincy Cubs, the Class A team of the Chicago Cubs. I had my picture in the paper, along with our pitcher Bill Travers and the Warriors' new manager, Sandy Johnson. The story described me as the "rifle-armed Darrell Porter, the No. 1 draft choice of the Brewers a year ago." I liked that description: "rifle-armed." I was determined to live up to my billing.

I didn't. I wouldn't say that I slipped into a slump: I started out in one! In the first two weeks or so, I was 0 for 15! I don't remember what was particularly wrong, but the stats speak for themselves. Boy, talk about being discouraged!

Then in early May we traveled back to Clinton for a series of games with my former team, the Pilots, who were now a co-op team—a team made up of players from different major league organizations. I don't know whether it was playing against my former team that did it, or what. All I know is I broke out of that slump with a bang.

After three scoreless innings, and with two men out in the fourth, I drove in two runs with a fly ball that the left-fielder lost in the lights and missed. Then, in the seventh, we scored two more runs. When I came to bat, I was beginning to feel good. After they pitched me a couple of balls, high and outside, I finally connected solidly and drove one 350 feet over the right-field fence!

The final score: Danville 5, Pilots 0. Something told me I was out of that slump for good!

We did really well in the first half of the season. By mid-May we were in the midst of a hot winning streak that lasted for ten games. Before it ended I had hit my sixth home run of the season.

By the middle of June the Warriors were leading in the Midwest League's South Division with thirty-three wins and only thirteen losses. But three weeks later, we were trailing the league co-leaders, Quincy and Quad Cities, four games. On July 8, in another game with the Pilots, I cracked my seventeenth homer of the season, and we beat them 10–4.

We eventually pulled ahead and won the first-half pennant in the league. I was so proud to be with a top team!

One of the most exciting things that year was an exhibition game between the Brewers' major league team and the Atlanta Braves. The Braves had originally been Milwaukee's team, before moving on to supposedly greener pastures in the South. Folks in Milwaukee were really burned up over the desertion, and resentment was still running strong several years later.

The controversial game was scheduled smack in the middle of the season, and it was to be played at Milwaukee's County Stadium. (They had no axes to grind in Atlanta, so it wouldn't have been nearly as much fun playing it there!) Oh, let me tell you, those Milwaukee fans were out for blood!

Imagine my surprise—shock, actually—when I was called up to catch that game! It was to be my first appearance in a major league stadium. To say I was on cloud nine would be an understatement. I was on cloud *twenty*-nine!

My first time up, I got a single. Then I got another hit, and I picked a guy off at first and threw another guy out at second. I was two for three, and I felt I had performed well. We won the game, 1–0.

Just about that time, I heard reports that Frank Lane had been approached by the Orioles, who offered to deal four players for me, including veteran pitcher Dave McNally. When Lane declined, the Orioles' scout stood there open-mouthed. That ended the conversation. Lane explained to reporters: "Darrell's a major leaguer behind the plate, and he'll improve his hitting. He's a potential superstar." I wish I could have shared Lane's confidence in my abilities. But I was still only in Class A ball.

In the second half of the season, things didn't go well for the Warriors. By mid-August we had dropped nine of the last ten games. Now, at that time, the military draft had been reinstated, and my birthdate was ninth on Uncle Sam's list. I was ordered by the Selective Service to take a physical. They found I had high blood pressure—160 over 80, something I had been aware of since my high-school football days.

After checking me a few more times, Uncle Sam shipped me back to Danville, a 4-F. I must admit I was relieved.

The Warriors continued to struggle for the rest of August, and we managed to get into a one-game play-off for the South Division championship, which we lost, though we gave a good account of ourselves. The Warriors drew almost eighty-six thousand fans that year, which was some kind of record, all the more remarkable since it was only their second season. That loyalty from the people of Danville really helped us do as well as we did.

At the end of the regular season, I was honored at a Fan Appreciation Day as the Most Popular Warrior of the season. I had hit twenty-four home runs, had a .271 batting average, and had driven in sixty-nine runs. It wasn't a great year, but I had improved a lot.

The frosting was put on the cake when, about a week before the end of the season, our coach came up to me after a game and said, "Hey, Darrell, guess you won't be going home right away."

"Why?" I asked, startled.

"Because you're going to Milwaukee! They want you to catch for 'em."

"You're kidding!"

"No, I'm not. Better call your folks and let 'em know."

What a thrill to be called up to play the last month of the major league season! Of course, it was a tryout. I could be back in the minors the following spring. But then again, maybe not.

Still, I had mixed feelings. I had been counting on going home in September; I was psyched up for it. I really missed my family and friends. Besides, I was physically tired. Having prepared myself to hang up my catcher's mask, I was now going to have to put it back on, so to speak. Then suddenly it hit me—I was scared again. I was doing well in Danville, but would I fail and lose all my confidence in Milwaukee?

I flew up first class. Tony Siegel was there to meet me at the airport. Shades of Baltimore.

Much as I loved going first class with the major league team, I knew it could be temporary, like all the other times. It wouldn't be smart to get too used to steak, if they were going to put me back on a hamburger diet. I kept telling myself they had only called me up for additional experience. It was better not to think beyond that.

Had I been able to see into the future, I would have been a lot more confident. The fact was that I was to stay in the minors only one more season. Most guys struggle up through the minor league divisions three, four, even five years before making it to the majors—an unbelievable grind—if they make it at all. As it turned out, I was one of the fortunate ones. On the other hand, I was afraid I wasn't ready, and in retrospect I certainly wasn't.

It seems that Manager Dave Bristol, however, the guy who had chewed me out the previous spring while I was standing naked as a jay-bird in the shower, had dreams of bringing up another Johnny Bench—and I was it. It's strange, but for years I had been compared to Bench, the great catcher of the Cincinnati Reds. He was from Oklahoma, too. The comparison was flattering, but it was one more pressure I had to live under.

So it was that on Thursday, September 2, 1971, I made my major league, regular-season debut. I didn't do well my first time out. I was 0 for 3.

Later my first week, things got worse. We were playing the Royals in Kansas City, at their old stadium. They stole about nine bases off me. To cap it all, in the ninth inning with the game tied, their Amos Otis (I think it was) stole third. My throw to try to catch him was wild—it ended up in left field—and Amos scored the winning run. I was crushed. In the clubhouse, I hid in the bathroom and cried silently. *What am I doing here?* I thought bitterly.

But also that first week, in a game against the California Angels, I got my very first hit in the major leagues, driving in two runs in the first inning and contributing to the Brewers' 6–4 victory. I was pleased over that, let me tell you! A few days later I hit my first home run.

About a week and a half later, I wrote the following letter to the family, in which I did some restrained bragging. I also filled them in on my new salary, which I thought was pretty good:

I guess you've already heard about my 1st homerun. It was a good feeling. We were behind 4–3, so I tied the game. We went on to win on Dave May's double....Well, here's a little money I thought I'd better send home. I'm making $1,074.48 every two weeks. Not bad, huh? I bring home $748.25.

Although it's great playing up here, I'll certainly be glad to get home. I don't think I'm going to winter ball. If I can think up an excuse. I'm exhausted with baseball presently.

I went to the doctor here and had a complete physical, and guess what he found out? He found I had high blood pressure! Isn't that something? I couldn't believe it. Ha! Ha!...They didn't put me on anything though. The doctor doesn't think there's anything wrong with me....

Well, I'll close for now, I've got to hurry to the park.

I love you all,
Darrell

P.S. Tell Jim & Pat hello for me. And tell Jim I heard they had fire trucks on the golf course, 'cause he was burning them up! 78, wow!

Actually, the blood pressure never did give me any trouble afterwards, and, who knows: if it hadn't been for that somewhat negative health thing, I might have been drafted. At the very least that would have put my career on hold, and it might have changed the whole course of my life.

12

Teri

I returned home at the end of the Brewers' regular season, feeling better about my career and myself. It wasn't definite that I'd get moved up to the major league team permanently, but it was a possibility. I did know that I was going to the big league training camp the next spring. One step at a time was my motto.

I spent a couple of weeks unwinding, visiting with the family. I was drinking a little beer. Life was great!

One night at a party, my buddy (I'll call him Dave, to protect the guilty) turned me on to Quaaludes—or "ludes" to druggies. It was a good-sized pill. "What is it?" I asked nervously. I mean, trying pot was one thing, but pills? That was for *junkies*, wild people.

"Look, D.P., it's not bad for you. It's only a muscle relaxer," Dave assured me. "Shoot, man, doctors give it to people with strained backs! It's *medicine*, man! It ain't gonna hurt you!"

I wasn't totally convinced, but everybody else at the party seemed to be doing them, so I figured I might as well. Whenever there was a contest between peer pressure and doing what was right, peer pressure won out. I wanted to fit in.

I took the lude. I was sold on them instantly. Quaaludes made me feel wonderful! Like beer—only better! Better than pot, which still didn't do much for me.

Quaaludes. Oh, wow! As soon as the drug kicked into my system, I got a fantastic "rush." Then my head seemed to get a little numb, but pleasantly so.

"Oh, Dave!" I cried. "I feel just like I'm a-gonna float clear off the flooooor!"

"Hold old D.P. down, Dave!" somebody laughed.

I was just floating and grinning. I felt totally relaxed. It wasn't scary at all, just a relaxed, pleasant sensation, which is why Quaaludes are classified in drug circles as "downers." They make you feel relaxed and mellow.

Of course, I felt a little guilt after the effects of that first lude wore off. I always felt a little guilty after trying something new. It was as if, with each step I took into the world of drugs, I had to satisfy my conscience by feeling guilt. Guilt is supposed to serve as a brake, to stop people from doing what's wrong. But I turned it upside down, so that having felt a few pangs of guilt, I was free to get on with my pleasures. And at each step along that gently descending path, I also convinced myself that whatever drug it happened to be, it wasn't so bad. How could it be, when everybody was doing it and it made me feel so good?

At any rate, I began taking Quaaludes occasionally, and only in the off-season. Never while playing—I'd have been zonked out on the field if I did. They eventually became my "drug of choice," as they say in drug circles. With a lude nothing bothered me. I mean *nothing*. With them I reached some kind of heaven on earth.

One night my buddy Joe Smart and I went to a local bowling alley. I remember it was my turn. I had the ball in my hand and was just about to make my approach when I saw this girl. Well, I almost dropped that bowling ball on my toes.

"Hey, Joe, who's that?" I asked. She looked vaguely familiar, but I was sure that if I had ever seen her before I would have remembered. She was wearing white jeans and a dark blouse. I swear, she was the prettiest girl I had ever seen . . . about five five with shoulder-length dark hair, a natural Jane Fonda type.

"Oh, that's Teri Brown," Joe replied.

I gawked. "How come I've never seen her before?"

"Oh, she's been around. Come to think of it, she used to like your brother Eddie, when they were in junior high."

I just couldn't stop looking. All at once that bowling alley seemed like a palace.

"Her father owns a jewelry store, Floyd Brown Jewelers," Joe was saying.

She had a great figure, and her eyes, even at a distance, were large, dark, and expressive. I think I began to fall in love with Teri right there, with people laughing and talking and bowling balls knocking down pins. She made a strike, right to my heart!

We didn't meet that night. She didn't even seem to notice me. All I could do was stand and stare, though I would have loved to talk to her.

My chance came a week or so later. I made some inquiries and found out that James Pilkington's brother, R.B., was a good friend of Teri's. I got R.B. to take me over to her house one night to meet her. I called her the very next night after that and made a date.

That date, as with many first dates, turned out to be awkward, with the two of us guardedly getting to know one another.

Teri Brown came from a different world from mine. I was just an Okie from the wrong side of the tracks. Her family was well-to-do. The jewelry store had been founded by her grandfather and was now owned by her dad, Floyd Brown.

Floyd and Teri's mother had divorced when Teri was just two, and his second wife, Martha Lee, adopted Teri and her two older brothers, Michael and Jeff. So Teri had two mothers, a rather confusing state of affairs, complicated by the fact that Floyd and Martha Lee divorced when Teri was twelve.

Floyd was an executive who led an active lifestyle. He couldn't spend a great deal of time with his three children, but he loved them and took them on many, many trips. Teri, it seems, had been everywhere—Los Angeles, Hawaii, Las Vegas, Europe. She grew up going to art museums, the theater, and the ballet. Her twelfth birthday party was held at a swanky nightclub. At fifteen she was more sophisticated and mature than I was at nineteen.

Regardless, we began to see each other regularly. We went bowling, to the movies, and to football games to see my little brother Eddie play. (Eddie was now the Spartans' quarterback and Mr. Southeast High!) I felt so good when I was with Teri, as if I was somehow more complete. And when we'd say good night, I felt as if I was dying a little, like a piece of me was being taken away.

In spite of her family's relative affluence, Teri had not been totally happy. I could tell from the way she spoke that her father's two divorces in the space of ten years had been traumatic for her and had left scars. Then, when she was just seven, her older brother Michael had been killed in a fall from a horse. I couldn't bear the thought of Teri's being sad or unhappy. I was so in love with her. In time, she came to love me, too.

My folks were crazy about her. She and my sister Pat got along great. By Christmas we were already talking about marriage. In spite of her youth, Teri, as I've already pointed out, seemed very mature. She felt she had already been everywhere, seen everything, and done everything. She said she was ready to settle down. We set the wedding date for May 30, 1972. Teri would be sixteen then; I would be twenty. Also, I would be finished with spring training, and I hoped I would be in the major leagues by May. The timing seemed perfect.

In March, I reported to spring training at Tempe, with the major league team. In April, I left camp as a big-leaguer. I had finally made it! Manager Dave Bristol, still smarting over the fact that the Brewers had finished in the cellar in the Eastern Division the previous fall, had hopes that I had matured over the winter. The idea was that I'd share catching duties with veteran Ellie Rodriguez. Ellie needn't have worried. Early on I strained my throwing arm and was out over a week. When I came back, the muscles were still sore, which affected my throwing. That bothered me, because throwing was always my strong suit.

To make things worse, I went into a terrible hitting slump. I couldn't understand it. I was fouling off the kinds of pitches I usually hit. And my old weak spot, the change-up, was there to frustrate me. I knew I shouldn't try to pull it or hit it too hard, but most of the time I'd overswing, or jerk my head and wind up looking into the dugout.

My batting average sank and sank until it was in the .100s.

Everybody was telling me not to be so down on myself, offering me all kinds of advice about how to get out of that slump. For a while I tried to hit everything out of the park, like a wild man.

One day, when I was feeling particularly frustrated, one of my teammates called me over. "Here, big guy," he said in a whisper, "try *this!*" He slipped me a capsule that looked like a Contac, except it was green.

I took the little green capsule, a "greenie" he called it. (It was an amphetamine, classified in the drug culture as an "upper" because it speeds up your system and makes you feel energetic.) It was my first encounter with drugs while playing baseball.

And it did seem to give me energy. In a few minutes, I was full of vim and vigor. I felt great. It was like, "Go get 'em, Tiger!"

It was all for nothing anyway. Just when I thought I was starting to hit well, Dave Bristol called me into his office. He told me they were going to send me down to the Triple A team in Evansville, Indiana. I was stunned. I was frustrated. I had really failed this time. But I was relieved, too, that I was getting out of a high-pressure situation.

"We want you to work on your hitting, Darrell," he explained. "Look, I know how disappointing this must be for you, but I'm sure with a little bit of additional work, the next time you come up, it'll be for good."

I consoled myself with the thought that it would give my arm a chance to heal completely. And Dave was right, I would get in some good solid work on my hitting. So it was with mixed emotions that I packed my bags and flew to Evansville.

13

Triple A

Being sent down wrecked our plans for a May wedding. Here I was—supposed to make it to the majors that spring, so we could be married. Now things were all loused up. I was back in the boonies.

Things weren't much better in Evansville, as far as my playing went. Worse maybe. In my first twelve times at bat I failed to get a hit.

Finally in a four-game series against the Tulsa Oilers, I had not one but *two* game-winning homers. I also broke up a no-hitter by one of their pitchers with a home run in the eighth, then tripled in the eleventh, and scored the winning run.

"I've always been a slow starter" was the way I explained the change to reporters. They asked me about how I felt being sent down. "I try not to be impatient," I said. "I'm only twenty, and I have a lot of time. But I want to be in the major leagues next year, and I'll be very disappointed if I'm not up there in two years." (I always had an inordinate desire to succeed mixed with my fear of failure.)

I said I was sure that working in Evansville under a manager who was a former catcher (Del Crandall, who had been with the Braves) had helped my catching tremendously. And it had.

Under Crandall's guidance, I gradually worked the soreness out of my throwing arm. My batting average stayed rotten, only .195—except when we played Tulsa.

We were scheduled to play a series against the Oklahoma City 89ers in early June. I really missed Teri, and she missed me too. (I had a high phone bill to prove it, too.) I talked it over with her, and we decided to get married anyway, while I was in town to play those games. We set the date for June 2, 1972.

The ceremony was held in Martha Lee's back yard. It was a simple affair, with just the two families and a few close friends. Teri didn't wear a traditional wedding gown, but she was all in white, a real vision.

It was a religious ceremony, but I didn't feel particularly inspired about the spiritual aspects of the thing. I was hardly conscious of God as we took our vows. All I knew was that I was marrying the girl of my dreams, and that was enough for me.

I was playing a game that night, so after the reception we went to the ballpark. I can't say my mind was on the game, what with my bride up in the stands, rooting for us. I don't even remember whether we won. That night we checked into the bridal suite at the Lincoln Plaza Hotel.

I was really happy. We both were. Though I didn't know it at the time, when Teri married me she secretly gave up her plans for a career in business, something she had always dreamed of. When she said, "I do," she shut down those dreams and made a vow to herself to be a good wife and a good mother to our children. We were going to live happily ever after.

Teri traveled back to Evansville with the team. We got a nice little apartment and set up housekeeping, though the place was sparsely furnished. I think we had a lawn chair in the living room, along with some rented furniture. What did we care? We were in love!

I still had some of my $70,000 signing bonus left, and I made more than most of the guys on the team, about $1500 take–home a month, so we did quite well.

Teri didn't know how to cook. Some of the other wives showed her how to make bacon and eggs. She experimented. On me. Seriously, I tried to encourage her, even when the results were less than perfect. She tried so hard to be an ideal wife, and that's not easy to do at sixteen.

One night we had baked chicken. A really strange smell hit my nose when I walked in the door. "Hey, darlin', that smells really good!" I lied, giving her a hug and a kiss.

"I don't know," she said, "smells kind of funny for some reason."

"It's going to be just fine!" I assured her.

I sat down while Teri served the chicken, which certainly did look all golden brown and delicious. "Oh, this is fine!" I said, taking a bite. And it really was! I ate what was on my plate, then began cutting a little more—which pleased Teri to no end. When I sliced through the rib cage, that strange smell hit me again, only now it was *bad*.

All this weird-looking stuff started bulging out of that chicken. "What's this?" I asked her. Teri leaned over to look, her face crimson. She had left the innards in that bird! No matter, though, that the girl had trouble cooking. She was beautiful and I loved her. Oh, how I loved her!

About two months after we were married, I brought a bag of pot home one night. I wondered what Teri's reaction would be. "Honey," I said, "look what the guys gave me. Shoot, I never have tried this stuff before!" The lie rolled off my tongue easily.

"Darrell, I've seen pot before," she said with a who-do-you-think-you're-trying-to-kid look.

"Ever smoke it?" I asked, undoing the bag.

"No, and I don't intend to start," she said quickly, then turned and walked to the window. With her back to me she added, "If you *have* to do it, I guess I can't stop you."

Hey, I thought, *at least she's not giving me a hard time about it!*

That joint was the first one I had ever rolled. It looked like a corkscrew. But I smoked it. It was the first of many I would smoke at home. I guess I wasn't thinking too much about Teri's feelings. She was only sixteen, and I was calling the shots.

That pot had a scary effect on me. Until then I had never really been high on pot. I got a very strange feeling—something I had never felt before. I was sure somebody had spiked the grass with LSD or mescaline or one of those really high-powered hallucinogenic drugs.

"Oh, honey!" I moaned. "I—I've got to go to bed! Sleep this off! Something's wrong with the pot." Teri helped me to the bedroom. I closed my eyes. Maybe I was going to die! *I was falling into a deep black hole.*

When I opened my eyes the next morning, the sun was streaming into the room and my head was perfectly clear. (That was the great thing about pot: there was never any hangover.) I decided whatever that weird sensation was, it must just be the normal pot high that I had never felt before.

The experience made me curious, and I wanted to experiment. The next night I smoked two more joints, and I felt really great. I wanted to stay awake, enjoy it, really flow with that high, with Teri by my side.

When I looked at the ginger jar lamp on the end table, I was delighted and intrigued by its graceful shape. It stood there, totally composed, self-contained, and perfect, its base resting gently against the polished wood of the table (also graceful and self-contained). I had never realized how distinct and defined an object can be from its surroundings. Before I tried pot, all the furnishings in a room tended to blend together for me. In fact, I hardly noticed them at all. Now, my senses seemed to be open, and I was seeing things in a totally new way.

Before long, smoking pot became an almost nightly ritual with me—dinner and then a joint or two.

I began to have some really fun times with people while I was doing pot. It used to make me feel happy—silly, actually. I never thought about it as being bad for me at all. The only twinge I might have had was wondering what my folks would say if they knew their all-American boy was doing pot.

However, there were bad trips too. One night, for example, we were having dinner at a restaurant. It was one of the first times I was high in public. All at once it seemed as though our table was on a dais or pedestal of some sort, because we seemed to be up above everyone else, looking down. It was very disturbing. People were looking at us and snickering. I was sure they knew I was stoned. It was my first bout of marijuana-induced paranoia. There would be others.

But, as I say, for the most part, in the beginning getting high on pot was sheer pleasure. Besides, everybody was doing it. You were square if you didn't.

Triple A

Pot didn't affect our marriage in the least—or so I thought. I didn't *think* it affected my game either, because I only smoked it at night or after a game or on my days off. The only thing I'd take on the field was an occasional greenie.

I did so well in Evansville that toward the end of the summer there was talk that I'd be sent back up to Milwaukee come spring. And this time for good.

We returned to Oklahoma City. We had a fun fall and winter that year. We went everywhere, did everything. We were a very popular young couple, the perfect couple: the beautiful girl and the professional athlete on his way to the major leagues.

Teri and I were looking forward to moving up to Milwaukee in the spring. It had to happen now; the time seemed so right. It would be the fulfillment of all our dreams. Or so we thought.

14

In the Majors

The sports columns kept quoting Brewers president Bud Selig's refrain: "This is the year we're expecting our farm system to bear fruit." He had been saying it all winter.

"We've been bringing along a bunch of talented youngsters," he crowed, "and now we think they are capable of making a contribution."

The "talented youngsters," also described by one sports columnist as the Kiddie Korps, included guys like Gorman Thomas, Pedro Garcia, and me. I was being described as a "can't miss" prospect after my season of sharpening up at Evansville. I still had my doubts. Thomas, an outfielder, and Garcia, second base, had played with me in Danville for the Warriors. Like me, Gorman Thomas had been a number one draft choice (in 1968).

Dave Bristol had gotten the ax. I liked Dave; he really believed in me. And now he was gone. But Del Crandall, who had managed me in Evansville, was brought in. That was to my benefit, because he had been a pretty good catcher in his playing days and had worked with me part of one season.

Again, as in the previous spring, I was pitted against incumbent catcher Ellie Rodriguez. But instead of becoming rivals, we tended to complement one another. Early in the season, Crandall platooned us, putting me against right-handed pitchers and Ellie against lefties. Ellie was the more consistent hitter and had the experience, while I hit with more power. It worked nicely.

Ellie had broken his hand in spring training, and when he returned, his hitting was off. But by early June, he was hitting so well (.286) that Crandall used him steadily and made me the designated hitter, which I didn't mind at all because I wasn't getting to catch that much anyway. Besides, I enjoyed being the designated hitter. If it weren't for that, I'd have been warming the bench. I had lots of time to make it as the regular catcher, too. I wasn't itching to push anybody out.

And I did really well as designated hitter. Crandall was making all the right moves with the team, too. In May and June we went on a winning streak, which I reckon made Bud Selig sleep easier at night. The Kiddie Korps wasn't making a liar out of him.

By July, Rodriguez's batting began to slip. Crandall decided to switch us around: I became the regular catcher and was used steadily in the line-up, and Ellie was used occasionally as designated hitter.

It was my big break, and I rose to the occasion. By the All-Star break I had forty-six hits, and half of them were for extra bases.

Although Ellie admitted in print that he'd rather catch than hit, he seemed happy for me. He told reporters we were the Dynamic Duo, like Batman and Robin. (He made me Batman because I was bigger.) But in spite of the brave face he put on things, Ellie must have been worried. There was talk that he would be traded to the Angels and I would become the Brewers' number one catcher. Sure, I wanted the spot. It was what I had been working for, dreaming of. But I didn't want it at Ellie's expense. Eventually, though, that's just what happened.

In spite of our early promise that year, the Brewers didn't finish so well. Pitching was our weak spot in 1973. Management had traded away veteran pitcher Jim Lonborg for Don Money and two other players, and our current ace, Bill Parsons, was doing poorly. Things got so bad that pitching coach Bob Shaw was fired and replaced by Al Widmar.

Meanwhile, Teri was struggling to adjust to life in the big leagues. She found it wasn't as friendly as it had been in the minors. Back in Evansville, all the players had lived in the same apartment complex. When the team went on the road, the wives would support one another. When we would get back, there would be a barbecue—just like a big, happy family. But the major leagues tend to be more businesslike. People keep their personal lives to themselves. So she was lonely.

One of Teri's problems was that she had never developed outside interests. When we were away on road trips, she would hang around the house, reading, watching TV, or doing exercises. Then, when we'd come home she would be all ready to go out, do the town. Only I'd be tired and would want to stay home and relax. It was our first source of friction. We just couldn't seem to get together on it. I found out some of the other players had similar problems with their wives. And people think ballplayers have easy lives!

When the team was on the road, Teri seldom called me, and I wondered why. The truth was she was afraid to call. She had mixed with other baseball wives enough to know all about ballplayers fooling around when they were playing away games. Typically a wife would call the hotel room after a night game, and if her husband wasn't in, she'd go bananas. And the next day she'd be on the horn screaming, "Where were you last night?" It would drive the wives crazy. Teri wouldn't call, because she didn't want to fall into that trap. She didn't want to know what I was doing while we were on the road.

When I'd come home, there would be a lot of kissing and hugging. In a way, those forced separations kept things fresh and romantic between us. We didn't see one another often enough to get bored.

Another source of friction began to develop when Teri would come to the home games. Since assuming the number one catcher's spot, I was getting more and more attention from the press and fans alike. I was becoming something of a celebrity around Milwaukee.

Of course, the fans were always all over us players, especially the women. Some of them were pretty bold. They'd do things like kiss me or playfully slap me on the fanny. And Teri would be standing right there. Nobody ever asked who she was, and I guess I rarely told them. Surrounded as I was by the adoring mob, I didn't even notice she was being excluded. I was having a good time. It was fun being admired and courted by the fans, especially the pretty ones.

Once, a blonde with a tight dress and a really good figure pressed herself against me and purred, "Oh, Darrell, I don't seem to have a scrap of paper on me. Will you autograph my breast?"

"Over my dead body, lady!" Teri shouted. I hadn't seen her standing behind me. She was really ticked off. The blonde just ignored her. I laughed it off.

When we got home, Teri tore into me. "Why do you let them talk to you like that, honey? 'Sign my breast'! Trouble is they don't respect you . . . poking and pinching you like you're some choice cut of meat!"

"Oh, come on, Teri!" I protested. "It's got nothin' to do with respect. They like me is all. Shoot, they're just fans, honey. A ballplayer is expected to be nice to the fans. It's my job!"

"Darrell, I don't mind you being admired. You're a big favorite in Milwaukee and a handsome guy, and I'm proud of you. And I don't mind you signing autographs. But that doesn't mean they have a right to make cheap, suggestive remarks. Don't they have husbands or boy friends for that?"

"You're exaggerating!" I said.

"I'm *not!*" Teri cried, all flushed and angry. "And what about me? You let some . . . some tramp talk like that to you, with me standing right there. I'm your wife! If you don't respect yourself, respect me!"

With that she ran into the bedroom and slammed the door. I couldn't understand what all the fuss was about. It didn't mean anything to me. Why should it bother Teri?

I finished my first full season as a major leaguer with a respectable .254 batting average, sixteen homers, and sixty-seven runs-batted-in. I returned to Oklahoma City that fall in triumph. In less than three years I had made it to the majors and was the Brewers' starting catcher. Not bad for a guy just twenty-one.

I began to be a little more open about my drinking. I would even show up at my parents' home a little tight. Shoot, I was never sloppy drunk like Dad. I think I was trying to show Mom that. I was saying by my actions: *Hey, I can handle this. I act like a human being when I drink. You won't see me fumbling and stumbling.*

As for Dad, I not only drank in front of him, but I began to smoke pot, too. I was telling him in effect that I was a man and not under his thumb anymore. I know he didn't approve, but he had no room to talk. I was saying to him: *I am a professional ballplayer now; I support myself. You can't tell me what to do anymore! Check me out! I'm gonna do this, and you can't stop me!*

Whatever my motives, my power-play had its desired effect. Dad said nothing about my drinking or pot smoking, though at times there was a baffled, almost hurt look in his eyes.

My sister, Pat, had a lot to say, though, especially after she found out both Jimmy and Eddie were smoking pot, too. "You guys are real idiots!" she'd shout. "Smoking that junk! Darrell, you oughta be ashamed! That stuff ain't worth a flip, and you know it! Deep down inside, you know it ain't!"

"Oh, Pat, grass ain't so bad!" I'd reply, as if I was talking to a child.

15

Cocaine

One night I was at a house party. I was really feeling good. A friend who was pretty wasted sidled up to me, waving a little glassine bag full of white powder. "Here, D.P., try this! It'll blow your mind!"

It was cocaine, or "coke," the Cadillac of narcotics, the drug of choice of the jet set, also known by a variety of code names—"blow," "ski," "snow," or simply "C." I had never done it before.

I watched my friend carefully divide the powder up into little rows called "lines." Then, rolling a $100 bill into a little cylinder, he leaned over the table. Pressing his finger against one nostril, he inhaled the line up his nose.

"Ah, great stuff!" he said, sitting up. "Here, try it."

I tried it. By that time I'd try anything new anybody offered me. Tight as I was, I felt kind of foolish, getting down on my knees and leaning over the coffee table to sniff the white powder.

It made my nose tingle, and I had an urge to sneeze but didn't. That was all. Nothing else happened except for an alert feeling.

"Shoot! This stuff ain't worth a flip!" I said. "How much you pay for this?"

"Seventy-five a gram."

"How much is a gram?" I asked.

"Much less than an ounce."

"Well, how much is an ounce?"

"Anywhere from twelve hundred to fifteen hundred. If you got the bread, sweetheart."

Fifteen hundred! I couldn't believe it. For the money, it sure didn't do much. What a waste! Who were they trying to kid!

But, of course, my indignation didn't stop me from trying it again on another night at another party. It was available, so why not? The first few times I felt practically nothing.

They say that coke isn't physically addicting—that is, you don't get chills and cramps, and you don't puke on yourself, like a heroin addict, if you can't get a fix. But it is psychologically addicting. If you can get it, you'll do it all you can. And pretty soon, if you do it enough, you *have* to do it. The main reason most users aren't cocaine addicts, in the strict sense of the word, is the expense.

It's hard to describe how coke makes you feel. The main sensations are energy and a sense of calmness. After a while, it made me feel good, even superior. Numero Uno . . . very confident! I'd be active, buzzing with energy. Go, go, go! And really talkative. I felt as if I was a brilliant conversationalist. (And I was the guy who got D's in English!) Oh, you're very pleased with yourself when you're high on coke.

The excitability and the sense of calmness might sound contradictory, yet both moods exist together with cocaine. In the novel *Cocaine*, the author speaks of "fireworks in the brain . . . my heart beating away like a sewing machine and on top of everything else that serene feeling," or words to that effect. Cocaine users will tell you there's nothing like the high it gives you.

I quickly discovered that liquor and cocaine made a powerful combination. The coke gets you up, the booze brings you back down again. You could go back and forth like that all night. And I was so *aware*—aware of my profound thoughts, my clever thoughts, dancing thoughts, tripping lightly through my brain and off my tongue, wittily, without a slip. Just dazzling! I was aware of the people around me as never before; I could empathize with them, gauge their thoughts and reactions, anticipate their comments and responses. And I could hold their attention with my brilliant talk.

The high lasts from fifteen to thirty minutes, depending on the dose.

But then you come down. The immediate feeling is a mild depression. The drug makes you go so hard—you think so hard, you feel so hard—that it burns you out. The next day you feel exhausted. The more you become addicted to coke, the harsher the comedown. You don't simply come down—you crash!

I wasn't off the wall with cocaine when I started. It's a social drug. I did it at parties and on weekends. But, hey, all the best people were doing it—I mean movie stars, executives. And I wanted to be like those people, the jet setters, the high-society types, the beautiful people who frequented expensive clubs and chic discos. I wanted to be cool. I began to snort the stuff through rolled-up hundred-dollar bills. What could be cooler and more "in"?

I also wanted to be liked. I wanted to fit in, *really* fit in. And coke did that for me. I wanted to be macho—not in the sense of tough or manly, but in the sense of being a guy people would point to and say, "Hey, there's Darrell Porter! Oh, he's a neat guy, a fun guy! He's the kind of guy I want to be like."

I didn't think of myself as a person who did bad things (like committing a felony by using cocaine). I wanted everybody to be happy. I tried to be kind to others. So, when my friends wanted a little toot of coke, I'd be the first to say, "Okay, let's go have a good time, on me!"

All of a sudden, however, I developed a low boiling point. I didn't know why. One night toward the end of the 1974 season, we were playing a double-header in Cleveland against the Indians. We had won the first game 6-2. We were on our way to losing the second game, and it was the seventh inning.

It was a rotten night all around. In a stadium that could hold 82,000 people, there were exactly 757 fans. One of them was a drunk who heckled me all night. Every time I stuck my head out of the dugout he was telling me how lousy I was playing. He had another guy with him and a girl. Maybe he was showing off for the girl. I didn't need the guy's needling: I was 0 for 3, and I had gone hitless in the first game as well.

So with two outs in the seventh inning, our George Scott grounded out to end the inning. As I walked back toward the dugout from the on-deck circle, this drunk shouted: "Don't worry, Darrell! You'll get a chance to make the first out in the eighth!" As he said it, he flipped beer across the dugout roof, splattering me.

Now, I had been thinking how I could get this guy all evening, mapping a way to reach him. So when he threw the beer on me, that was it—I put one foot on the rail surrounding the dugout, then leaped onto the dugout roof.

The guy was running up the steps in an instant, and I began to slip and slide on the beer covering the roof. I knew I couldn't reach him, so I grabbed his buddy and drilled him one. The girl began to scream. Then my teammates and the cops were on the dugout roof trying to pull me off the guy. And *they* were slipping and sliding in the beer. I got thrown out of the game.

At first I refused to talk to reporters. I sat facing my locker, sipping a mug of beer, wondering what was wrong with me. Finally I told them I was sorry for my conduct. "I made a mistake," I said, "and it will never happen again. But fans have to understand what it's like to have a bad day and have to listen to a lot of guff. They were on me bad all night. I've taken it before, but something happened. Maybe it's the long season, I don't know."

It never occurred to me it might be all the garbage I was dumping in my system.

At any rate, the cops came into the clubhouse and questioned me. After they left, Tommy Ferguson, the Brewers' traveling secretary, came in and said, "Come on, Darrell, you're going with me. Don't bother showering."

He hustled me back to the hotel. He was afraid an arrest was imminent. I quickly showered and dressed in Tommy's room, then grabbed my bags and was whisked to the airport. They shipped me to Baltimore.

The next day, the *Milwaukee Journal* carried a headlined story on the brawl. There was a two-column picture of yours truly being subdued by teammates and the cops. But in the Cleveland papers, the woman mayor of the town, who was at the game, stoutly defended me. She said she would have done the same thing. That may have kept the guy I slugged from suing me. Anyway, except for a fine and a three-day suspension, nothing more came of it.

The significant thing about the incident, I think, is that my personality seemed to be changing. All my life I had been a shy, gentle kind of guy, never a brawler. Now, all of a sudden I was ready to tear a fan's head off. But I soon forgot about it.

The one really bright spot in the 1974 season was my being named to the All-Star team in mid-season. It was a great honor and a big thrill for a young player in only his second full major league season, even though I didn't actually get into the game.

I don't want to give the impression that my drinking and drug use were flagrant in those early years. It wasn't an everyday thing. But in 1975, something happened to change that.

One day after I returned home from a hunting trip, I got a call from Eddie. He said he had to see me. I went over to the house.

"D.P., I hate to be the one to tell you. Shoot, I don't know how to begin."

"Spit it out!" I told him. I was growing alarmed. What could it be that had him so tied up? You'd have thought somebody died.

"While you were away, we were partying...me and this girl, and Teri...was...with this guy. The two of 'em were kissing."

"Eddie! What are you saying! It ain't true! Not Teri!"

"D.P., I wish it wasn't true. But I was there. I saw it."

"Who was the guy?" I asked, almost dizzy with shock.

"Al. You know Al. It was him."

Oh, dear God...Teri...Teri! I was sure I had to be dreaming. I was totally ripped apart.

"What else did they do?" My voice was thick with a need to cry, but no tears came.

"Nothin'—that's it," Eddie said.

"Yeah, I'll *bet* that was it!" I said. "He take her home?"

"I don't know. I don't *think* so."

I was weak and sick. I thought I might vomit.

"Thanks, Eddie," was all I could manage as I pushed past him and out the door.

"You gonna be all right, D.P.?" he called after me, concerned, as I plunged down the steps toward my car, lurching like a drunken man.

Shock. Total shock. Teri. My beautiful angel...with another guy! A mountain was on my chest. I couldn't breathe. *It can't be real*, I thought. *I can't take it...I can't stand this.*

I drove home. Gradually shock and despair turned to rage. It was building in me like a volcano about to blow.

I hated Teri so much then that I could have killed her with my bare hands. How could she have done this to me? To us? She had smashed what we had to smithereens.

As soon as I walked in the door, she knew something was wrong. I didn't mince words: "Eddie told me you were fooling with Al...says you were with him at a little party. Is it true?"

She looked as if I had just slapped her.

"No...I didn't! Darrell, I swear to you, I didn't."

"You calling my brother a liar?" I spat out. "Why should he lie?"

"If Eddie says I was fooling with another man, then he's a liar!" she shouted.

"He says the guy kissed you, you were kissing him! Eddie says Al took you home. Is that when you went to bed with him?"

"It's not true!" she cried, tears in her eyes. "I've never been unfaithful to you, I swear I haven't!" She buried her face in her hands and wept.

"That's right, cry! You oughta cry! Only reason you're cryin' is because I found out!"

She looked at me, stricken, "It's just not true!"

"Well, if you didn't sleep with the guy, what *did* you do? Were you playin' tiddlywinks maybe?"

"Okay," she said, swiping at the tears almost angrily. "I was there. We were all feeling good."

"So?"

"So...I let Al kiss me. I was lonely is all. It was just a little kiss! Darrell, you're never home! You're always off hunting or fishing! Do you ever stop to think about me? About what I want?"

"I *loved* you!" I cried. "I don't know what you're talkin' about!"

"And I love you...and I swear I never cheated on you! Okay. I did wrong, I let him kiss me. But that was all, I swear!" She was looking at me with her tear-stained face, like a child wanting to be picked up and hugged and told that everything is all right. I hardened my heart. All I felt was rage.

I had never hurt her before, but now I grabbed her shoulders and shook her until her teeth fairly rattled. "Is that all you did? Is that ALL?" I roared. Her head snapped back and forth, her long hair whipping around her face. "Get out of my sight!"

I pushed her, and she staggered back against the end table.

There was a look in her eyes I had never seen before, a look of fear. She backed away, fumbling with the top of her blouse, where the button had torn away.

"Can you...," she said, her voice shaking, "...can you honestly say to me that you have never been with another woman since we've been married?"

"You dare ask me a thing like that, after what you've done?"

Then, turning, I stormed out of the apartment. I drove over to a friend's house, and we got ripped. But even the liquor and pills couldn't blot out the pain, the rage, and the grief that were tearing at me.

Teri, Teri, my heart cried. *My angel, my life! What have we done?* Inside, something was broken and bleeding. I was wounded beyond all healing.

16

The Death of a Marriage

MILWAUKEE, 1975–76

Although we stayed together, I could not forgive Teri. No matter that I had no proof of her infidelity and that she denied it. My ego and my pride were shattered. I no longer trusted her or believed in her. Oh, I *needed* her, but I *hated* her, too. The contradiction ripped me up.

I had never confronted Al about it. He had been my friend, but I was too ashamed.

I became increasingly irritable and short-tempered. When the fans screamed at me, I'd scream right back at them, trading insult for insult. I began to swear, mildly at first. Soon I was freely using all the four-letter words.

From a carefree, outgoing guy, I turned into a withdrawn, almost paranoid wreck. I felt worthless, and the worthlessness was that my wife had chosen another man over me—or so I believed. And how many others had there been? The thought made me shake.

Teri began visiting a girlfriend and her husband. I was sure she went there to see the guy's brother. At the time it never once crossed my mind that my fears were ungrounded, that maybe she really was only going over to visit Maureen and Leon.

I never meant to be unfair. All I knew was that I wanted a wife I could trust, who wouldn't even think of any man but me.

The worst thing was that we couldn't discuss things, talk them out. And if problems aren't aired and discussed, they don't go away, they only fester. If only we could have been open with one another. If only we could have communicated.

Things got so bad between us that we separated briefly. Somebody wrote once that it's easier to be miserable without somebody than it is to be miserable *with* them. Not true. I couldn't stand being apart from Teri. I asked her to come home, and she did. We were miserable together. We were miserable apart.

The 1975 baseball season was in full swing. I didn't care about baseball. I didn't care about anything. My playing was off. Brewers' president Bud Selig asked what was wrong with me. They suspected marital problems, of course. Selig asked if perhaps I wanted to "talk to someone" (translation: "We think you need to see a shrink, kiddo"). I said I supposed I did. They sent me to a psychiatrist.

I had good intentions, but I went with the wrong attitude. I thought, *I can't really be honest with this guy. He's working for the team. He'll go right back and tell the front office. I'm not going to tell him everything about Teri, and there's no way I'm going to tell him about the drugs. No way!*

That's a stupid way to go to a psychiatrist who needs to know what you're thinking, what's bothering you, in order to help. I wasn't ready for it. I went a few times to keep the front office happy, then quit.

I couldn't stand the pain of my failing marriage and my smashed ego. My solution was to get heavier into drugs. I found they gave me at least temporary relief from the pain. And my general attitude on and off the field was rotten.

I began to do weird things. In the trainer's room was a whirlpool. I was so out of my mind that I would climb the ladder and do flips into the tub—which was about the size of a small barrel. It's a wonder I didn't break my neck.

Then there was the day I went to the ballpark with a splitting hangover from a party the night before. "Hey, Tiger. That was some performance last night!" one of the guys said. "It's a wonder you didn't catch cold!"

He said it in a kind of leering tone, and I didn't like it. "What the h—— you talkin' about?" I asked.

"You mean you don't remember? You were dancin' on the table in your Jockey shorts! " He began to laugh.

Now, I'm a very private guy, and I would never dream of doing such a thing. I slammed the guy up against the locker. The other players pulled me off him.

"You crazy?" he shouted. "You oughta go back to that shrink you were seeing!"

It was only later that it hit me that I didn't remember anything about the party. It was all a blank. That shook me up.

Things continued to deteriorate between Teri and me. We hardly ever talked. I hated her for deliberately making me into a nothing.

When we did talk, it invariably led to arguments. When we were in Chicago, we went to a club one evening. Then some of my teammates came in and sat near us. After about five minutes they called me over and asked if I'd be willing to take Teri somewhere else. They wanted to get a little action going.

When I told Teri we were leaving, she was livid. She chewed me out all the way to the coatroom. I hoped the guys couldn't hear. "They have no right to break up our evening like this!" she fumed. "I don't understand you, Darrell. Why didn't you tell them to get lost?"

"Look, it's no big deal. And keep your voice down! We can have a good time somewhere else just as well."

"Yeah...while they play around on their wives?"

"Just shut up, Teri, will you? What they do is their business."

"Well, I sure hope they return the favor to you some day, when *you're* out tom-catting!"

I could have hit her then.

As you might guess, the 1975 season was not one of my banner years in baseball, nor was it a good year for the Brewers. Later, Teri and I were getting ready to go to Oklahoma after Christmas. We had stayed in Milwaukee after the season. It was early 1976. "It'll be good to see the folks again," Teri said.

"I don't want you to come with me. I'm sorry," I told her. "I want to go home alone."

The truth was that having sworn Eddie to secrecy, I couldn't let my family and friends know my wife had made a fool of me.

Teri looked at me, her face blank. I wanted to hurt her, and I had.

"Well . . . if that's the way you want it," she said, her voice matter-of-fact. "I'd better get supper on."

I went to Oklahoma City, and Teri went to Minnesota to visit a girlfriend. After a few days I began to wonder what she was doing up there. This girlfriend of hers . . . I knew she was a baseball-Annie type. Sure as shootin' she'd try to get Teri involved with some ballplayers there.

I was waiting for a call one day from Teri. Finally the phone rang. It was only Jeff, Teri's brother. All I needed was a crazy kid tying up the line.

Jeff was a couple of years older than Teri. He had been taking some drugs. About six months earlier he began acting strangely, so Floyd sent him to a fancy hospital to detox. I felt sorry for him. But I didn't need his problems at that moment.

"Darrell, I have to talk to you, right away," he said.

"I really can't right now, Jeff." I put him off.

Why wouldn't people leave me alone? Didn't I have enough pain, enough problems of my own?

Four days later, Jeff went into the garage of his father's home and closed the door. He got into his shiny, expensive car and turned on some music. Then he turned on the motor.

Teri got the call from Floyd while she was in Minnesota. Then Floyd called me. I was at the house the next day when she arrived. Ignoring me, she went to Floyd. Martha Lee, her face swollen from crying, gave me a sympathetic glance and pat on the arm.

Teri buried her head on Floyd's shoulder and cried for her dead brother. "It can't be true!" she sobbed. "Not Jeff! Oh, Daddy, it can't be!"

When I tried to go to her, she turned away. "Don't touch me!" she hissed. "You don't need me, and I don't need you!" She was like stone.

Oh, how I wanted to take her in my arms and hold her! I wanted to say, "Hey, I need you and I love you, and I just can't stand any of this anymore! Please don't shut me out . . . not now, not when we're both hurting so much! There's too much pain! Let's not add to it! I love you so! We need each other. I need you, like I need my life!"

111

But I said nothing. My stupid pride wouldn't let me say it. And so it wasn't said.

Everything seemed to be falling apart at once. I was crushed by the knowledge that I hadn't helped Jeff when he needed it. But my own pain had been so great, I couldn't bear his, too. Now he was dead, and it was too late. And it was too late for Teri and me. Somehow Jeff's death was the final, agonized blow.

A day or so later, just before the funeral, Teri asked me for a divorce. "Let's end it now, before we hate each other."

"What'll you do?" I asked.

"Dad needs me here now. You don't need me."

Maybe that was my last opportunity to tell her it wasn't true, that my whole heart and being were crying out for the comfort of her arms. But again I said nothing. She said nothing. And so we saved our precious, precious pride. And we killed the marriage. Although I blamed Teri, I felt it was *my* failure, my ultimate failure. The divorce became final during the next season. I think it's significant that Teri didn't ask me for a dime in alimony.

I returned to the Brewers for the 1976 season. I did poorly, as you might imagine. I was in such emotional pain that I thought of killing myself, but not seriously. There were always pot and Quaaludes, beer and cocaine to dull the agony of living.

I virtually withdrew from all personal contact with my teammates. I couldn't let anyone know what I was suffering. I had my pride. And real men didn't cry.

One guy knew—Jim Colborn, our pitcher. He lived next door to Teri and me, and he knew what had happened. He had a pretty good idea about the drugs, too.

"Darrell," he told me, "you've got to face where you are right now. That's reality. You've got to be conscious and aware of what's happening. You can't be drifting off in space somewhere. You've got to face the pain!"

"I can't!" I told him. "Why should I face it?"

"Because you're never going to get over the pain until you face it, until you *feel* it! You've got to feel the pain!"

I couldn't accept that. It was too crazy. Why feel pain when there were Quaaludes, when one snort of coke could knock it out? That would be plain stupid!

Oh, I wanted to get straight. I wanted to be able to face life. *But I couldn't stand the pain.*

Later, much, much later, I would be able to accept Jim's wisdom. But right then I hadn't fallen far enough.

I had so much anger in me—against Teri, myself, baseball. One night I went to a striptease joint, hoping to find some companionship. At the end of the evening I was still alone, and they were closing the place. I was really mad and frustrated.

On the way home, this guy was just crawling along in front of me, and that burned me up even more. When we got to a red light, I jumped out of my car and ran up to him. He was trying to roll up his window, but I got the door open. He had a buddy with him, but I didn't care.

"You lousy, s——!" I screamed. Then I drilled him one, and he went half over the back seat. I kept screaming at him. Two more of his friends came, but I was acting so crazy they weren't about to tangle with me. When the guy pulled himself back into his seat, the eye that I punched was all droopy and crooked. His friend in the car sat there shaking.

"Guess that'll teach you, you little b——!" I snarled, slamming the car door.

As I drove home, I felt suddenly drained. Remorse and guilt swept over me. I could see the guy's eye, all bloody and crooked. *What did I do?* I thought, horrified. *That guy did nothing to me! You can't control yourself. You're flipping out!* I was so sorry. If only I could have found that man I'd have apologized, told him I didn't mean it. Only it was too late for that.

As I've said, I had a terrible season in 1976. So did the Brewers. Actually, I didn't care about baseball anymore. I began to wonder if I ever had. I hit a dismal .208 that year and had only five home runs and a measly 32 RBIs. Del Crandall had been replaced as manager by Alex Grammas. Grammas and I were in constant conflict over my lackluster catching. I accused him of not paying enough attention to me, a claim he hotly disputed.

I was traded at the end of the season to Kansas City, along with my friend, pitcher Jim Colborn. After my departure, Grammas badmouthed me to the press saying: "Not only was he so bad hit-

ting, but defensively he hurt us worse." He said I let too many opposing players "run the bases at will," adding, "had we been able to
throw out half the runners, we'd have won a lot more games. Not
only would they steal second, but they'd wind up at third, because
of bad throws." Reading that really hurt me. It was another torment I didn't need.

The trade was not a surprise, but still it gave me a jolt—KC after
four years with the Brewers.

But there was a bright side to it: here was my chance to start all
over again, with a new team in a new town, where nobody knew
me. I would put my past behind me and begin fresh. It would be a
whole new life!

What a fool I was! I guess I was blaming everyone else for my
problems: Teri, my teammates, her family, my family. I never once
thought that *I* might be to blame. I was going to Kansas City all
right—and I would cart along all the junk festering inside me. You
never get away from it all; you just take it with you.

That fall I dated Teri twice. I'm not sure why I did that. Maybe I
couldn't accept the finality of the divorce. Maybe I wanted to see if
there were a few embers still glowing. Why couldn't relationships
end cleanly, dramatically, like they did in books and movies? We
just prolonged the agony.

Then I couldn't let well enough alone. I dated Teri's best friend in
Oklahoma City. I guess that was some kind of payback. I knew it
would eventually get back to Teri. It's just that I didn't count on being around when it did.

One night I was at this gal's house when the doorbell rang. It
was Teri. I tried to lie my way out of the obvious. When you're on
dope, you become expert at being devious. But Teri could see
through me by then, and she wasn't buying it.

If she had had a gun, I'm sure I wouldn't be alive to write this
book. Teri seldom cussed. But that night I think she called me
every four-letter word in the book—plus a few I'd never heard.
Punched me out, too. Then she had a few choice words for her so-
called best friend—who from that minute was her *ex*-best friend.
When she stormed out of that house, she nearly broke the door off
the hinges.

17

Goin' to Kansas City

I may have told myself I was going to have a whole new life in
the spring, but in the winter of 1976, in the wake of my split from
Teri and the trade to Kansas City (announced on December 6), I
went hog wild. It was nonstop parties, drinking, and drugs—always drugs. Anything to shut out the disillusionment, the pain—
anything to erase Teri's lovely face from my mind.

We did a lot of hunting that fall and winter, my brothers,
buddies, and I. But half the time I was wiped out on beer a
Quaaludes, or beer and pot, or beer and coke.

On one occasion, when our car broke down on an isolated road
one of the guys (who was as drunk as a skunk) decided to hitch-
hike to the nearest gas station. When a woman came along the
road in the opposite direction, he threw himself on the hood of her
car yelling, "No. No! Thataway! Go thataway!"

We thought it was funny, but it got us thrown in jail for a couple
of hours. The arresting officers were good old boys, though, and
as soon as they found out who I was, they let us go with a gentle
warning to cool it in those parts.

The corker was the time we got up at 4:30 A.M. to go duck hunting. I had some Quaalude in powder form, so we made our own
capsules—and we made them really big. Then we washed them
down with beer. In just about five minutes those things kicked in
and, man, we were totally out of control.

Sunrise found me doing fifty-five miles per hour down a little dirt road, and I was weaving all over the place. "Better let me drive, D.P.," one of the guys drawled from the back.

"Naaaah!" I slurred back. Just then we went across a little board bridge with no rails. The wheels were half off and half on that bridge (we checked the tire marks on the way back). Had we gone over, it was a long way down, and we would have smashed into a solid clay bank below.

"Better let me drive, D.P.," the guy in the back said again.

"Naaaah. I wanna," I replied, my head practically on the wheel.

A hundred yards farther down the road, we ran out of luck. All of a sudden everything was in slow-motion and I was off the road, hitting a row of saplings. I mowed them down; they snapped off, one after the other, and went right over the top of the car!

The car finally came to a stop.

In the middle of a pond.

When we wrestled the doors open, water poured onto our laps.

"I told you to let me drive, D.P.!" my buddy from the back complained, as we stumbled through the waist-high water and weeds, mud sucking at our calves.

Just then four carloads of coyote hunters came by. We were stumbling around in our muddy clothes, trying to act straight and not quite succeeding. We looked pretty pathetic, I guess. They hauled us out of the drink.

We drove on to the lake and set up two blinds, one on each shore. It was a bluebird day, with the sun shining—the worst kind of day for duck hunting (which, ideally, is overcast and mucky so that the birds will come in seeking shelter).

Anyway, we were so messed up that we spent the day firing our shotguns at each other across the lake. Like a bunch of dumb, overgrown kids. It's a wonder we didn't put our eyes out with the pellets. I was normally so cautious with guns.

In the spring, when I reported to the Royals' training complex at Fort Myers, Florida, I put all that stuff behind me. I had a growing sense that I was really messing up in baseball, the one thing I could do and do well. That last season with the Brewers, I'd started sneaking under the stands to light up a joint—something I'd never done before. No wonder I hit .208 and got traded! Well, now I knew: I couldn't do marijuana on the field and play good ball. The two don't mix. I also knew I couldn't do cocaine at all during the season. All that stuff I'd been giving the reporters about Grammas not paying enough attention to me was just a crock. It was *me*. I had messed up, but good!

I *had* to do better. And more than my job was at stake. With Teri gone, there was a big hole in the middle of things. Life had no meaning for me, no purpose. Now baseball would be my purpose. Achieving excellence in the game would be my aim, my goal in life. Then I would be happy.

I went to spring training telling myself, *Boy, I'm going to work my butt off! This is my chance to reestablish myself, to find out just how good a ballplayer I really am!*

Coming to the Royals was like being reborn. Or, as I told reporters, it was like "going from an outhouse to the penthouse." There was an enthusiasm, a joy and love of baseball that I hadn't felt in years. I couldn't help catching the spirit.

I quickly learned that the Royals had a "family" approach to the game. There was a camaraderie among the players that had been lacking in Milwaukee. The players studied one another's performance and offered praise or constructive criticism. I liked that. It meant we cared about one another and the good of the team.

In one of the early exhibition games I hit the ball in the gap, and the grass just sort of grabbed it. I played it safe and stayed on first. When I got back to the dugout, one of the guys told me, "In this club, Darrell, you take a chance and go to second on a ball like that."

At the bottom of these criticisms was an aggressiveness, a drive to win. That was okay with me, because I was out to win, too. But it could smart sometimes.

A few days after I was told about not going to second, I figured I'd put the advice to work and stretch a single into a double. Instead I got hung up between first and second and wound up being tagged out. My teammates kidded me about getting "the piano off your back." At least I had tried. I never was the fastest thing going. Oh, those guys kept me on my toes, right from the start.

The Royals' management wasn't naive. They knew I was a calculated risk (which is probably why they only signed me to a one-year contract). So did everybody else. *The Sporting News* referred to me that spring as the "Royals' Number One Riddle." But Manager Whitey Herzog believed in me, despite my poor record in 1976. (He knew nothing about the drugs, of course.) Whitey thought the change of teams would rekindle the potential with which I had started out, back in 1970. He told reporters he was banking on the fact that I could add badly needed power to the Royals' line-up.

I don't think I disappointed him. In my very first game for the Royals, I doubled down the left-field line, not once but twice. Then, a few days later in a game with the Tigers, I socked a two-run homer. In the same game my buddy Jim Colborn showed his stuff by giving up only five hits in six innings to lead us to a 5–0 victory.

The season was off to a flying start, what with four straight wins right off the bat (if you'll pardon the pun). My playing continued strong, and I was named the Royals' Player of the Month for April.

In early May, things turned with a vengeance. The team went into a terrible slump, losing fifteen out of twenty-five games. To make things worse, our star third baseman, George Brett, was out for ten days when he developed a hyperextended elbow.

Even though the team was doing poorly, by this time, *I* was doing so well that I gained a confidence I had never had. But it was more that that—it was a cocky aggressiveness.

Toward the end of the month we were playing the Texas Rangers and were getting whipped. It was the second of two games (we had won the first).

I had taken an instant dislike to the Rangers' center-fielder, Juan Beniquez, because he was too fast and was stealing bases on me. *Making me look like a fool.* Beniquez wasn't just a player on the opposing team. To me he was an enemy. The fact is, I hated his guts.

Without my realizing it, the drugs were beginning to trip me up. Oh, I had carefully scheduled them all right: greenies on the field, an occasional Quaalude, a little pot. Only after a game, so as not to interfere with my playing. And they didn't, I thought. At least the stats were good. But nevertheless they were wreaking subtle havoc in the cells of my brain, in my personality. And only Satan was checking those stats.

Every time Beniquez would come to the plate I'd mutter, "Okay, you S.O.B., you'd better get ready to *die*, 'cause we're gonna drill you in the head with one of these pitches. We're gonna drill you, and I ain't gonna tell you which pitch it will be, so you'd better be ready."

I thought I had him intimidated in the first game, but in the second game he slammed a three-run homer in the third inning. Boy, was I burned up! I stepped up the muttered threats.

At one point our relief pitcher Marty Pattin actually came within inches of beaning Beniquez with a fastball, though whether it was on my instructions I honestly can't remember.

Anyway, when I came to bat, Rangers' pitcher Bert Blyleven threw a ninety-mile-per-hour fastball into my thigh. Hurt! I thought I was shot! I limped to first, where I exchanged a few choice words with Blyleven. Then I saw red and started running toward him.

Instantly both benches emptied, but after a few tense moments, play was resumed.

The next day Blyleven bragged publicly in an Associated Press story carried in all the papers that he had deliberately hit me. "They [the Royals] were throwing at us all night. It just so happens that Porter was the one, and he's the catcher—and he was calling them. I thought it seemed like the time to be wild. I didn't throw at his head."

Oh, you bloody b——! I thought, as I read it. Whitey was furious, too, and he hinted to reporters that Rangers' manager Frank Lucchesi had put Blyleven up to beaning me the minute we brushed Beniquez. He said he saw the two of them with their heads together, hatching the plot.

When we went to Arlington, Texas, in May I had revenge in my heart. During the first game of the series, I stood on our dugout steps and shouted obscenities at the Rangers. My teammates thought it was great fun, but the rage in my heart was murderous.

I was looking for trouble, and I got it soon enough. A little into the game, when George Brett and I got Bump Wills in a run-down between third and home, Wills turned and came charging right toward home plate on the inside of the baseline, my territory. He rammed right into me, looking for an interference call.

119

He must have hit his head on my shin-guard when he went down, because he was holding it. I was delighted. "Take *that!* I yelled. "How do you like it down there?"

With that he turned over and smiled. "Hey, Porter," he said, "I thought it was a pretty good play!"

"Yeah, I thought it was a good play, too, you S.O.B.!" I growled. "But you're out, so just get your ass back to the dugout! Move it!"

As I turned to point, I saw their entire bench charging me—all twenty-five players. Leading the pack was Willie Horton—monstrous Willie Horton, known far and wide as the "terror" of baseball. Oh, Willie had fire in his eyes!

Oh, Lordy . . . what have I got myself into here! I thought.

I remembered what Dad always told me: "If you have to fight a big guy, get the first lick in."

That's what I did. I charged old Willie and all twenty-five Rangers. I took one swing at Willie, but I just grazed him. Then he hit me, and the fight was on!

Our guys jumped in, and it was a real donnybrook. I was down, then I was up, then I was down. Somebody was pounding on the back of my head. I twisted around and saw it was the Rangers' coach, Pat Corrales. I popped him one, and he went down. Then I jumped on him and hit him twice more. When I got off him, Whitey shouted at him: "Corrales, you're a no-good S.O.B.! You're a coach, and you should be out there trying to break things up! Instead you're taking cheap shots at my players! You should be suspended!"

That fight lasted for twenty-five minutes—one of the longest brawls in recent baseball history. The fans loved it.

I got thrown out of the game. Pete LaCock got thrown out. The Rangers who were ejected included Manager Frank Lucchesi, Coach Pat Corrales, Bump Wills, Claudell Washington, and Horton.

We won twice that night: 6–5 in the game and 5–2 in the basebrawl!

After the game I got word that Willie Horton was going to meet me when our bus unloaded at the hotel. I was scared. As usual, my anger had passed, and I was wondering how it all happened. Thank God he never showed up.

Later, my brother Jimmy and his wife and my date and I decided to go out. Wouldn't you know, of all the places in Arlington, we had to pick the cocktail lounge that was the Rangers' hangout!

I was sitting with my date near the bar. "Hey, Horton, there's your friend!" a voice said. I was in the act of lighting a cigarette when I heard that, and I broke the darned thing in half! I looked up, and there was Willie, standing not more than four feet from our table, looking out over the crowded dance floor. He stood there a few minutes, then walked away. Had he seen me?

I was as nervous as a cat. After a few minutes, we decided we had better go to some other place. Guess who was sitting by the exit? Willie Horton. Well, I went strolling by there with my date, trying to be nonchalant, sure that he was going to catch me outside and pound me into jelly. But for some reason, he didn't. I suspect that Willie didn't want to tangle with me, any more than I wanted to tangle with him. I think the fact that I had charged him gave him pause. I guessed Dad was right about getting in the first lick.

The next day Bump Wills was quoted in the newspapers as saying "Porter's got a big mouth."

I had a big mouth all right, and a lot of anger and hate was coming out of it. Outside I was disciplining myself, but inside I was seething with all kinds of conflicts and hates—against Teri, baseball, myself. And I couldn't handle it. The drugs were making sure of that. It was all bound to erupt in outbursts on and off the field. I could no longer understand myself. It was all too complicated. Better not to think about it, better to concentrate on my playing. Winning would make it all come out right . . . somehow.

18

How the West Was Won

I was doing well. By mid-June my batting average was .274, I had six homers, and I had driven in thirty runs. But the Royals, who had won the American League West Division title the previous year and had been the preseason pick to win again, were in real trouble. On June 16 we lost 7–0 to the Yankees and were out of first place by seven games, behind first-place Minnesota. We were three games below .500.

The guys were grumbling because no deals had been made before the trading deadline to improve our situation. Whitey Herzog told reporters, "Yeah, they're down. But these players can't keep feeling sorry for themselves. They can't make excuses for what deals haven't been made. They've got to go out and play."

A reporter asked me what I thought the trouble was. "It's hard to say," I replied. "We just can't seem to put it all together. Like one game we'll get great hitting but no pitching. Then, we'll get the great pitching but won't score any runs. And when we get these things going, it seems our defense falls apart."

I wasn't as polite about it to my teammates. We were facing a weekend series with the Twins. If we lost, the scales would be tipped against us. It was crisis time. I took it upon myself to call a clubhouse meeting.

"Shut the door!" I barked at the clubhouse guy. "I don't want the press or anybody in here!" The other guys could see I was dead serious. Angry. You could have cut the tension with a knife.

I stood in the middle of that room and laced into them: "When I came here, they told me this was a good ball club, a championship team. You guys ain't no championship team! You stink! You're awful, if you ask me!" I called them every name in the book.

Then I turned my guns on the pitching staff. "You guys let people intimidate you! START DRILLIN' 'EM! Pitch inside! Knock a few of 'em down!"

I aired them out. And they took it, probably because they felt it was true.

Sure, I wanted the team to win. I had to be the *best* catcher on the *best* team. I wasn't about to let those guys jeopardize my success. We had to win—the division title, the pennant, the World Series. I couldn't be satisfied with less.

I'm not going to say the little talk did it, but things began to turn around, starting that weekend with the Twins. We took all three games. That pulled us back to the .500 mark and put us in the race. We began to play aggressively and win consistently.

In late June a critical point was reached when we won nine out of twelve games on a road trip. The Angels, the Mariners, the A's, the Rangers, the Indians—all fell before the Royals. We were closing the gap—four games out of first.

Fresh from that triumphant tour, we returned to Kansas City to face my former team, the Brewers. I wish I could say I clouted a home run that day (or two or three), but the day would belong to George Brett. Brett, who had been hospitalized with his bad elbow, had returned to action that very day.

The Brewers were trouncing us 7–2. Then we squeezed out a few runs. In the seventh, we tied the score when pinch-hitter Amos Otis slammed a two-run homer.

An inning or so later, with Frank White on second, Whitey Herzog brought Brett in to hit. Herzog hadn't intended to use George right away, after his ten-day absence, but things were crucial. Brett didn't let him down, driving a single up the middle, bringing White home. It was a Royals 8–7 win.

"Brett could hit snowballs on Christmas Day!" a delighted Whitey Herzog told reporters. He could, too. Secretly, I was beginning to resent George Brett because I thought he was getting all the glory.

I was doing all right myself: a .280 batting average, eight homers, and thirty-six RBIs. But I wouldn't be satisfied until I was Numero Uno.

In mid-July, a three game weekend series with the Yanks was a repeat of our sweep of the Twins that had begun the turnaround. We beat the Yankees 7–4, 5–1, and 8–4.

In the first game I got a single and a double. In the second game, I lined three singles. Although the temperatures on the field reached 135 degrees on the third day, the fans jammed Royals Stadium to see the home team. The attendance for all three games broke some kind of record.

Those three games gave us our sixth straight win and put us within two and a half games of the division-leading Chicago White Sox.

At the end of the month, we traveled to Chicago to face the Sox in a four-game series. As I walked out on the field the first day, I immediately noticed the usual banner hanging on the outfield wall: "Welcome annual pennant chokers." Those White Sox fans, always merciless to Kansas City, were out in force (46,000 for the first game). They roundly booed the Royals and cheered the Sox all the way. After we dropped the first game 11–8, they surrounded our bus and began chanting, "Na-na-na-na, Na-na-na-na, hey, hey! Good-by!"

We lost the second game 6–4, which had Chicago fans delirious. They were in a frenzy. Talk about being in the enemy camp! It was unnerving, let me tell you.

We finally split a double-header (Sox 5–4, Royals 4–8) before fifty thousand screaming fans. I was so sick of those Chicago fans! Adding insult to injury, the White Sox held the games up by taking bows after each home run they hit! I stood on the steps of the dugout and screamed at them. I was carrying on like a crazy man. I think I *was* a little crazy. Once I started yelling I'd totally lose control. It's a wonder I didn't have a stroke.

To my teammates it was great fun, all part of the hoopla of baseball, the rivalry between teams. They didn't suspect that the obscenities, the venom and hate I was venting, had very little to do with baseball but a lot to do with the corrosive effects of drugs and my deep inner torment.

Dropping those three games to the Sox put us behind five and a half games.

Back in Kansas City, after losing to the Twins and winning a pair off the Blue Jays, we hosted the White Sox in early August. We were out for blood, a payback for the humiliation they had put us through.

We staggered them in the first game 12–2. Our guys got seventeen hits in that game, including home runs by Otis, Mayberry, Brett, and yours truly.

In the fourth inning their first baseman collided with me in an abortive attempt to score from second. I was mad as could be.

I took it out on their pitcher, Bart Johnson—I nailed him in the back with my forearm when he was covering first base on a grounder I hit to the right side. Johnson was furious, because he had just recovered from serious back surgery and was scared to death about getting hurt again. He was out to get me from then on.

When I came out to warm up in the sixth inning, he made his move, charged up to the plate, and drilled me a good one. I was already sorry I had nailed him, and I didn't fight back, but we both wound up getting ejected anyway.

Later Whitey minimized the fight: "Darrell plays hard and never lets up. He just got upset." Whitey was always protecting me. I think he admired my feistiness, never dreaming it was the tip of the iceberg.

The next night we beat the Sox again, 6–3. Brett hit a three-run homer—his seventh in eleven games, in front of forty thousand adoring Royals fans. I was 1 for 3.

In mid-August, we made our decisive move: we went on a ten-game winning streak that vaulted us into a three-game lead. For the first time, retaining the division crown was a real possibility.

In September we moved into high gear, winning our first fifteen games. We left the competition in the dust.

On September 21, we clobbered the Twins 10–5. Among the sixteen hits we racked up were three each by Brett and Otis and my home run. That homer was doubly sweet for me, because that crucial win—and an equally crucial loss by Chicago—knocked the White Sox out of the running.

Two nights later we did it: the Royals defeated the California

Angels 13–7 to clinch the Western Division title for the second year in a row.

After the game it was pandemonium in the clubhouse. I grabbed Joe Burke, Royals' general manager, and gave him a bear hug. I felt so great being part of a winning team for a change!

In the next days, sports pages all over the country carried stories describing "How the West Was Won," "The Winning of the West," and "How A Team's Agony Became Ecstasy." Everybody loves an underdog—and that's what we had been. From seven and a half games back in June, in just two and a half months we had struggled through to victory.

Joe Burke listed three reasons why he thought we clinched the title again. "First, the talent was there. The players were capable of winning and they did. Second, the club has great spirit and camaraderie. The players enjoy being together, and they play together. Whitey and his coaches have great rapport with the players. Third, the fact that we didn't make a lot of changes, just for the sake of change. The players felt secure. That's important."

We couldn't have agreed more.

The papers made much of the fact that my being traded to Kansas City had resulted in my bouncing back from one of my worst years ever to one of my best. I had finished the season with a .275 batting average, sixteen home runs, and sixty RBIs. *The Kansan* crowed: "Porter enjoyed his best year at the plate. He set personal highs in hits and doubles as well as proving himself one of the outstanding catchers in baseball."

I told reporters that the two biggest thrills of my career were catching in the All-Star game in 1974 and being traded to the Royals. And I meant it.

19

My First Play-off

Now we faced the Yankees in the league championship play-offs—a best-of-five series starting in New York in early October.

My brother Eddie was scheduled to be married in Oklahoma City on October 8, in the middle of the play-offs, but I flew Mom and Dad to New York for the first two games. They had never been to the Big Apple before, and they were thrilled.

The Royals had lost the play-offs the previous year, and we didn't intend to fly to New York to lose again. We felt we were ready for the Yankees. We were going with enthusiasm, and, as Hal McRae put it, "We're more mature. We have more confidence." But Whitey Herzog said it all when he told the press: "I hope we play as well as we did last year in the play-offs—*but win!*"

In the opening game, Yankees' pitcher Don Gullett walked our shortstop Fred Patek, first thing. Then McRae slammed a homer, giving us an early 2–0 lead.

In the second inning I walked, and Frank White connected for a single that sent me to second. Then Patek hit a hard ground ball along the left-field line that looked like a ground-rule double. So Yankee left-fielder Lou Piniella lightly threw the ball back toward the infield, giving me and Frank the chance to score easily. When Piniella found out the ball was still in play, he nearly died. But it was too late—we had already crossed home plate.

Gullet got McRae for the final out, but that was the last we would see of him. With his bad shoulder acting up again, he took himself out of the game. Yankee Manager Billy Martin was really ticked off at Gullet for not telling him about the problem before giving up four runs in two innings, according to the next day's papers. (Gullett said he had thought he could work out the stiffness.) His bad judgment was a good break for us.

By contrast our Paul Splittorff, a left-hander, was in complete control. In eight innings of pitching, he allowed only a two-run homer by Thurman Munson in the third inning. Earlier that same inning we had forged ahead, 6–0 on a single by Al Cowens and a homer by John Mayberry.

Cowens hit a homer in the eighth, making the score 7–2. The highlight of the game came in the ninth, with two Yankees on base and no outs. Willie Randolph grounded to George Brett, who tagged third for an out, then fired the ball to second (for out two), and Frank White relayed the ball to first—in what was almost (but not quite) a triple play. That finished the Yankees off. As Maury Allen of *The New York Post* sarcastically observed, "It was embarrassing enough as it was."

Meanwhile, up in the stands, Mom and Dad were having their own problems with the Yankees—fans, that is. When my folks, wearing their Kansas City Royals hats, took their seats, the sea of Yankees' fans surrounding them gave a Bronx cheer and began to needle them. It was kind of scary, particularly after all the bad things the folks had heard about New York. (Would the Yankee fans mug them?)

A kid about sixteen began talking to them—arguing actually. But as soon as he found out they were Mae and Ray Porter, he yelled: "Hey, shuddup, youse crumbs! Dis here is Darrell Pohtah's muddah and faddah! So will youse please pipe down, already?"

For the rest of the game Mom and Dad were treated like visiting royalty. Then that young Yankee fan escorted them back to the hotel (to make sure they wouldn't really get mugged, no doubt). The next night he was waiting for them when they arrived at Yankee Stadium for game two. Mom and Dad exchanged addresses with the boy, and they got a nice little correspondence going after they returned home. They almost made him into a Royals fan—but not quite.

In the second game, we jumped ahead 1–0 in the third inning on a walk, a single by Frank White, and Fred Patek's sacrifice fly. When the Yankees came to bat, Cliff Johnson had one of the longest at-bats of the season, because his eyes repeatedly teared in the cold October night. He finally hit a foul that corkscrewed up behind home plate. I ran so many circles chasing it that I tripped and fell—and missed it.

After Johnson called for towels to wipe his eyes, he connected on the next pitch and sent the ball over the center-field wall for a 1–1 tie. I felt horrible for not making the play to retire Johnson. We could have still been ahead.

Next, Willie Randolph singled, our Andy Hassler balked him to second, and Bucky Dent got a single, bringing in the run. The Yanks were leading 2–1.

We managed to tie things up again in the sixth on a controversial play: Hal McRae had walked. Then Fred Patek hit a fly off the right-field wall. McRae charged toward second, sliding at second baseman Willie Randolph to take him out of the play. McRae was called out, but in the collision they both went down—McRae was on top and took his time getting up. Meanwhile, with McRae out and the basepath clear, Patek rounded second and third and managed to score in all the confusion.

Randolph had been hurt and limped off the field. The furious Yankees came out of the dugout and cussed McRae. Billy Martin insisted on an interference call to void the run. But in spite of his bellowing, the umpires let the run stand.

When reporters later asked Martin about "bad blood" erupting, Martin snapped, "After a game like that you can be sure there won't be any good blood."

In spite of McRae's feistiness, the Yanks pulled ahead and stayed there. Ron Guidry struck out seven of us and allowed only three hits. The Yankees took it, 6–2.

The play-offs moved to Kansas City for game three. The largest crowd ever at Royals Stadium—41,285—turned out to see us meet the enemy.

The Yankees hadn't arrived in KC until five in the morning and might have been tired—at least that's what one of their players told reporters.

At any rate, in the third inning we drew a walk; then I singled, as did Fred Patek. When the inning ended, we had scored twice. Then the Yankees scored a run in the fifth, when Nettles singled and Piniella doubled.

We scored two additional runs in the sixth off relief pitcher Sparky Lyle, the big hit a pinch double by Amos Otis. With two more insurance runs, we took the game 6–2.

The Yankees and their supporters were all gloom and doom after the game. "YANKS MAY BOMB OUT TODAY" read *The New York Post* headline the next day. Maury Allen wrote of the sound of "hollow bats" and "bittersweet tears."

They had reason to cry. For the crucial fourth game, Ed Figueroa would be starting for the Yankees—his first game after having been out over a week with a strained muscle, which, he admitted, wasn't quite healed.

A lot more was riding on the game than who was going to play in the World Series. Rumors were flying that Billy Martin would be o-u-t as Yankees' manager if they lost.

Larry Gura was our starting pitcher for the game, which was played on Saturday, October 8, at Royals Stadium. Leading off for the Yankees was Mickey Rivers. On the first pitch he smacked a double, and a few minutes later he scored when Thurman Munson forced Graig Nettles at second.

In the Yankees' second inning Willie Randolph scored on a double by Bucky Dent, who later scored on a single by Rivers.

The Yanks scored again in the third. Gura allowed Munson a double and walked Reggie Jackson, so Whitey replaced him with Marty Pattin. Lou Piniella promptly hit a single off Pattin, scoring Munson. The score was now 4-0, Yankees.

But in the bottom of the inning, we scored three runs against the ailing Figueroa (whose side had begun to ache) when Reggie Jackson missed Fred Patek's fly ball to right field for a triple, opening the way for Frank White and George Brett to collect key RBIs.

Willie Randolph scored an unearned run in the fourth, after having been moved around the bases by Bucky Dent (who sacrificed him), Rivers (who grounded out), and Nettles, who scored him with a single. The Yankees were now leading 5-3.

Billy Martin sent in Dick Tidrow to relieve Figueroa after Fred Patek doubled home a run with one out in the fourth. Bad move:

White doubled off Tidrow, bringing in Patek. After a ground out, Tidrow walked Hal McRae. It was crisis time. We had two outs with runners at first and third, and the Yankees were leading by only one run. Martin called in Sparky Lyle.

Smart move: Lyle retired us on George Brett's fly to left field. We didn't score for the rest of the game and got only two more hits.

I know when I came to bat in the fifth, I could actually see the rotation on the sliders Lyle was pitching us. You should be able to hit it then, but we sure couldn't. The best contact we managed off him was in the seventh—Hal McRae's fly to left field—but even that one Piniella snagged up against the left field wall. By the time I came to bat again in the eighth inning, I could no longer see the rotation: Lyle was getting better as the game progressed. "It was tough," I later told reporters.

The Yankees got an additional run in the ninth inning, making the final score 6-4 and forcing a fifth game (in a best of five series) for the second year running.

Even Whitey praised Sparky Lyle's performance: "He was amazing!"

For the final game, Martin announced that Ron Guidry would start for the Yankees. Paul Splittorff would start for us. In a surprise move, Martin benched Reggie Jackson, presumably because of Jackson's poor fielding and his seeming inability to get a hit off the left-handed-pitching Splittorff.

Things started off promisingly: in the first inning, Hal McRae singled. Then, while Mickey Rivers fumbled around in center field with George Brett's line drive, McRae scored and Brett was safe at third.

Maybe Graig Nettles, the Yankee's third baseman, was remembering the McRae-Randolph incident in game two, because he kicked Brett as he slid into the bag at third. George leaped up and popped him one.

Both benches emptied, but the umpires managed to get things under control. Then Brett scored on an Al Cowens bouncer to third, and we were ahead 2-0.

In the third inning Mickey Rivers singled. Then, after stealing second, he scored on a single by Thurman Munson. That cut our lead to 2–1.

When we next came to bat, Hal McRae scored again, this time from second base on another single by Cowens, making it 3–1.

Mike Torrez relieved Guidry, who was tiring. We never scored again in the game.

In the eighth, Randolph hit a single for the Yankees. Then Whitey relieved Splittorff with Doug Bird, who managed to strike out Munson. Next, Piniella singled. Ditto, Reggie Jackson, who was pinch-hitting for Cliff Johnson, which drove home Randolph. The score was now 3–2 Royals, with Yankees at first and second.

Then Chris Chambliss smacked the ball toward right field. Frank White stopped it and fired it to shortstop Fred Patek for the force-out to end the inning.

In the ninth, Paul Blair got a single. Then Roy White, pinch-hitting for Bucky Dent, walked. At this point Whitey sent Larry Gura in to relieve Dennis Leonard (who had replaced Bird), because Mickey Rivers was coming to bat and Whitey thought he might bunt—and fielding bunts is one of Gura's strong suits. Instead, Rivers smacked a single to right that scored Blair, bringing White to third.

With Willie Randolph's sacrifice fly off our third pitcher in the inning, Mark Littell, the Yankees led 4–3.

They added one more run in the inning, and the final score was 5-3.

It was all over. The Yankees had beaten us once more in the American League Playoffs and won the pennant.

It was a bitter, bitter pill to swallow, after struggling so hard all season, coming from behind the way we did, coming so close, two years in a row! I told *The Sporting News*: "Maybe once we get going [next season], I'll be able to forget losing the way we did....My stomach still turns over thinking about how close we came. Maybe I won't be able to forget about it until we get into a World Series."

In addition to the loss of the play-offs, I wasn't really satisfied with my season, in spite of all the good things said and written about me. My thirteen (or was it fourteen?) errors annoyed me. Nor was I satisfied with my .275 batting average. Shoot, at the start of the year a .270 looked good, but now I was thinking about a .290 or .300. The only thing I was happy with was my throwing.

(left to right) Me, Jimmy, Pat, and Eddie in 1956.

Mom and Dad in the Clinton, Oklahoma, city park in 1947.

The men in our family in April 1961. Dad is in back, then (left to right) Jimmy and me, and in front, Denny and Eddie.

My friend Tommy Adams and me (on the right) getting ready to go to the high school prom. The year was 1968 or 1969.

Jimmy in his baseball uniform in 1964.

Here I am at age 14 with the Yankees, my prep ball team. (I'm on the left end of the back row of players.) This was my first official baseball uniform.

Shooting a free throw as a high school senior in January 1970.

The clean-cut Southeast High School star in the spring of my senior year. (Copyright 1970, The Oklahoma Publishing Company. From the **Oklahoma City Times**, 5/22/70.)

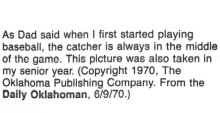

As Dad said when I first started playing baseball, the catcher is always in the middle of the game. This picture was also taken in my senior year. (Copyright 1970, The Oklahoma Publishing Company. From the **Daily Oklahoman**, 6/9/70.)

Working out in the summer of 1972 with the Brewers' Evansville minor league team. Standing with me is Al Widmar, pitching coach. (Dave Lucas, Evansville **Press**.)

Teri and I as happy newlyweds in 1972. (Copyright 1972, The Oklahoma Publishing Company. From the **Daily Oklahoman**, 6/5/72.)

As a major league catcher for the Brewers, I was no longer the clean-cut kid of my high school days. (Milwaukee **Journal**)

Sliding practice in spring training during my early days with the Brewers. (Milwaukee **Journal**)

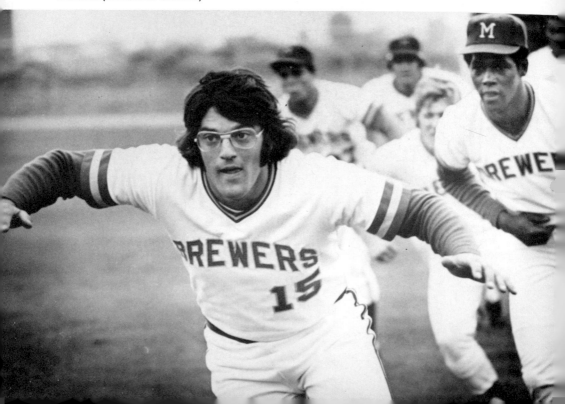

After my workout on my first day back from The Meadows, I tipped my cap to those wonderful fans who stayed to watch and gave me a warm ovation. (Jim McTaggart, Kansas City **Star**)

Some of those great fans and their supportive sign on that first day back, April 26, 1980. (Jim McTaggart, Kansas City **Star**)

As a Royal with Manager Jim Frey and George Brett. (Fred Kaplan)

I was the picture of miserable dejection after our loss to the Phillies in the first game of the 1980 World Series. My base-running blunder was partly responsible for our defeat, and I was crushed. (Jim McTaggart, Kansas City **Star**)

There's always a lot happening at home plate. Here, as a St. Louis Cardinal, I'm tagging Bill Buckner of the Chicago Cubs in a May 1982 game. (UPI)

Sometimes the action gets rough. On this play I was separated from my cap, my glasses, and, unfortunately, the ball (lower left corner) by a sliding Atlanta Brave in a May 1982 game. (UPI)

My crouching, weight-on-the-back-foot stance may look funny, but it works!

My inexpressible joy after the last out of the 1982 World Series is captured in this now-famous picture as I jumped onto and hugged Bruce Sutter. (Bill Stover)

The people of St. Louis celebrated our World Series victory by jamming the downtown area to see us in a parade. It was a day I'll never forget. (Bill Stover)

Deanne won my heart by showing that in addition to being beautiful and charming, she could fish, too!

Deanne and I on our wedding day with the minister who married us, Kenneth Tucker.

Proud new parents with our little bundle of joy, Lindsey, born March 31, 1982. (Morris Sealy, Independence **Examiner**)

I enjoy being a Cardinal, but I enjoy being a daddy even more. (John Schaefering)

The Porter family in the fall of 1983. God has been very good to me. (Bill Deerfield)

I had my best year ever with that.

You see, doing well was no longer good enough for me. I was obsessed with becoming the best in every department.

Who can fault you for wanting to improve yourself, to be the best you possibly can be? No one.

Now, winning, being perfect, is okay, if your motives are right. But there was something a little twisted about my motives. I was pursuing success for the wrong reasons, to squelch the hate and anger in me. It was like scratching poison ivy.

Not to belabor the point, but even if my desire to win had been pure, winning, being number one, is not a big enough goal for a man's life. That may sound strange coming from a professional athlete, but it's true.

I returned home to Oklahoma City to visit the folks and unwind. I did a bit of hunting and fishing and partying, then returned to KC to do some promotional work for the Royals.

I loved the Royals, and I planned to be with them a long, long time. I found I loved Kansas City, too, and wanted to make it my permanent home. So that winter I bought a house, and I asked my brother Eddie and his wife to live with me. They did. Later, Denny moved in, too.

That fall and winter I did my share of boozing and drugs (always the drugs). I remember one night when I walked into a bar with my half-sister Barbara's husband, Wayne.

We were sitting at a table having a pitcher of beer. I had just done a little cocaine and was flying.

A big guy was playing a little guy in pool. The big guy had a big mouth, too—kept putting the other guy down in a really insulting way. Finally I spoke up.

"Hey, you play a pretty good game of pool—with your mouth!"

The big guy was getting ready to take a shot when I said it. Instead, he straightened up and leaned on his pool stick.

"Put your money where your mouth is, turkey!" he drawled. "I'll show you how good I kin play!"

"No...no!" I said, dismissing him. "I don't need any trouble. Just play your game."

Nothing more was said. We drank a couple more pitchers, and I did a little more coke in the john. We closed the place up.

As we were all heading toward the door—weaving, actually—I was itching to smash somebody. (I was feeling that way a lot lately.)

"You called me a turkey before," I said to the big mouth. "I'd appreciate you not calling me that again."

Fixing me with beady eyes, he sneered, "I'll tell you what—not only are you a turkey, you're a turkey sissy!" And he brought up his beefy hands and clapped me hard on the ears.

I let out a stream of obsenities and drilled him one in the mouth. He moaned and started to go down, spitting blood. I hit him three more times. He hit the floor like a sack of chicken feed—or maybe cement—and lay there like a dead man.

I stood over him, cursing. He didn't move.

"Hey, D.P.!" Wayne said, grabbing my arm. "We'd better get out of here! You can't afford any trouble!"

I shook him off. But I was still straight enough to know he was right. We cut out of that place.

This was all just fun and games to me. When I wasn't carousing, fighting, and doing drugs that winter, I was working out with weights and playing basketball. I guess I was schizoid—baseball was one world and partying was another. I didn't see the discrepancy between my wild partying and my disciplined workouts.

Baseball was the thing I was really living for—my goal. The Royals had opened that door for me once more. Whitey had told me midway through the 1977 season that he wanted me to be one of the four top catchers in the league that year. Then he added that the following year he wanted me to be in the top two. And the year after that, he said, he expected me to be the best.

I could hardly wait for spring training time to roll around again! I wanted to prove Whitey right!

20

Frustrated Again

"I tell you one thing, I sure won't stay up worrying about anything tonight."

It was June 4, 1978, and I was being interviewed by reporters after rapping a perfect 5 for 5 against our old nemesis, the White Sox. It was a career high for me. I had hit two triples, a double, and two singles in that 13–2 rout of the Sox, driving my batting average up to .306.

I needed something like that game really badly at that point.

I had begun the season determined to outshine my 1977 debut with the Royals. And I had done beautifully for the first month; I was again named Player of the Month for April.

Then came May. One morning I woke up, and it just wasn't there. I went into a slump. In a few weeks my batting average was down fifty points. And there was nothing I could do but suffer and hang in there.

When things turned around again, what reporters described as my "rampage" started modestly enough. In the third inning of that White Sox game I managed to get a single that brought in a run and gave us a 4–2 lead. Then, in the fourth, I got hot and doubled. The triples came in the sixth and the eighth. I needed a homer to hit for the cycle, but my last time up I only singled.

But I was out of that slump and stayed out of it. The proof is that Whitey Herzog worked me to death that season. I logged the most playing time of any catcher in 1978, with 150 games. I earned the team's Player-of-the-Month award twice. In addition to that 5 for 5 showing, I had a four-hit game and four separate three-hit outings. Though my batting average was only .265, I was becoming a consistent run-producer. I reached career highs by slamming eighteen homers and driving in seventy-eight runs. The frosting on the cake was my being selected to catch my second All-Star game, which was played in San Diego. (I got to pinch-hit, with two outs in the ninth, and made the last out of the game! Bad as that was, it was an improvement over my 1974 All-Star debut, when all I did was warm up everybody else in the bullpen and never got near a bat!)

The Royals did really well in 1978. By July we were in the race for the American League West title against the Rangers and Oakland. It was nip and tuck, with the standings changing almost daily. Just like 1977.

A month later, in mid-August, we had done it: we were in first place! We dropped out only briefly in September, when our whole batting line-up seemed to go into a slump.

Then, like magic, between September and October we once more snatched victory from the jaws of defeat to win our *third straight* title. Our pitching was largely responsible. (It had been great all season.) Dennis Leonard won twenty-one games; Paul Splittorff, nineteen; Larry Gura, sixteen; and Rich Gale, fourteen.

And for the third time in three years, we would be meeting the Eastern Division champions, the New York Yankees. We were hungry to win the pennant, having been beaten twice in a row in playoffs that went the limit of five games. Nobody, but nobody, believed we had a chance, not even our loyal Royals fans.

The first game, played at Royals Stadium, should have been a snap for us. The Yankees were tired, coming as they did straight from their playoff victory over the Boston Red Sox the day before. Their star pitchers, Ron Guidry and Goose Gossage, were recuperating from their labors, while our best pitcher, Dennis Leonard, was well rested.

The Yankees were obliged to pit rookie Jim Beattie against us. But Beattie, a six-six former basketball player from Dartmouth, surprised everyone—including the Yankees—by allowing us only two measly hits in five and a half innings. Then relief pitcher Ken Clay, another youngster, took over and held us hitless for the rest of the game!

"I'll tell you," sighed Whitey Herzog, "when you get [just] two hits, you're gonna get beat."

Then, adding insult to injury, Leonard and the rest of our well-rested pitching staff gave up sixteen hits, including three by designated hitter Reggie Jackson, one of them a homer.

It was not just embarrassing; it was humiliating. Not only was our hitting bad, but we were making all kinds of errors. In the first inning second baseman Frank White muffed a double play. Then Amos Otis bobbled the ball on a hit and made a bad throw to the infield.

In the third inning Pete LaCock fielded Lou Piniella's pop foul—then dropped it. Al Cowens misplayed a ball off the right-field wall by Graig Nettles, turning what should have been a double into a triple. Then I had a passed ball, and George Brett had a ball kicked out of his glove on a play at third base.

I'm not sure now exactly when it happened, but in one game that might have been this one, I gave Leonard a signal that resulted in Jackson's hitting a homer. Then, in the very next inning, when Reggie came to bat again, for some reason I gave Leonard the same sign—and sure enough, Jackson clobbered the ball again. I was shocked. How could I have forgotten that Reggie had hit that same pitch out of the park just the previous inning? What was happening to my memory?

The final score was 7–1. "It was the flattest I've ever seen my club," Whitey said after the rout.

The second game belonged to our pitcher Larry Gura. Gura had a score to settle with the Yankees' off-again-on-again manager, Billy Martin, who had insulted him constantly while he was on the Yankees, particularly over his tennis playing. (Martin said it was a "sissy" sport.) Gura had been traded to the Royals in 1975, and Martin continued to taunt him. In the 1977 play-offs, for instance, when Martin heard Gura would pitch the crucial fourth game, he had suggested he might send a limo to pick Gura up to bring him to the ballpark, ". . . so he won't get hurt."

Well, he who laughs last . . .

In game two, Gura allowed only two runs in six-and-a-third innings and had Martin laughing out the other side of his mouth. Added to that, our line-up had Yankees' pitcher Ed Figueroa baffled and frustrated. In the first two innings alone we got five hits and five runs off Figueroa, a twenty-game winner.

By the seventh inning we were leading 5–0. Gura was replaced when the Yanks got four hits, producing two runs. When we came to bat, Pete LaCock got a double off Dick Tidrow, and Clint Hurdle banged a triple. But the corker was little shortstop Freddie Patek, who slammed a homer into the stands near the left-field line. Patek was so taken by his own performance that he stopped midway around the bases to watch the ball sail into the stands.

In the same inning Willie Wilson and Thurman Munson nearly came to blows when Wilson gashed Munson's chin in a collision at home base. There were one or two other such incidents when the sparks flew, showing both teams were in dead earnest.

We won the game 10–4. The turnabout surprised everyone. I think we were so mad over our humiliating defeat in the first game that it got our adrenaline flowing. Said George Brett: "Maybe they came out thinking we were pushovers."

Even Whitey was puzzled by our performance: "That's the way we are," he said with a shrug. "I never know what they're going to do. We're a model of inconsistency."

The playoffs moved to New York for game three, which turned out to be an exercise in total frustration for us. We started off doing well. George Brett hit three home runs, but then the Yankees dogged us: we would score, then they would score. We were leading on three separate occasions, but we couldn't keep the lead.

In the third inning, after Brett put us on top 2–1 with his second homer, Amos Otis was on first and there were two outs. When I came to bat, I hit a liner into right center that Mickey Rivers tried to catch. Evidently he fumbled around with the ball, because when he started trotting toward the dugout with it, the umpire frantically signaled that it wasn't a catch.

Meanwhile Amos Otis was having a memory lapse—thinking there was only one out, he took his time trotting from second. He could have scored by the time Rivers realized his mistake, but he was so slow that Rivers had time to fire to third and Otis was tagged out. "I ain't got nothin' to say!" Otis later snapped at reporters over his mistake.

In the fifth inning, Patek gave the Yanks a run when he had Piniella trapped in a rundown between first and second and zinged a wild throw, missing first baseman Pete LaCock by a good twenty-five feet and sending the ball into the box seats behind first.

In the sixth, LaCock banged out a triple, but he didn't make it home. Clint Hurdle struck out, and Al Cowens dribbled the ball back to the mound and got thrown out, leaving LaCock frozen at third.

By the eighth inning we were ahead 5–4. Then, with two Yankees on base, Whitey was afraid to pit lefty Paul Splittorff against power-hitter Thurman Munson, so he brought in right-hander Doug Bird. It turned out to be a disaster. Munson clobbered a 425-foot, two-run homer—the game-winning hit. It was a close 6–5 contest.

We had one more chance to turn things around. Game four started out on a good note for us, with a triple by Brett, who scored.

It was our only run of the evening.

In spite of phenomenal pitching by Dennis Leonard, who at one point retired thirteen Yankees in a row, Ron Guidry proved more effective. Only one of our players got as far as third base for the remainder of that sad game. Oh, I had a hit—a single. So did Pete LaCock.

It was all over. The Yankees beat us 2–1 and captured the pennant from us for the third straight year.

In the inevitable post-mortem, I told *Sports Illustrated*'s Larry Keith that "very little separates these two teams." His reply (in print) was: "... but that small difference is what makes KC a good team and New York a super one." Touché.

I was establishing a pattern. I played hard during the season, carefully regulating my intake of drugs so as not to interfere with my playing. But in the off-season I went wild—as I had done the previous year.

I remember one night I was driving my sister Pat and her kids home from Mom and Dad's. I had been drinking all afternoon and had tooted some cocaine. Coke always gave me the feeling that I owned the world. I was going down that highway doing at least eighty.

I decided to have a little fun with Pat and took my hands off the wheel. "Looookee!" I slurred drunkenly.

"Darrell! Just put your hands back on that wheel! You crazy or something?" Pat cried.

I just turned and gave her a stupid grin and pushed the van up to ninety. Her eyes were wild with fright.

"Darrell!" she screamed. "You drunken, drugged-up fool! If you want to kill yourself, then do it! But don't kill me and my children! Do you hear me!"

The more she pleaded, the faster I went. I'd grab the wheel for a second or two, then let it go again. But when the kids began crying, that got to me. I put my hands on the wheel and slowed to forty-five or so. Pat glared at me but said nothing all the way to the house. When she got out she hissed, "Don't you *ever* do that again, you d—— fool!" Her hands, as she fumbled in her purse for her house keys, were trembling with fear or rage—or both.

Heck, I was only trying to have a little fun. She couldn't take a joke. Women!

That same winter in Kansas City there was another incident in which a guy ahead of me in traffic wasn't moving fast enough— like the guy I had punched out in Milwaukee in 1976. I got on this other guy's tail and followed him for miles. He kept trying to lose me in traffic, but I was right on him, thinking how I was going to punch the living s—— out of him once he stopped. Suddenly, he pulled into a vacant parking lot. I pulled up about fifty yards away, got out, and started toward him.

His door opened, and he got out of the car and faced me. He had a gun in his hand, and it was aimed right at my belly. My mouth went dry.

He must have seen my out-of-state license plates, because he said, "I guess you Oklahoma boys don't know who you're tanglin' with, when you try messin' with us Missouri folks. Now, git back in your car before I blow your G—— d—— brains out, Okie!"

Drugged-up as I was, I took his advice and sped out of there!

21

Financial Troubles

Spring 1979, my third season with the Royals. It was going to be the best year of my major league career, as 1972 was for me in the minors. At least I wanted it to be. I vowed to break my neck trying—and maybe a few others, too.

Things didn't start out too well in spring training. I was plagued with injuries—a sore right shoulder, a pulled leg muscle.

As a result, I didn't get to play too much—eleven exhibition games in which I had twenty-five hits, including a homer and five RBIs. But I did get a lot of extra batting practice. So although I went into the regular season in April feeling a bit out of shape as far as my catching went, the extra work in the batting cage showed: in my first week I was 6 for 13, with seven RBIs. At the end of the month I was chosen Player of the Month for April, the third time running. The sports pages were crowing: "Porter Packs an Early Punch."

By our eighteenth game, I was really feeling my oats when we played the Indians.

I broke Mike Paxton's shutout in the fourth inning with a homer—my second of the season. I also knocked out "three little Indians" trying to steal second—Bobby Bonds in the third inning, Paul Dade in the seventh, and Horace Speed in the eighth.

One sports writer remarked that picking off those three Indians made it appear as if I was "on the business end of a Winchester rifle in the frontier days." We won the game 5-4.

I told the press, "I enjoy throwing guys out, as much as I do getting a single or a double." I said that my arm still felt weak from that sore shoulder, but I felt my throws were accurate.

Whitey Herzog had nothing but praise for me, something I still craved. "No doubt about it, Porter's the best catcher in the league," he crowed to a reporter. Then, after a moment's reflection he added, ". . . maybe in all leagues. He was last season." (When Whitey said that, I was batting .379 and had hit safely in fifteen of seventeen games.)

By mid-May I was doing so well that my name was being bandied about by sports columnists for a berth in the All-Star game. I was batting a career high at that time of .322, in 143 at-bats. I had five homers and thirty-seven RBIs. My pitchers were saying I called a "mean game." Oh, I was feeling good about myself, let me tell you. Everything was right on schedule!

A week after the voting for the 1979 All-Star team began, five Royals moved into first place in their positions: Fred Patek, Amos Otis, George Brett, Frank White, and guess who?

By the end of June, my batting average had dipped a bit—to .305, and although I had racked up nine homers, fifty-three RBIs, and had scored fifty runs, myself, the only thing in which I was leading the league was walks. I was exercising more self-discipline than usual and not swinging at the bad pitches I used to chase.

By late June, with a 10–3 victory over the A's, and the Rangers' victory over the Angels, we were tied with the Rangers for first place in the western division.

When a reporter asked me for a comment, I replied, "What's to get excited about? It's only June, not September. We've been there before."

July proved me right. Our hitting was still terrific, but our pitching collapsed. It was awful. At one point we lost thirteen out of fourteen games. One sports writer compared the embarrassment over our pitching to having an uncle in the family who likes wearing high heels and dresses. As catcher, of course, I felt partly to blame. I felt like yelling or punching something. We had been in slumps before, but never anything like this one.

Meanwhile, more personal problems were surfacing. Wouldn't you know it, just when I thought my drugs were under control, my finances were in shambles. After Teri and I split, I let everything slide for a long while. I didn't care about anything, not even money.

So I lost track of how much I had (as if I ever knew). I had made loans to family members and friends (even to friends of friends). I had gotten involved in a number of investment schemes that turned sour. I lost chunks of money, but I didn't care. Besides, I liked being thought of as generous to my family and friends— money was made to be spent, shared. And I did both freely. Shoot, there was always lots more. My salary with the Royals was $150,000 a year.

After forty thousand dollars went down the drain in a deal involving a leaky swimming pool in a mobile home park (including a ten-thousand-dollar tab for pickaxing a city water main), Dad thought it was high time I got a good financial adviser.

My half-sister Joy and her husband did business with Bill Katzbeck, a sharp young guy who has his own insurance business in Pittsburgh. So they introduced me to Bill, who expressed an interest in becoming my agent.

At first I was leery. Although I had always been a friendly, outgoing guy, strangers had begun to make me nervous. Before long, though, Bill and I became fast friends. I decided to retain him. Once I did, I felt better knowing I had someone with expertise to negotiate my baseball contracts and handle my TV and magazine testimonials and other similar matters.

Bill told me I needed someone to handle the money itself, to put it to work with some sound investments. He suggested Frank Knisley, a vice-president with the Pittsburgh National Bank. Knisley, Bill assured me, was a top man in financial management and estate planning, an expert in the field who had made several of his clients millionaires. Most important of all, he said, Frank Knisley was honest.

Again I was dubious. It meant another total stranger on the scene, poking around. Besides, things financial were over my head, always had been. I preferred things to be in a comfortable muddle; the details were too complicated, boring, and maybe a little scary. Still, I agreed to meet with Bill and Frank when the Royals were in Cleveland to play a series with the Indians. We met at my hotel.

I found Frank Knisley to be a corporate big-shot type—very methodical and practical appearing, low-keyed and unemotional, too. His interest in athletes probably stemmed from the fact that he had been a college football star in the 1940s.

Knisley told me the story of a top basketball player he had handled—or, more accurately, had *attempted* to handle. The basketball star, he said, was like a child in a candy store—totally unreliable and undisciplined. Money in his hands was like water in a sieve, except it ran through twice as fast. He couldn't even be relied on to return a phone call. Knisley ended the story by saying the big basketball star was now stone broke.

"Mr. Knisley," I said when he had finished the sad tale, "you're talkin' about *me*. I've done some of those very things, like not opening important letters, not returning calls."

"That is exactly why I don't think we can do business," he replied. "Darrell, I wouldn't sleep nights if we couldn't work together in solving your financial problems."

"But I do need help," I said. "I do want to change."

"Okay, what are your assets?" he said crisply, taking out a pad and pen. "List them for me."

I gave Bill Katzbeck a pleading look. He just shrugged.

"Uh, I have $50,000, I *think*, in a checking account," I replied.

"And your debts are what?"

I felt trapped. "I'm not ... uh ... sure. But you can ask my CPA. He's in Kansas City. I'll give you his name and number."

Frank took the information, then put away the pad and pen. He sat back, crossed his legs, and studied me. I felt like a bug on a pin.

"Darrell," he said at length, "how long does a man last in the major leagues?"

"Ten years or so."

"Well, you're halfway through that, aren't you? And you've already let several hundred thousand dollars slip through your hands. And what do you have to show for it?"

The air-conditioning was going full-blast, but suddenly I was sweating.

"Tell me, Darrell," he continued, "when your baseball career is over in say five years, what kind of job are you prepared to take?"

The question hung heavy in the air. I thought I didn't like this guy. I felt like I had been called to the principal's office.

"I . . . uh . . . I've never done anything but play ball," I replied sheepishly.

"Well, what do you know about truck driving?"

"Gee, I don't think I'd care to do *that!*"

"Oh? Well, then, what about being a short-order cook in one of those diners?"

Now I was really getting burned up. I was a major league star. Just who did the man think he was talking to? But I felt guilty, too. The man made me feel guilty.

A few weeks later, I contacted Frank Knisley again and asked him if he would handle my finances. He agreed he would—with the strict proviso that, once invested, I would not touch the principal and wouldn't even use the earnings unless absolutely necessary. "The idea, Darrell," Frank explained, "is to accumulate enough principal so that the earnings generated can keep you living at the economic standard you're now used to for the rest of your life. Even if you never work another day."

"Sounds great," I replied.

"Yes, but it won't be easy. It means living within your means. Now, if you all at once want to invest a chunk of money in some harebrained scheme, Darrell, be my guest," he said. "After all, it's your money. But if you do, we part company. Is that understood?"

It was going to be tough, but I agreed to everything.

Of course, Knisley almost had a stroke when he learned I hadn't paid my income taxes for 1977 or 1978, because my record-keeping was about as organized as a wastebasket. But he managed to straighten that mess out and keep me out of jail.

Even after we thought we had my finances all shipshape and well ordered and businesslike, things had a way of coming out of left field. And Frank would be burning up the phone lines. "Darrell, you mean to tell me *that* wasn't paid?" was his favorite barb.

"Darrell, *please* start opening your mail!" ran a close second.

But I began to feel better, knowing I had found a good agent and a crackerjack money man, both of whom also became good friends.

22

All-Star Catcher

By July 1979, I had slipped behind Carlton Fisk by over eighty-three thousand votes in the All-Star voting. Sid Borgman of *The Kansas City Star* waxed indignant: "If Darrell Porter doesn't pull more votes than Carlton Fisk or Thurman Munson as starting catcher...the system of allowing fans to pick the starting teams should be stuffed." Just where, Borgman failed to specify.

But when the dust settled, the Royals had done it! *Three* of us had done it. I would be starting catcher, Frank White would be on second base, while George Brett would be on third. In the final vote I collected 2,046,505, while runner-up Thurman Munson had 1,806,261. I quipped to reporters: "I want to thank all the Kansas City fans for stuffing the ballot boxes!" Modesty with a touch of humor, don't you know. But inside I was crowing!

The fiftieth All-Star game was played July 17 at Seattle's Kingdome before a sellout crowd of nearly sixty thousand. Interest was especially keen because the American League was determined to break the National League's All-Star winning streak of seven straight games.

A high-scoring game was expected, not only because of the heavy hitters playing, but also because of the small size of the Kingdome—316 feet at the foul lines and 356 feet in the power alleys. It was an indoor stadium that produced 127 homers in the first half of 1979 alone.

I was thrilled to be playing my third All-Star game on the same

146

team with guys like Tommy John and Ron Guidry. But for all the hoopla, it turned out to be far from the most exciting game on record. It *was* the longest—three hours and eleven minutes.

There was an initial flurry of excitement in the first inning with a run-scoring triple by the National League's Mike Schmidt (Phillies) and a double by George Foster (Reds), which were followed in our half of the inning by a two-run homer by Fred Lynn (Red Sox).

The unscheduled bit of craziness came when Morganna (known as the "Kissing Bandit" of baseball) dashed onto the field in the first, wearing short-shorts, and bussed George Brett.

My most exciting moments of that long, long game came in the sixth inning. I doubled to right field, which sent Rick Burleson of the Red Sox to third. Reggie Jackson then bounced to second, and I foolishly got caught in a rundown between second and third and got tagged out. Then Bruce Bochte (of the home town Mariners), batting for Frank White, singled, driving Burleson home.

By the eighth, the score was tied 6–6, after Lee Mazzilli of the New York Mets clobbered the ball for a 316-foot homer for the National League. In our half of the inning, with two American League players on base, we might have gone ahead had either of the base-runners scored. But they were both gunned down (in separate plays) by outfielder Dave Parker of Pittsburgh.

In the top of the ninth, American League pitcher Jim Kern of the Rangers walked Joe Morgan of the Reds, then balked him to second. He then intentionally walked Dave Parker, who was followed at bat by Craig Reynolds of the Houston Astros, who fouled out. Next, Kern walked Ron Cey of the Dodgers.

With bases loaded and only one out, a master hand was needed, so AL manager Bob Lemon summoned Ron Guidry from the bullpen.

It was a tense few moments, let me tell you. But instead of striking two men out, as we hoped, Guidry walked Lee Mazzilli, bringing Joe Morgan home and giving the NL a winning score of 7–6.

That was a tame finish to a game that had begun to get interesting.

Coming out of the All-Star break, the Royals had plenty to worry about. Jimmy the Greek was saying we were a 100 to 1 shot to retain our American League West title. And, beginning July 27, we were facing a grueling thirty-seven-game marathon against our six division foes. And we were still in fourth place.

I was bidding to make the record books as the walking-est guy in baseball that season. I had just passed my seventy-fifth walk in 101 games. My goal was one hundred, I told reporters. "Yeah, sure, why not?" I told them with a laugh. "I might as well get into the records that way. If it's in the books it counts. That's what matters."

I did go on record saying I wasn't about to swing at any more bad pitches. I had been swinging at too many really rotten pitches, and I was tired of it.

Also, I was feeling rotten. My eyes were irritated; I couldn't see the ball well; and I had some kind of bug in my system. But I refused to give in; things were just too critical to slough off now. So I struggled along with the team.

On August 2, 1979, something happened to cast a shadow over the baseball season: Thurman Munson was killed when his private jet crashed. He was thirty-two.

Thurman had a reputation for being unfriendly, but to me he was always a nice guy who offered sound advice on my hitting. One sports writer characterized him as a man "of fierce integrity on and off the field."

Gabe Paul, a close friend of Munson's and president of the Cleveland Indians, summed up Thurman Munson like this: "He was one of those guys who worked hard at refusing to let people think he was a nice fellow. But under all the toughness, he was a very nice guy. If you were his friend, he'd go the limit for you."

The outpouring of grief for Munson within baseball and from outside was tremendous.

But life goes on. Ironically, while the team sweated to pull ahead in the race for the pennant, I was having my best year ever, despite temporary setbacks. I was batting .294 and led the league in bases on balls, and I was league runner-up in on-base percentage. In addition, I had now collected thirteen home runs and seventy-four RBIs in 361 at-bats. Whitey wasn't working me quite as hard as he had been the previous season. By his own admission he was resting me a little more. It helped.

My goal was to hit twenty homers in 1979. Until now, I had always thought of my range as being fifteen to eighteen home runs a year, but having hit eighteen in 1978, I was setting my sights higher.

The Royals continued to struggle. It was mid-August. We dropped a three-game series in Milwaukee, just when our competition—the Angels, the Twins, and the Rangers—was also losing series. Here we had a perfect chance to pick up some ground but failed to do it. (Then again, we didn't lose any ground either!)

But it was aggravating. And we were slated next to play a four-game series against the Orioles, who were leading the American League East.

Those games turned things around for the Royals. We took three out of four from the Birds. Suddenly we were just four and a half games out of first place. Would it be a repeat of 1977, when we came from behind to win the pennant? It was hard to believe that just four weeks earlier we had been ten and a half games out of first place.

We had thirty-nine games remaining in the season, including two road trips in the final six weeks. Fourteen of the twenty final games would be played at Royals Stadium, which gave us some hope. Could we do it?

In a 10-9 victory over my former teammates on the Brewers, which put us within one and a half games of first place, I had one of my best performances of the season. In the first inning I drove in two runs with a double—becoming the eighth catcher in American League history to drive in ninety or more runs in a season. In the bottom of the tenth, with bases loaded and one out, I slammed a drive off the right-field wall. I barely missed a grand slam—something I would have dearly loved to do while playing against my former club. I think that hit drove in the winning run.

A few days later we met the Yankees. It was crisis time, and I rose to the occasion, as did every other Royal. In the first inning, with two men on, I took my position at the plate in my awkward-looking open stance. The one that works. I belted a three-run homer. It was my sixteenth of the season.

In the fifth inning, we were winning 7-0. By the time the dust settled we had won 8-3.

Meanwhile, the first-place Angels took a drubbing at Cleveland—7-1.

We had a feeling of déjà vu—as if we were living 1977 over again. After two months of struggle, we were suddenly a half-game ahead! Kings of the (western) mountain again! And I had contributed heavily to the victory.

Whitey Herzog wasn't about to count his chickens, however. "You never know in this game," he said. Then he reminded us of what had happened to the Angels, who thought they had it made earlier in the season. We still had a month to play. A lot could happen.

I was garnering praise from every quarter. Sports columnists were predicting I would have my best season ever. I should have been jubilant, for that, after all, had been my goal all along.

Yet I felt a strange sense about it all, almost as if the Darrell Porter about whom everyone was crowing was somebody else. I was alien—detached from that successful Darrell Porter. *He* was the one who had been starting catcher in the All-Star game. *He* led the Royals in RBIs; *he* was second on the club in game-winning hits, the AL leader in walks. *He* was the catcher Whitey Herzog had called "the best in the league."

The feeling of having failed somehow was so strong that I began openly talking about it. "I'm getting ready to go over one hundred RBIs," I told one reporter, "and yet, it doesn't seem exactly like it's sufficient. . . . I would be going bananas if the other guys weren't going good and we were losing. I'm my own worst critic." My teammates dismissed it; they thought I was being modest. Sports writers wrote good-naturedly about my having "a few bolts loose" to talk that way. Whitey Herzog turned it into a virtue when he said, "Good players never think they're doing good enough."

How could they know that something more serious was going on— something that no amount of praise, camaraderie, or good-natured backslapping could heal?

There were other things. The fans and people on the street were making me more and more nervous and apprehensive. People tend to stare at you when you're a professional athlete, and you get used to it or at least live with it. But lately there was something in the smiles of strangers I didn't like at all. It seemed they were amused about something and they weren't letting me in on it.

I began staying in more and more when I wasn't playing. I enjoyed being at home with my brothers, just drinking beer and doing drugs. There were so many people out there . . . so many strangers, and so much pressure to perform. The only place I felt really relaxed and safe anymore was at home or on the field.

Of course, it wouldn't do at all to let anyone know what my fears were, what I was really thinking or feeling. I carefully maintained my public image, my cheerful professional personality.

On September 25, in the 158th game of the 1979 season, we met the Angels at Anaheim Stadium for the second in a final three-game series. The deciding series.

They had won the first game, in what one writer described as a "chilling" 4–3 victory.

Now, Angels' pitcher Frank Tanana, who had been plagued by injuries, was in top form. In the second game, he held us to five hits.

Our pitching collapsed again. The Angels got eleven hits off Craig Chamberlain, Paul Splittorff, and Dan Quisenberry. The final score was 4–1.

It was all over.

Although there was one game remaining in this series, the Angels were now five games ahead. They had clinched the western division title.

The next day, the newspapers carried a two-column picture of yours truly waiting at Kansas City International Airport for a ride home. That forlorn picture captured my mood perfectly—isolation, loneliness, defeat.

It was some consolation that I had enjoyed my best year ever. But the Royals had lost the division race for the first time in four years. I had tried, sure, but I was partly responsible for the failure of our pitching staff. More than once I had called a stupid pitch, only to watch the ball disappear over the wall or up into the stands. *I had let the team down. I had failed again!*

To add salt to the wounds of defeat, on the final Sunday of the season, before a packed Royals Stadium, the Oakland A's stole the runner-up spot from us when they beat us 6–5.

Even before the dust of the season settled, rumors were flying that Whitey Herzog's head was on the block.

Whitey talked with Joe Burke. Burke confirmed it: Whitey wouldn't be rehired.

When I heard the news on TV, I was furious. "I think it's dumb!" I told reporters. "I can't believe it!"

Then I launched into a tirade against the Royals' management, accusing them of making Whitey a scapegoat for the Royals' failure to capture the pennant. "That's the only thing they can be doing!" I fumed, adding, "I hope Whitey goes to the National League. I'd hate to have that guy managing against me!" The next day the story appeared on sports pages across the country. I didn't care.

It was so unfair! Whitey had taken our team and turned us all into winners. He had won three straight western division championships. Now, because he lost one, they had booted him. Baseball!

There have been few managerial dumpings that proved more unpopular with the fans and the media. TV stations and newspapers joined me in blasting the Royals for days. They had special condemnation for Joe Burke, for his refusal to give a reason other than that it had been "for the good of the team."

It took me several days to work up the courage to call Whitey. "I just don't know what to say," I told him. "It's not fair. G——d——! It's just not fair! What the h—— do they want?"

"Darrell," he replied in an almost optimistic tone, as if he was talking me out of a slump, "you and I know these things happen all the time in baseball. There's nothing we can do about it."

I could have cried. I told him how much I appreciated all he had done for me.

"I didn't do it," he replied. "You did. You made the plays, not me."

"But I couldn't have done it without you."

"You're just coming into your own, Darrell," he said. "Your future is unlimited. Your best years are ahead, believe me."

He didn't know what I was really like inside. I was a failure. I was weak. He didn't know about the drugs. What would he think if he knew? He would hate me. He would be horrified.

"I won't be your manager anymore, Darrell," Whitey was saying, "but I'll be watching and thinking about you.

"Hey, kid, we had some great times, didn't we? Just look at what we did. We don't have anything to regret or to apologize for."

I was glad he couldn't see me . . . the tears in my eyes.

We talked a few more minutes, shared a couple of laughs over old times. Then we wished each other good luck and said good-by.

I had an urge to call him back . . . to tell him what my life *really* was. But I knew I couldn't. It crushed me to realize I could never share my inner torment with anyone. Oh, how I wished there had been a moment, just one moment, in all of the past three years, when the wall I had carefully built around myself had come crashing down.

The irony was that Whitey wouldn't have heard me. "You're doin' okay, kid. Hey, you're doin' okay," he would always say. "You're my catcher!"

But just the way he would say, "You're my catcher," had the power to restore my faltering confidence.

It was Whitey Herzog more than anyone who had helped me feel I was regaining some of the manhood I seemed to lose when Teri went out of my life.

It was with a deep, grievous sense of loss that I realized Whitey was out of my life, too. Maybe, just maybe, more than a baseball season was coming to an end.

23

On the Brink

I had reached my goal, the goal I had set for myself two years earlier when I came to the Royals. It had taken dedication, discipline, and hard, unrelenting effort. But I had done it. I had exceeded all my previous accomplishments: 20 home runs, 112 RBIs, 121 walks, league leader in on-base percentage. Also, I was only the second catcher in the history of baseball to drive in 100 runs, walk 100 times, and score 100 runs. What else was there to do?

I hadn't won the league's Most Valuable Player Award. (It went to Don Baylor of the Angels.) I ended up tenth in the voting for the second year in a row, and I felt I should have finished much higher. But if other people didn't give me the credit I deserved, at least I had the satisfaction of knowing I had accomplished what I had set out to do. I had come in first among catchers in all categories. I was the best.

So why wasn't I happy? I was *supposed* to be. Here I was living the dream of every American kid: I was a professional baseball star, one of the best in the game. *Why wasn't I satisfied? Why did I have the haunting feeling that all the glittering prizes weren't enough?*

I was like a mountain climber who, having struggled to the top of the highest mountain in the world, stands on the summit and suddenly realizes it's all over. There are no more mountains to conquer. What a desolate feeling that is. *My goal was supposed to make*

154

me happy, but it didn't. I had been cheated.

That was when I began to come apart at the seams.

After having strictly abstained from cocaine consumption for the entire season so that it wouldn't interfere with my game—my goal—I now plunged back into my habit like a glutton going off a diet—or a dog returning to its own vomit.

Within days of the season's end, I was consuming more than a gram a day. About the same time, I was wrestling with a growing feeling of insecurity. Always before, even in my deepest depressions, there was comfort to be found in my home, safety behind tightly locked hotel room doors. But it didn't seem to be working effectively anymore, my habit of withdrawing from everything and practically everybody. I let the phone go unanswered as a wasteful pattern of empty, aimless days and nights set in. Get up and make coffee, do a Quaalude, drink beer, sniff cocaine, and smoke cigarettes.

How striking, I thought one morning, *that the Royals know nothing about my drug use. Or do they?* Surely if they had suspected anything, they would have said something. Or was it their plan not to say anything until they could catch me at it? I told myself I was being stupid, imagining things.

But fear of discovery, always a worry, was becoming obsessive. October's anger turned into the deepening despair of November. I think I sensed the toll that guilt and shame and a five-year drug dependency were beginning to take, because I circled November 4 on a calendar. That day, I promised myself, I would start toning down all the drinking and drugs to a reasonable level.

The night of November 4 the news flashed around the world that more than fifty Americans had been taken hostage in Iran. Fascinated, I kept the television on most of the night, hungry for news of the hostages. I thought I had some idea of how they might feel, imprisoned against their will by forces stronger than themselves.

A week later I went elk hunting in Montana with a buddy, Jerry Pemberton, and some other friends, and for the first time since the end of the season, I felt happy and comfortable. There's a lot of solace to be found for a country boy like me in the rugged wilds of the Rocky Mountains. But I was ill at ease when Jerry and I began the long drive back to Kansas City, because I had arranged to stop in Denver and pick up some cocaine. Even though he and I had been tight friends and drinking buddies for years, I had managed (I hoped) to keep the darkest side of my life from him. As we neared Denver, I asked if he could keep a secret.

"What are you talking about, man? You know I can."

"I want to stop in Denver and make a phone call," I said. "I'm gonna try to get hold of a guy and buy some ... uh ... cocaine. You mind stopping?"

"H——, no."

We got to Denver about dark. As usual, it wasn't as easy to get the stuff as the supplier told me it would be, and the hours dragged on while we waited at a pay phone. Jerry had fallen asleep in the van before I had what I came for. We set out for Kansas City with Jerry at the wheel. I told him I'd wait until we were out of the city limits before I took some, but I broke down in the suburbs. I lay back and let the drug take charge. First came the amazing sense of well-being and contentment; relaxation, a new surge of energy. I found a good country-western station on the radio dial as we glided down the highway. Jerry didn't say much, but I felt resentful of him for watching. About ten minutes after the first rush of pleasure, the tenseness set in. I opened a beer for Jerry and reached for another snort of cocaine for me.

"Say, Pimbo, you know, I don't want you getting the wrong idea," I said. I couldn't look him in the eye. "I don't do this sort of thing all the time. It's just that I haven't had much in quite a while, you know."

"Sure, D.P., it's okay," he said. "Don't sweat it."

We drove all night and got to Kansas City about midmorning. The seven grams I'd bought in Denver for six hundred dollars were gone. I used the last little bit just before we got to the house, and I wished Jerry hadn't witnessed any of this. I told him this batch would definitely be the last coke I did for a while.

"This stuff is all right for a time, but you take so much and the effect starts wearin' off. You toot and toot and toot and hardly feel a thing," I lied.

Jerry went back to Indianapolis the next day, and I needed more coke. I never bought drugs in quantity. I was afraid that if I bought too much at once, I would go hog wild and snort it all up at once. Every time my supply ran low I was on the phone to sources for another small buy. If I was careful, I usually had enough to get high during the drive to replenish my cache.

But now I had a new problem. My doctor in Kansas City said he was stopping my prescription for Quaaludes.

"You've been taking them pretty steady for quite a while now, Darrell," he said. "I think we ought to stop for a while. If you need something else for your high blood pressure, we'll try it."

"Fine," I lied. "I've been thinking about quitting them. I think it's a good idea."

The next morning I got on a plane for Oklahoma City, where I knew there were cooperative doctors. I always had two things going for me when it came to conning doctors into prescriptions for Quaaludes. I was in a high-pressure occupation, and I had that convenient history of high blood pressure. I called Tom Spencer, an old high school buddy, from the airport and told him to pick me up at the doctor's office in forty-five minutes. At 10:00 A.M. we were in the airport bar. We each took two Quaaludes and drank a beer. We downed two or three more beers while waiting for my plane.

We were both wasted when we staggered out of the bar and bumped into two cops. The sight of the two uniformed policemen terrified me, but I didn't show it. The prescription, although it was perfectly legal, felt like it was burning a hole in my skin. Tom became belligerent, and the cops decided to arrest him for public drunkenness.

"You can't do that!" I protested. "He's a friend of mine!" By now the cops had checked our identification and recognized me. I guess my name was still almost as familiar in Oklahoma City as it was in the glory days of my high school career.

"You can get on that plane, Darrell," the cops said, "or you can accompany your friend to jail." Maybe I *should* have been arrested. Because I was a baseball star, people let me get away with murder.

I got on the plane. I'd never felt such fear of getting arrested. It was stark, unreasonable fear. I was still shaking when I got home two hours later and told Eddie about it. The thought of being jailed for drugs or drunkenness was unbearable.

So why did I keep doing it? I asked myself over and over, but it would be several months later, in a place I'd never heard of before, that I found the answer.

One night Frank Knisley called to clear up a business matter. I was zonked out and didn't want to be hassled. "Uh, hold on a minute, will you, Frank?" I said, and left him hanging. Poor Frank waited, and waited, and waited. I had put on my coat and gone out to get a six-pack. An hour or so later, Denny saw the receiver dangling and put it back on the cradle.

Then there was the weekend at Cape Hatteras. I had gone there to do some surf fishing. I was spaced out as Bill and Frank drove me from the airport; I was talking a lot of gibberish in the back seat. They thought I was just tired.

I had never been surf fishing before and waded out too far. Bill and Frank were alarmed. They called me in and warned me that if my waders were to fill with water and I got knocked down by a wave, I'd sink like a stone. I just laughed and waded out even farther. *So what if I drown?* I thought, as breakers boomed all around me. *All this s—— will be over once and for all!*

Later, Bill prepared dinner at our lodge. In the middle of the meal I excused myself and went into the other room. When I reappeared, I was moving and talking in slow motion. The transformation was startling. Not only that, I was paranoid.

"Ohh," I droned, "you're gonnna rippp mee offf, Fraaank!" And I kept repeating it.

When Frank got back to Pittsburgh, he told his oldest son how strange I had been acting.

"Dad, it sounds to me like the guy's on Quaaludes," his son volunteered. Quaaludes? Frank had never heard of them before. It was his first inkling that I had a drug problem.

Christmas was miserable. I flew home but hardly spent any time with the folks, which hurt Mom's feelings. One evening when I was home, we were talking about my season, and I was telling my half-sister's husband I had hit .291, hammered 20 home runs, and led the league with 121 walks.

"O.K., but what about the twenty-one passed balls?" It was Dad, of course. I left a short time later and spent the night with Joe Smart.

Christmas Day, Mom was cooking our holiday dinner. I wandered into the kitchen. Oh, that turkey smelled good! And a mince pie and an apple pie were baking in the oven too. Mom was peeling turnips; she looked up and smiled as I came in. "Won't be long now, Darrell!" she said. "Hungry?"

"Yeah," I replied, sitting down on a stool.

She wiped her hands on her apron. "You look real tired, Darrell. You've been staying out awful late. You're not gettin' your rest."

"Mom, I feel like I'm going crazy!" I suddenly blurted out. I lowered my head and began to cry softly.

Then her dear arms were around me, and she was saying in my ear, "You aren't doing any such thing! You're just tired is all! It's been a long, hard year for you. You just need some rest! You'll be just fine! There . . . there."

"Mom, you don't understand," I sobbed. *How could she? How could I tell her that when I wasn't home I was popping five Quaaludes a day and snorting cocaine every half-hour?*

Christmas dinner was delicious.

The next week, I didn't want to go to the annual fishing tournament my family and friends have at Lake Taneycomo in central Missouri. I was beginning to really hate being around people. Even friends were like strangers. But I decided at the last minute to go.

I didn't want anybody to know I had cocaine so I sneaked toots behind closed doors. We were drinking gallons of beer every day. My Quaalude habit was picking up steam, too.

We were staying in a cabin owned by a sales representative for an outboard motor company, as his guests. One afternoon we were in the boat, with me manning the motor and steering. Jerry, with his back to me, offered to pass me a sandwich. "No thanks," I said. Ten minutes after doing a Quaalude, the last thing I wanted was something in my stomach to dilute the effect of the drug.

We moved on through the water and spoke little. Shortly, Jerry reached into the knapsack and pulled out another sandwich. Still without facing me he asked, "You sure you don't want one of these?"

"No thanks." We glided on across the water. I gazed at the clouds.

"Darrell!" Jerry's voice exploded in my ear.

"What the h—— are you doing?"

I looked ahead suddenly, and there was a big, low-hanging tree limb right in front of the boat. We both ducked instantly or we would have been decapitated.

I gunned the motor, and the boat lurched forward. Jerry almost toppled out of the boat and cussed me while he regained his balance. Lake Taneycomo is actually a dammed-up river, several miles long but not very wide. I sped the boat full blast down the long, narrow body of water.

"Hey, take it easy, man!" he yelled. "You're gonna drown us!" It's a wonder either of us got home alive.

24

Paranoia

Sneaking cocaine between beers and Quaaludes that night, I felt miserable. Jerry and I went to the lounge at the local Holiday Inn. I hadn't been there ten minutes when the outboard motor salesman walked up and asked if he could join us.

"Sure, have a seat," I said, hating his intrusion. He unleashed a constant chatter about baseball, and I kept trying to anticipate what his next question would be. I wished he would leave. A few minutes later I excused myself and got up. The dimly lighted room seemed to shimmer. I had the feeling the guy was starting to figure out how drunk and drugged-out I was.

I remember asking somebody where the men's room was. I don't remember anything else.

Jerry's face shone through the haze.

"Darrell, what happened! Oh, for G—— sake, what happened?" It was Jerry speaking in a hoarse, panicky whisper.

Slowly, a dim awareness came back to me. I was seated on a toilet. Pot was scattered at my feet. I was holding a half-rolled joint.

"Hey, Pimbo. I just thought this would make us nice and mellow!" I said, or something equally idiotic.

"Darrell? Are you all right? Where did all this blood come from?"

My right hand was throbbing. The knuckles were bruised and bleeding. Staggering to my feet, I looked around and saw the mirror was splattered with blood. Bloody paper towels were thrown everywhere. Jerry opened another toilet door and found a guy about my age sprawled half-unconscious on the toilet seat holding a blood-soaked paper towel against his mouth. He looked terrified.

"C——, Darrell, what did you do?" asked Jerry.

I kept mumbling over and over, "He was bad-mouthing me. I didn't want to hit him. I really didn't! I didn't want to hit him."

Jerry said something to the guy, then started pulling me out of there.

"Let's go, let's go, D.P., for G—— sake! What if a cop came in right now, with blood and pot all over the G——d—— place? Come on!"

He got me away, and we sped back to the cabin. Jerry fell down twice trying to carry me up the steps to the cabin door.

The next day he left for Indianapolis.

"Hey, man, I'm sorry, but this is just getting a little too rough for me, buddy," he said before he left. "Darrell, I think you need some help. Why don't you go back to Kansas City and talk to a doctor or something?"

"Get the h—— out of here!" I yelled. "I *know* I did a dumb thing last night, but it won't happen again!"

I fished another day before I drove back to Kansas City, worrying all the way about the guy in the men's room and what would have happened if anybody but Jerry had walked in and found us. *Who was that guy, anyway? Why did I hit him? Was he gay? Did I hurt him bad?*

Maybe he recognized me. I switched off the radio and tried hard to think. *What, in God's name, was the matter with me that night? I don't go around starting fights in bars!* I closed my eyes and tried to pray.

"Dear Lord, I know I haven't prayed in quite a while now, and I've really strayed from Your way. But I need help, Lord. I need help!"

But no inspiration came. I felt abandoned, frightened, and foolish. *That's it. I'm not taking any more cocaine. As soon as baseball starts, I'll be all right! I'll finish what I've got and that'll be the last of it.* A late-model sedan had been behind me for several miles, and I kept glancing at it through my rearview mirror. Suddenly, my breath caught in my throat. The car was following me! I was so scared I could hardly keep the van on the road.

It must be the police! The guy I had the fight with must have recognized me and filed a complaint! I slowed to about forty, and the car pulled alongside and passed. A woman about sixty years old was behind the wheel. Still I could not quell my fear.

I stopped and searched the van, finding some pot in the glove compartment and two Quaaludes on the floor. Cupping them in my left hand, I pulled back onto the highway and watched for a chance to heave it all away. Suddenly, in the rearview mirror, I saw red lights flashing; a Missouri highway patrol car came roaring up behind me!

My knuckles turned white on the steering wheel, and I think I almost fainted. My foot pressed hard against the accelerator, and the speedometer jumped past sixty.

You stupid s——! I thought. The patrol car was getting closer! I started to stick the marijuana and Quaaludes in my mouth to swallow it all. *No, throw it out . . . throw it as hard and as far as you can!* An image flashed through my mind of my standing beside the highway in handcuffs. I froze and kept my eyes glued straight ahead as the patrol car whizzed around me and disappeared.

All strength and will was drained out of me. *Oh, Lord,* I thought, *this is miserable!* With another furtive look in the rearview mirror, I rolled down the window and threw the stuff away.

I got home about noon and walked into an empty house, but I still didn't feel safe. Fifteen minutes later I had checked and rechecked every window, making sure each was securely locked. The sight of the red light coming at me from behind would not leave my mind's eye. *What if they were after me? Were they still after me?* I called Wanda, my supplier.

"Listen, after January 1, I'm not buying anymore," I told her. "This stuff is startin' to mess me up too bad." I tried to make my voice sound hard. "I don't want anymore after January 1. That's it. I'll be seeing you around."

It was five days after Christmas, a Sunday. I was alone in the house and my right hand was swollen about twice its normal size, aching and throbbing.

I stared at the digital clock that sat on top of the television: 2:31 P.M. . . . 2:32 . . . 2:33 . . . I closed my eyes and drifted slowly into a fitful sleep. A sudden noise outside the window woke me. I bolted off the couch.

I dropped to the floor, waited, and listened. Silence. I crawled to the corner of the picture window and listened again. There it was again, a suspicious noise coming from the patio! *Somebody's out there!* I thought. *Did they see me?*

On my hands and knees, I parted the curtain near the floor and peered outside. Late-afternoon shadows were beginning to lengthen across the patio, but I saw nothing. Then I noticed it—a piece of newspaper blown against a patio chair flapping in the wind.

I went upstairs to bed and pulled the covers tightly around my chin. I lay there as the room grew dark in the twilight. Was the noise I heard really the newspaper? How could I be sure? After a while I fell into a deep sleep.

I was drinking coffee the next morning when the jangling of the telephone made me jump. Denny answered it upstairs and said it was for me.

"Tell 'em I'm asleep. I don't care who it is!" But it was an acquaintance calling with word of a new shipment of prime marijuana, Denny said. So I took the call and agreed to buy one thousand dollars worth. The guy brought it over that afternoon, and Denny, Eddie, and I lit up. It was special Hawaiian-grown, a type seldom available in the Midwest. Most pot is brown and coarse, but this was light green, almost powdery. It induced a relaxing, pleasant high. We sat and smoked, not saying much. But twenty minutes later I was edgy and jittery again.

"I think somebody followed me home from the lake yesterday," I told them. Eddie seemed fascinated, Denny skeptical.

"You sure? Who?" Denny asked, challenging me.

"H——, yes, I'm sure! And yesterday I heard *noises* outside on the patio! 'Course it might have been a piece of paper blowing against a chair, but I couldn't tell. I think there was somebody out there."

"D.P., why would anybody be following you? What would they want?"

"The only thing I can think of is they wanted to catch me with some dope. For a couple of months now I've had this feeling somebody was watching me, following me."

"You're just stoned," said Denny.

"My a——! I'm tellin' you, somebody is out to *get* me!"

"Who, for C—— sakes? Who?"

"Well, I think it must be the Royals. I think the Royals know what I'm doin'. They want to catch me!"

"What would they do if they caught you?" asked Eddie.

I gave him a look of utter disgust.

"I suppose they'd give me a fat new contract—then run out and tell everybody in the American League their All-Star catcher gets off on cocaine."

"Aw, you're crazy!" said Denny. "Besides, it ain't nobody's business what you do on your own time."

I took a Quaalude, opened a beer, and kept smoking the grass. Before long, I was bored with it. I snorted the last of the coke. The next day I spent about five minutes trying to talk myself out of calling Wanda. My right hand was still so sore and swollen I had to dial her number with my left.

"Wanda?...Darrell. Say, I just found out I've got a bunch of friends coming in for a few days. What you got?" Wanda said she couldn't help me. She was all out.

"Okay, no big deal," I said with forced cheerfulness.

If there is one thing all drug dealers have in common it is this: If they don't have what you want, just wait a few minutes and they're positive they'll get it. Without fail, they promise to come up with anything you need right away. Just wait a little while, they'll say. It won't be long. I'll make a couple of calls and get right back to you. They all say the same thing, and Wanda was no different. I did a Quaalude and waited for the phone to ring.

I washed it down with two beers and called Wanda.

"I told you I'd call, soon as I heard anything," she said. "It won't be long, I promise."

Five minutes later the phone rang, and I pounced on it.

"Darrell?" A man's voice.

"Yeah." It was Bruce Carnahan, the Royals' assistant public relations director and one of the best guys I've ever met in baseball. I was thinking, *Bruce old boy, you got no idea how badly you've disappointed me.*

165

"I just wanted to remind you about the luncheon this afternoon at the Stadium Club," he said.

I'd forgotten all about it.

"Sure," I said. "I was just getting dressed. Is everything all set?"

Feeling angry, disappointed, and imposed upon, I practically sang into the phone. "What time am I supposed to be there?"

"We'd like for you and Brett to get here no later than 11:30. The luncheon starts at noon."

"O.K., Bruce, I'll see you in a little while!"

I frantically called Wanda.

"Hey, man, I told you I'd get back to you as soon as I had anything! I've got some calls out now, and it won't be long. *I'll call!*"

The digital clock said 10:30. I had to be at the stadium in an hour. At 10:45 I called Wanda and got a recorded message. She'll call, it said. I started to leave the number at the Stadium Club to tell her to have me paged during the luncheon.

Oh great! I thought. *I'll have my cocaine supplier call me at the Stadium Club while I'm sitting there with the Kauffmans and the Burkes and all the fans and team officials.*

But I couldn't leave and take a chance of missing her call. It wasn't a conscious decision to forego the luncheon. I just sat there the rest of the afternoon working myself into a seething, boiling mass of hate and anger. *Just stand everybody up, you good-for-nothing s——! What'll they all think? Oh, well, George Brett will be there, and everybody knows George Brett is the only member of the team who plays championship baseball!*

That didn't help. I kept picturing Joe Burke and Ewing Kauffman (owner of the Royals) looking at my empty chair. I thought about Carnahan and could just imagine his throwing up his hands and pleading, "I called him this morning, honest I did! He said he would be here. Maybe he had a wreck or something." Minute by minute, the afternoon crawled along.

Why didn't Wanda call? G—— d—— her! She made me miss that luncheon! Well, maybe Wanda would like for me to take my business elsewhere.

The phone would not ring. What if the Royals had been suspecting I was a drug user? Missing the luncheon would make me look even more suspicious. What if they figured out why I wasn't there?

As desperate as I was to keep the line open, I called the public relations office at the stadium.

"I'm sorry I couldn't make it," I lied, "but my van wouldn't start. The battery's been down since last weekend. Somebody left the headlights on and ran it down. I'm sure sorry." I hung up quickly before the secretary could transfer me to anyone else.

Finally, about four o'clock Wanda called.

"How much do you want?"

"Just enough to get me through the weekend with these guys coming in. I told you, I'm gonna start getting ready for spring training."

25

The Drug Addict

There is a special kind of humiliation know only to the alcoholic and the drug addict. It is the spirit-withering disgrace of submission. On January 3, three days past my self-proclaimed deadline for quitting, I was down to about two more toots of coke. What was I going to say to Wanda? More to the point, what was she going to say to me? She'd laugh.

It is a depth all addicts sink to at one time or another. When your mind and body begin screaming for the drug to which you've enslaved them, things like self-esteem and self-respect go flying out the window—or maybe get flushed down the toilet. An addict, regardless of his accomplishments, talents, looks, or community status, is reduced to peonage when his supply is exhausted and he must return with bowed head to his supplier.

The supplier becomes the second-most important thing in the universe. God and family, friends and loved ones, are irrelevant—unless they get in your way. And then they are enemies to be stomped out. All you want is to put the chemical into your bloodstream, and no sacrifice is too great to accomplish that.

I was luckier (or maybe unluckier) than most addicts. I always had plenty of money to buy what I wanted. I was spared the disgrace of selling my possessions, of stealing, or of cheating. But when you're out of your drug and crazed with need, you become a beggar to your supplier. It's a degrading master-slave relationship with no room for doubt over who is the master and who the slave.

Tragically, many dealers in hard drugs get a perverse enjoyment from feeding on the misery of others. They become expert at taking advantage of this human bondage.

The starting catcher for the American League All-Star team dialed Wanda's number.

She laughed—but almost in sympathy at my weakness. She was a friend, and she didn't want to see me continue a habit she knew I wanted to break—needed to break. Again I conned her into getting me what I needed.

January 1980 was unusually snowless in Kansas City, but bitterly cold. I withdrew deeper and deeper within myself and would not leave the house for days at a time. On those rare occasions when I did venture outdoors, I always looked out the window first. One afternoon Eddie asked me what I was looking for.

"Eddie, there's a conspiracy. I know it. I just know it! People are watching the house all the time. I think it's the Royals."

I had enjoyed a beautiful anonymity in Milwaukee, able to go almost anywhere without being recognized. But everywhere I went in Kansas City, it seemed, someone pointed me out and struck up a conversation. A thousand times that winter I heard someone call my name in a crowded store or check-out line, but I quickly walked away, pretending not to hear. When I couldn't flee, I cut the conversation short to the point of rudeness.

The drug and alcohol thing was unbroken daily: Get up about noon, drink coffee, do a Quaalude, sniff cocaine, and drink beer.

One effect cocaine always had was to increase my appetite for beer. Mixing it with tomato juice, I could guzzle an entire case in a couple of hours while doing cocaine. And now I was up to five or six Quaaludes a day, more than ever. The doctor in Kansas City had cut me off, just as he had said. But I found another doctor there for what I needed, and Oklahoma City and my other source were only fifty-three minutes away by jet.

The only thing I took much interest in that winter was the plight of the Iranian hostages.

Following their story every day in the solitude of my house, a prisoner in my own home, I thought I must know what they were going through. Why didn't President Carter do something to get them out? I felt a kindred spirit to them. They were helpless; I felt helpless. But they were just temporary prisoners of fate and, hopefully, would soon be free. *But, hey, you will too*, I told myself.

In my pitiful, befuddled state of mind I had no way of realizing what was happening. I paced back and forth like a caged animal. I *was* a caged animal.

One afternoon a sportscaster in Kansas City requested, through the Royals, that I call him. I hated doing it, but I did. He wanted me to appear at a Muscular Dystrophy Association telethon he was emceeing the following week.

"I've got a fishing trip planned next week," I lied. "But if I get back in time, I'll be there." I knew I would never go.

Then why say you will? Everything was becoming a predicament. Even the simple decisions were tough. I felt physically vulnerable, unable to defend myself.

I went into the spare bedroom and sat down next to the window that looks out over the front of the house. *I'll wait here and see if anybody tries to sneak up*, I thought. *If a car drives up and turns off its lights real quick, it'll be them.*

I was still at the window at daybreak. The next night I was by my post again. Cars drove past about every thirty minutes or so, but every one that passed gave renewed life to my suspicions. Maybe they had seen me waiting at the window.

I stood up and strolled out of the room, pretending to close the door. Dropping to my knees, I crawled back to the window. A couple of minutes passed, then a car drove by very slowly. *It's them!* I crawled out of the room, then raced downstairs for my shotgun.

I rammed two shells into the breech and held the shotgun cocked and ready as I inspected every window and door. I took up my vigil at the window a couple more hours before finally going to bed. But first I made sure the shotgun was loaded.

A few days later, I watched part of the telethon on television. I hadn't gone fishing; I hadn't gone to the telethon. In fact, I hadn't left the house for almost a week. That night I made my usual inspection of the doors and windows before turning in.

But I still couldn't sleep. *How many can I take out with the shotgun?* I thought as I lay in the darkness. *If they come pouring through the bedroom door, I won't have time to reload.*

I went downstairs and scooped up a handful of billiard balls from the pool table. I took one in my right hand and felt its hardness. I visualized somebody coming into the room, and I leaned back as if to throw. I tossed the heavy, hard ball up and down, getting a feel for it. *About the same size as a baseball,* I thought, *but much harder and heavier . . . more lethal.* I calculated the distance between my bed and the doorway; then I put the billiard balls next to the loaded shotgun. *Shoot, if my right arm is strong enough to gun down runners at second base,* I thought, *I ought to be able to do some damage to somebody with these babies.*

When I went to bed the next night, I added to my arsenal—between the shotgun and the billiard balls a baseball bat now lay ready for action. *If they rush me in the night,* I thought, *I'll take out as many as I can with the shotgun. Then I'll stave them off with the billiard balls. And if there's any left I'll have the bat.*

Paranoia plagued me night after night until one evening I could stand it no longer. An overpowering urge to confront my enemies, to do battle with the unseen plotters, took control.

I'm tired of waiting for 'em to surprise me in bed, I thought. *I'll go outside and wait.* The long stone walkway leading from the drive to the front door of my house seemed like a perfect place to hide. After peering out the window and making sure no one lay in ambush for me, I slipped out the door and dropped to a crouch, the loaded shotgun cradled and ready.

The night was dreadfully cold. A few minutes later a car stopped in front of the house and parked just out of my sight. Every muscle in my body grew taut. *This was it. I'd have them.* I heard one car door slam shut. *Good, there's just one of them.* I heard footsteps rounding the corner of the driveway. The footsteps banged against the stone steps. I pulled back the hammer as a solitary figure walked toward me out of the shadows.

I leaped up and aimed the shotgun.

"Eddie! What the h—— are you doing?"

He looked at the shotgun and the wild look in my eyes and went pale.

"D.P.? Is that you? What are you doing out here with *that*?" He reminded me he got home from work every night about this time.

"Eddie, I'm tellin' you there's a conspiracy of people out to get me! By God, I'm tired of waiting! Let's go find out who they are."

At first he hesitated, but I was so insistent, he finally agreed. We got in Eddie's car because I figured they would all be on the look-out for my van. I congratulated myself on this clever move.

Eddie didn't know what to think as we drove away from the house.

"D.P., what about that shotgun? What are we gonna do if we get stopped by the cops with a loaded shotgun in the car?"

"Don't worry about that. I'll just tell 'em who I am and that we're looking for some people who are out to get me."

"For G—— sake, don't tell 'em *that*! Now, D.P., why don't we take the shotgun back home?"

"No!"

"Are you gonna shoot somebody?"

"Look, if you don't want to help, okay! You can just get out and walk home! But I know there's a conspiracy. There's an army of 'em, Eddie. They've got CB radios, and they call ahead. They know where I'm at every minute. They're out to get me!

"I think it's the Royals. They've found out what I'm doin', and they're out to get me before I embarrass 'em. You know how Kauff-man is always talking about community relations. What would Joe Burke do if people found out their catcher is a dope addict? I tell you, they've hired these people to get me. I think they've been watching the house every night."

It was past midnight now, and traffic in the northern, rural out-skirts of Kansas City had thinned to almost nothing. But soon we came upon a car.

"There's one of 'em there!" I shouted. "That's one of 'em, Eddie! Write down his license tag number, while I move up close behind him."

Eddie dutifully copied down the tag number while I trained my attention on the driver.

"I'm gonna pull around him now. Watch what he does. See if he talks into his CB." I passed the guy.

"He didn't look at us or do anything, D.P.," Eddie reported.

"That means he must have recognized us! They've probably got a description of your car, too. We'll keep going 'til we find out where their headquarters are."

In a residential area we passed a parked car and spotted a guy in the front seat who appeared to be asleep.

"That's one," I said. "That's gotta be one. They radioed ahead and told him we were coming up behind him so he pretended to be asleep." I touched the loaded shotgun lying in the seat between us.

Eddie gave me a funny look. Why couldn't he see what they were doing?

"I'll circle back behind him while you take down his number." It was dark, but our headlights splashed light upon the gray Mercury. I came to a stop behind the parked car. Eddie copied the tag number and looked uneasily at the shotgun.

"What exactly do you have in mind, D.P.?"

"Watch and see if he does anything. We'll check his tag number against other cars that follow us later."

"Darrell, let's put the shotgun in the trunk, okay?" I knew Eddie was concerned when he called me Darrell. Ever since we were kids, I was always "D.P." to him.

"Look, I'm not gonna shoot unless I have to," I said. "We'll see how many there are. If there's just a few of 'em, we won't need the shotgun."

We waited behind the parked car for several minutes, but nothing happened.

"Let's get out of here," I said. "They're wise to us now." I drove north toward Kansas City International Airport, sticking mostly to side streets.

My heartbeat quickened at the sight of every car.

"That's one of 'em there!" I said. "There's another! They know we're out lookin' for 'em now. They're keepin' in constant touch with each other through their radios. What we've got to do is find out where their headquarters is, their central lookout point. Shoot, it must be around here somewhere."

"What are we gonna do if we find it, D.P.?" It was about the fifteenth time he'd asked me. The loaded shotgun and my attitude were making Eddie very, very nervous.

"We're gonna kick their a——, that's what we're gonna do!"

"D.P., why don't we just go back home now? Okay, maybe there

173

is a bunch of guys out to get you. But I can't believe every car in Kansas City is part of it."

"G—— d—— it, there's an army of 'em!" I yelled. "A whole army!"

I followed a tan Ford for several miles, and I made Eddie write down the tag number.

"We'll follow him to the headquarters. We've got to find out where they meet. Then, by God, we'll kick some a——!" The Ford disappeared in a driveway, and a man about sixty-five got out. A few minutes later I pulled onto an access road that parallels U.S. Highway 291, heading toward the airport, away from town.

I immediately fell in behind a small red sports car.

About a half-mile ahead were lights, shining like a beacon in the dark night. A twenty-four-hour convenience store.

"That might be it! That might be where they meet," I said. "Get ready, man, we might have some trouble."

The sports car turned into the store parking lot, just as I figured it would. There were two men in it, and several cars were parked at the front entrance to the store.

I felt like a soldier heading into battle. *All right, you rotten b——s!* I thought. *I'm tired of being followed and hounded to death! If you want me, here I am. Come and get me!* I was ready to fight, ready to kill or be killed.

I stopped in the middle of the parking lot. My palms were sweaty, and my heart raced.

"I've got the gun, Darrell," said Eddie. He was pressed against the door, as far away from me as he could get, with a resolute look in his eyes.

"I'll blast 'em if we need to, don't worry, Darrell. But first, let's make sure who they are. We don't want to make any mistakes, do we?"

"Yeah, okay. Just be ready."

The two guys got out of the red sports car and started into the store. Then I saw a head pop up in the cab of a parked pickup.

"Look! Look at the s——!" I said.

"What the h——'s he doing?"

He wore a hat pulled down over his face. He looked straight at us, then looked away, and disappeared.

"Did you see that, Eddie? Did you see that? He saw us, and he ducked back down so we wouldn't recognize him!"

Inside the store, the clerk behind the counter and the two guys who got out of the red sports car were staring right at us!

Then I saw a fourth guy, somebody about my age, wearing a heavy parka that would be perfect for concealing weapons. He was in the corner of the store talking on a pay phone. And he was looking our way.

Tires screaming, I shot out of there and hit sixty within a block.

"That's it, Eddie! That's it! We've found their headquarters. Did you see the guy on the phone? He was calling somebody for reinforcements! And what about the guy in the pickup? He saw us, and then he ducked out of sight. That's it! I'm telling you, that's it!"

Eddie hardly knew what to think by now.

"Well, it did look suspicious, I'll admit," he said. "What are we gonna do now?"

"I don't know, but there's too many of 'em there now for us to take without using the shotgun."

"Let's drive around some more then."

We did—and followed three more cars. It was past 2:00 A.M., and we had been driving around more than two hours. Eddie kept suggesting we go back home, and finally exhausted, I agreed.

Before I went to bed, I checked all the doors and windows and made sure the shotgun was loaded and ready alongside the billiard balls and baseball bat.

I slept past noon. I got up and did a Quaalude, made coffee, and tooted my first cocaine of the day. *They'll move their headquarters for sure now*, I figured. *We should have confronted them.*

A sudden knock on the front door terrified me. I was alone, and I just froze on the couch. The knock came again, louder. I slunk back into the utility room and crouched in a pile of dirty laundry.

Whoever was at the door knocked once more. I listened hard and heard a car start and drive away.

Every noise made me jump the rest of the day and night. That weekend, the Royals were having their annual baseball awards dinner, and of course they urged me to attend. In the three years I had played in Kansas City, I had never been to one of their awards dinners, which is one of the best in any town in the league. For weeks my girlfriend had been telling me I should go. I had agreed to make it this time, but as usual, at the last minute I began thinking up excuses and arguing.

"There's a television show on that night I've been waiting to see," I told her. Anticipating what she would say next, I spoke up ahead of her, "It's a special about the Iranian hostages."

"Oh, Darrell, they have shows about the hostages on every night," she countered. "I want you to go for your sake, not mine. You never go out anymore!"

It was something she constantly harped on. Usually I became sullen and angry, and she would let up. But not this time. We had been planning for more than a month to go to the dinner with two friends of mine. He was the owner of a catch-all outdoors and army surplus store. I had been doing television and newspaper ads for him, and he had given Denny a job.

"We've been looking forward to this all winter," she said. "And you need to get out of this house, yourself. It'll do you good. We'll have fun and see a lot of people."

She didn't know, but every stranger's face was now a hideous mask of hostility to me. It was the worst thing she could have said. But, in the end, she forced me into it.

When the time came to leave, I was a hopeless bundle of raw nerve endings.

"Let's go and get it over with," I said. We met our friends at the Hilton Plaza Inn, where the dinner was to be held.

I was miserable the entire evening. I was one of the "feature attractions," although I had made it clear months earlier that I would not, under any circumstances, appear on the dais. Our table was near the front, and throughout the evening I kept up a light chatter with the well-wishers, old friends, and teammates.

I was doing all right until Denny Matthews, who does the Royals' radio play-by-play and always emcees the dinner, said something that made my skin crawl. I was only half-listening, but he mentioned my name in some sort of lighthearted vein and said something, I don't even remember what, that made me think he knew.

HE KNOWS! I thought. I fought an urge to get up from the table and walk out. Matthews went on to something else, but I could hardly control myself the rest of the dinner. Time crawled by, and every speaker seemed to talk forever. Finally, it was over. I grabbed my girl's hand and almost dragged her to the car.

"Did you hear what Denny Matthews said?" I asked as she got in.

"When?"

"What he said about me?"

"When do you mean? He talked about you lots of times."

She leaned across the seat and kissed my cheek.

It took us fifteen minutes to get out of the crowded parking lot and untangle from the knot of traffic around the hotel. I headed north on Main Street toward the Interstate 35 exit as the heater blew warmth through the car. It was a tightly locked island of security in a hostile world.

Maneuvering through heavy traffic, forced to stop at every red light, we drove on. The huge Crown Center Hotel complex was looming on our right when I noticed a light-colored Oldsmobile trailing about a car's length behind us. I counted three men in the back seat and two in front.

"Don't turn around," I said, "but I think that car behind us is following me."

"Following you?" She stared straight ahead with wide, innocent eyes.

I turned right at the next intersection, went a block, and turned left, heading north up Grand Avenue. The Oldsmobile switched lanes every time I did, and it was right behind us as we drove up Grand past the Kansas City Star building.

The Oldsmobile disappeared behind us in traffic, but in its place a pickup appeared as soon as we got onto the interstate six blocks farther north. Unreasonable, uncontrollable fear pays no attention to detail. It makes connections where there are none.

I snapped at my girl every time she attempted conversation until she finally lapsed into a hurt silence. I cursed under my breath for not bringing anything along to defend myself with. I thought of the loaded shotgun I had left under the bed.

Once home, I headed straight for the refrigerator and opened a beer. My date, her evening ruined, made one more futile attempt at conversation, then went home, leaving me, a rolling mass of emotion, on my couch.

A long, deep snort of cocaine chased away the fear, but twenty minutes later I was seething again.

By 3:00 A.M. I was working on my second case of beer, prowling the house, checking the doors and windows. I took up my vigil at the upstairs window and stayed there, cupping the glow of my cigarette in the dark so it couldn't be spotted from the bushes below.

Somebody had followed us all the way home. I was certain of it. And Matthews! *Oh, man*, I thought, *he knows*. What was it he said? I didn't remember, but I didn't need to. *This proves it*, I thought. The Royals are behind the conspiracy. By now, they must have advised the commissioner's office of what was happening. Bowie Kuhn, the tall, authoritative baseball czar, was always preaching about "the best interests of baseball." Huddled in the darkness, I hated Bowie Kuhn, Ewing Kauffman, Joe Burke, Denny Matthews, and everyone connected with baseball. I stubbed out the cigarette in an ashtray at my feet. *Oh, God*, I cried, *why didn't I go ahead and play football at Oklahoma?*

If I had played football, probably none of this would be happening to me. I would have been a quarterback in the NFL.

I stayed at the window about thirty minutes, then went back downstairs and peered out the back window at the lake, lights shimmering across the water from the opposite shore. Without turning on the kitchen light, I crept carefully back to the refrigerator and mixed beer with tomato juice.

I watched the sun come up from my lookout at the upstairs window.

Book 2

The Long Way Back

26

Reaching for Help

Miserable day and night followed miserable day and night. I would jump at every unexpected sound and order whoever was nearest the phone or the front door to lie and say I wasn't home.

I finally had the conspiracy figured out. The Royals had learned about the drugs and had probably told the commissioner's office. Highly trained detectives were shadowing my every move, waiting to catch me red-handed.

January turned into February. Spring training was drawing closer by the hour, it seemed. My brother Denny, a left-handed-hitting catcher just like me, was working hard to get in shape for a tryout with the Royals' rookie team in Sarasota, Florida. He kept urging me to jog and lift weights with him, so we both could be ready for the season. But I could never quite bring myself to start.

I had broken down and called Wanda again, and cocaine was coming in regularly. But I always sent Denny or Eddie to get it. I was spending at least two or three hours at the upstairs window every night, the loaded shotgun by my side.

The thought of spring training, where I would be surrounded by people making demands on me, was gnawing at me. Always before, I would start running and lifting weights a month before reporting date. Normally, I couldn't wait to put the frigid Midwest winter behind me and get to that warm Florida sun. But now I was pitifully out of shape and dreaded leaving home, as I'd never dreaded anything in my life.

In fact, I still can't remember leaving. It's not uncommon for a drug addict or alcoholic to go into a blackout. My girlfriend later said she drove me to the airport the day I left, but I don't remember any of it. It's lost to me. She said it was early one cold February morning, and we sat in the terminal, while I waited to board my flight. She recalled that I was nervous and irritable, and that I had said, "I wish I was going fishing instead."

Bits and pieces of those days flash through my mind even now in a mosaic blur of faces and images: my greeting Pete LaCock and his saying something about working out all winter on a new weight program, checking into the hotel and drinking that first night, putting on my uniform for the first time and its fitting too tight around the waist.

Then, with striking clarity, I recall Jim Frey walking up to my locker and introducing himself.

Frey was the new manager they had brought in to replace Whitey Herzog. *D—— them!* I thought.

I was polite to Frey, but that was all. I wished Whitey was back. I couldn't stand any of this!

When I went out on the field, I felt sluggish and out of it. Since I had sat on my butt all winter, the calisthenics just about killed me. There was no enthusiasm in my workouts, and I wasn't connecting with the ball.

Everything was wrong. The Florida sunshine that I usually loved so much was too hot. The crowds of fans, whom I usually enjoyed, struck me as so many flies buzzing around a garbage pile with their stupid shorts and fat bellies and their stupid, stupid cameras. I couldn't stand them.

And underneath it all was a gnawing fear, indefinable but very real, a fear that something awful was about to happen.

You're going to die like this, I told myself. *You're going to die unhappy and miserable, without hope, without God. And after you die, when you're in eternity, you're going to feel just as miserable as you do now. Maybe worse.*

I sought comfort at Baseball Chapel, but I found none. It's strange, but I had never stopped going to chapel—the services they have for the players before a Sunday game. Through all the bad years I had continued going, and the services had helped a little. It always gave me some small sense of hope in my hopeless situation. But now, when I needed something so badly, I felt nothing. When I prayed, it was if a steel door had shut down inside, cutting me off from heaven.

Jerry Terrell was our chapel leader. He was a born-again Christian, and a kind, caring guy. One Sunday, after the meeting, I told him I had a problem. I didn't dare tell him it was drugs.

"Darrell," he said, "whatever is bothering you, just give it to Jesus."

Give it to Jesus. What did that mean? How could I "give it to Jesus"? I couldn't make the first move, take the first step. *How was I supposed to do it?* Why were these born-again Christians always telling you that and then not showing you *how*?

One thing I did know: I had received Christ into my heart once. But now I was so lost I couldn't find my way back.

Yet in my confusion I knew in a deep-gut way the answer to all my problems and unhappiness was wrapped up in that Man, Jesus Christ. I *believed* that. But many years before, I had turned my back on Him, and now I needed Him so desperately, I couldn't find Him. *I couldn't find Him! I couldn't die without Him!*

"Help me, Christ," I prayed. But I felt nothing.

If only I could have felt *something*, but I seemed to be dead inside. My emotions, my feelings, were gone. *This was the end result of the "beautiful" cocaine high? To be dead inside? To be unable to feel either joy or sorrow, to feel only hopeless fear?*

I hated drugs! *Hated them!* They had promised me happiness, ecstasy, but instead they had plunged me into a living hell! And I was enslaved to the thing I hated; I needed drugs, craved them. I was caught—caught in a trap of my own making. I had conned people so well for so long with my false sincerity and my smiles that no one could see how desperate I was.

There seemed to be no help from any quarter, and I didn't know how much longer I could hold on, going out day after day in the hot sun, trying to pull it all together, trying to play baseball and endure the fans. *I had the dreadful feeling that in the next moment I would fly out of control and start smashing things, screaming.*

Jerry Terrell had been of no help. I had prayed, and even Christ was of no help. That was the last straw.

I was like a child who breaks his toy, willfully, methodically, deliberately. Then he looks up and wants the broken pieces glued back together and made right. And he wonders why it is not done. As if mere sorrow and regret over a broken toy—or a life—were enough.

I knew God was there and that someday He would lead me out of the mess I was in. But when? where? how?

The week after I spoke to Jerry Terrell, Don Newcombe, the former baseball great, came to talk to the team. His topic was alcoholism. He told us how drinking had wrecked his life and had shortened his career in baseball. He said that it was only by the grace of God and Alcoholics Anonymous that he had gotten sober and stayed sober.

He was talking strictly about drinking. But I saw myself in some of the things he described, especially about how it affected his marriage. I thought about Teri and me.

He gave us a list of fifteen questions about our drinking habits.

"Read them over," he said. "If you can answer three of the questions with a yes, then you may have a drinking problem."

I answered positively to about fourteen of those questions. I broke out in a sweat. I had never thought of myself as an alcoholic or, worse, a drug addict. I always put my problems down to other things—Teri, the folks, the ups and downs of baseball.

All of a sudden, sitting there in that room I said to myself: *I am an alcoholic and a drug addict!* I felt a little giddy.

I knew I wanted to talk to Don Newcombe, but I couldn't make myself do it. I was so far gone that making a simple, rational decision and then acting on it was impossible. I simply couldn't do it.

After the meeting broke up, we went out to begin our daily routine. I caught up with Pete LaCock. Pete was a nice, warm-hearted guy and a good friend.

"Hey, Pete," I said. "Can I ask you a favor?"

"Sure thing, Darrell, shoot."

"Well, . . . I think I have . . . uh . . . a drug problem." I said it very softly and looked around to make sure none of the guys had heard. "I . . . uh . . . I was wondering if you could talk to Don

Newcombe for me, tell him I want to see him?"

"Are you crazy? No way!"

Then, seeing my look of disappointment, he quickly said, "Hey, Darrell, you don't *have* a drug problem. Don't worry about it. So you've tooted a little coke . . . so what? Don't make trouble for yourself."

Here I was needing Pete to help me and he was dismissing the whole thing.

Grabbing his arm, I looked into his face and said, "Pete, I *do* have a drug problem, and I do need to talk to someone."

"O.K., O.K.," he replied, seeing how serious I was. "Sure. I'll talk to Don right now!" And he turned and hurried back into the clubhouse.

A few minutes later he came back out and said, "Newcombe said he'll talk to you in Jim Frey's office. Right now, if you want."

"Thanks, Pete." I hurried into the clubhouse.

Newcombe was sitting behind Frey's desk. I felt a little scared and shaky, but I was glad I was finally making a move, trying to do something to get some help. I was thinking, *This guy's been through it. He knows what it's like. He'll be kind and understanding.*

"What's the problem?" Newcombe asked me.

"I . . . uh . . . drinking and drugs," I said.

"*Drugs*? What are you doing?"

"Pot, Quaaludes, amphetamines, cocaine. . . ."

Newcombe's face lost its pleasant expression. "How long have you been into all this stuff?"

"About eight years. I've been doing it real heavy for about four. Yeah, I think about four years now."

"That's awful!" he exclaimed. "It's *terrible*! Here you are a major league ballplayer, with thousands of kids out there looking up to you, and you sit here and tell me that you're a drug addict? Snorting that s——! Rotting your brain out?"

Had he slapped me in the face I couldn't have been more shocked. I had thought he would be kind. I lowered my head and began sobbing.

"Porter, you are a jerk!" he sneered. "You are a real idiot! You ought to cry—you're a disgrace to baseball and that uniform you're wearing!"

Suddenly I was angry. "Well, you can just kiss my a——!" I shouted at him. "Here I come needin' help, and you give me all this stuff!"

"If you think I'm going to pat you on the head and tell you it's all right, think again, buddy!" he shot back.

"Now . . . I want you to go to Joe Burke and tell him what you told me. Here's my card. He can reach me at that number until 4:00 P.M. Then I've got to catch a plane to California. We've got to get you some place where you can get straightened out."

An hour later I was sitting in Joe Burke's office. I was still burned up about Newcombe's attitude, but I figured since I had gone this far, I had better see it through. In spite of Joe Burke's role in the firing of Whitey, I still liked the guy. He had always been decent to me.

I was so convinced that Burke and the Royals knew all about my secret addictions that I began by saying, "Joe, you probably know all about this."

Joe's face registered total surprise when I told him that his number one catcher was a dope addict.

"Listen, don't worry about it, Darrell," he said with fatherly concern. "We'll fly you back to Kansas City and have you see a doctor. Talk to him for a few days, and then come back when you're okay."

"That sounds fine to me," I replied. *And here I thought it was going to be awful.* "Oh, Don Newcombe wants you to call him. Here's his number." I handed him the card.

He called Newcombe. They talked for about ten minutes. "Yes, yes, I see," Burke kept saying, without looking at me. Then, "Hmmmm. Oh, I didn't know that . . . hmmm . . . I see."

When he finally put the phone down, he said, "Darrell, this is a lot more serious than I thought. Newcombe's arranged for you to go to a treatment center in Arizona." The concerned fatherly tone was gone. His voice had taken on an authoritative, no-nonsense ring. "You've got to get this thing taken care of. You cannot play for the Kansas City Royals again until you get a clean bill of health."

"What?" I shouted. "Are you kidding me? I hit 20 home runs last year. I drove in 112 runs! I should have been the MVP! I've done *everything* for your team, and you're sitting here telling me I can't play ball for this club?"

"That is *exactly* what I am telling you!" He was angry, but totally controlled.

He said I was to leave the next morning for the treatment center in Wickenburg, Arizona. The name of the place was The Meadows. He told me he would be in touch. There was nothing I could do but take it—it was the treatment center or lose my job.

I didn't even go back on the field. I went to the locker room and showered and changed; then I left the ballpark. Instead of going back to my hotel, I went to a religious bookstore and bought a Bible. I'm not even sure why I did that. I just had to.

I hadn't read the Bible in years, and whenever I did read it, the King James English was really hard to understand. Yet I *needed* it. Just the weight of it in my hand, the texture of the black leather cover, gave me comfort. The edges of the pages were trimmed with gold, making a beautiful golden band around the Bible when it was closed.

I went back to my hotel room and began packing. Then I called the folks in Oklahoma City. Dad answered.

"Dad, listen, something's come up," I said. "I ... I have to go into a drug rehabilitation center. I'm leaving tomorrow."

"What are you talkin' about? You kidding or something?"

"No, Dad, I'm not. I've got a serious drug problem. The Royals say I can't play for 'em anymore until I get it cleared up."

There was a silence at the other end of the phone. "I'm ... I'm sorry, Dad." I was near tears.

"Listen, Darrell, whatever's wrong ... whatever you have to go through, your Mom and I are behind you one hundred percent. You know that. I'm just concerned about your career."

"Dad ... I know all that. But I'm just going crazy! I have to do this. Look, if any reporters or TV people call you, just tell them you don't know where I am ... or say you have 'no comment.' Okay?"

"Sure, Darrell. I won't say a word, son."

"Thanks, Dad. I'll have to face all that in my own time, my own way. Well, I've got to get going now. I'll try calling you from the place. It's called The Meadows. But I don't think you'll be allowed to call me. At least not right away. Tell Mom I love her and not to worry. Say a prayer for me."

After we said good-by, I sat on the bed in that hotel room and bawled like a baby.

Before flying to Arizona, I first had to go to California, to talk to Don Newcombe and his associates. I apologized for the way I had spoken to him. I described my drug habit to them in detail—when I had started on each thing, how much I was doing of it, and for how long. Frankly, I was glad to be making a clean breast of things. It was almost a physical release. Newcombe thanked me for coming and wished me luck. The next morning I flew to Wickenburg, Arizona, and The Meadows.

27

The Meadows

The Meadows. Sounded like a real funny farm to me. I almost expected bars on the windows and guys in white coats. The place turned out to be a group of pleasant-looking, low ranch-style buildings, sitting in the desert in the middle of nowhere. It had been a resort or a dude ranch of some sort before its conversion into a drug rehabilitation center.

I was nervous, let me tell you. I didn't know what to expect. But I had always been good at conning people, and I started right away on the motherly-looking nurse who picked up me and this other guy at the airport.

The other guy, about my age, was drunk by the time the plane touched down: he was acting like a real turkey all the way out to the place. But every time he'd make a nasty remark, I'd give the nurse a wink—to let her know that she and I were the normal ones and we'd have to put up with this guy.

I had taken my golf clubs to spring training, and when I left, I brought them along. When we walked through the lounge area after arriving at The Meadows, there were snickers from the people sitting there. I assumed they were patients. *What the h—— are they laughing at?* I wondered, suddenly feeling paranoid. Later, they let me in on the joke. It was the golf clubs. The other patients were saying, "Man, this guy must think he's at a country club or something. Just wait!"

The Meadows was no country club. On my really bad days I thought it was kind of like a mini-Alcatraz, without walls or armed guards.

First thing I did was fill out a bunch of forms. After they gave me a physical, the nurse handed me a pair of pajamas.

"What're these for? I ain't sick," I protested.

"Never mind, Mr. Porter," she replied. "Just put them on, please." The fact is that all incoming patients at the facility are required to wear pajamas the first week, just to show them they *are* sick.

I went to the lounge and introduced myself to the others.

"Darrell Porter? *You're* Porter, the baseball player?" one guy asked. "You gotta be kidding!"

"Wish I was," I replied.

"Hey, you guys. This here's Darrell Porter, the catcher for the Kansas City Royals!" Other patients began to drift over. They looked at me with a mixture of awe and disbelief. *What was a major league baseball player doing at a dryout facility?*

I felt strange, standing there in my pajamas being stared at. The nurses came and broke it up.

After dinner that night, I wandered out onto the patio. Bobby, the turkey who had come in with me that day, was out there smoking a joint for crying out loud! I couldn't believe it.

"Want a toke, man?" he asked.

"No, none for me, thanks." I thought he was pretty stupid. Here he was paying five thousand dollars to kick the dope habit, and he was getting high! He had smuggled the pot into the place inside a dental-floss container. I figured he'd last a week maybe.

My first group therapy session the next morning had me wondering just how long *I* would last at The Meadows.

It was held in a little trailer. Maybe they thought the close quarters would make for togetherness. There were about six or eight of us. Our counselor (I'll call her Lois) was a heavyset woman with a short haircut. Oh, she looked really tough.

We sat in a circle, and the first thing everybody did was hug everybody else. I didn't go for that too much, especially with the other guys.

Somebody read something from a daily devotional book.

Then this Lois asked us one by one how we were feeling. When she got to me, I told her "fine" in a not-too-friendly way.

"Well, what is that 'fine' feeling?"

"I don't know. I just feel good."

"What is the 'good' feeling like?"

"Look, I feel *fine*! O.K.?"

"What's the anger all about, Darrell?"

"I'm gettin' mad, lady, because I'm tryin' to tell you I feel fine. But I don't know what the 'fine' feelin' is all about. I just feel O.K., you know? So lay off me, will you!"

"Who are you really mad at?"

"I'm mad at you, I told you! Why don't you ask the next guy how *he's* feelin' and just leave me the h—— alone?"

"Darrell, you don't even know me, so why should you be angry? Now . . . who are you *really* mad at?"

"J—— C——, I don't *know*!"

"Yeah, you do. You know."

Silence. I had had about all I could take.

"Darrell, you're not going to work at this program, are you?"

"I'm tryin'!" I snapped.

"Look, you're either doing or you're not doing. There are no 'tryings' here."

"I just got here, lady. Give me a break!"

"Just who do you think you are that I should give you a break?"

"I am Darrell Porter. I am a professional baseball player and the best d—— catcher in the American League. My manager said so. And who are *you*?"

"Listen," she said, shriveling me with a glance, "all you are, buster, is a drug addict, just like all these other people here. You are no different, and you are no better. So don't pull any of this baseball star stuff on me, *Mr.* Porter!"

She left me sulking and went on to ask the next poor guy how *he* was. And he had about as much luck explaining how he felt as I had. Oh, I wanted to get out of there!

Most of the patients tried to be open and frank, to describe their feelings honestly. I was determined not to listen. I was just going to sit there, my arms crossed, my legs extended, and stare at my feet. But, after a bit, I found myself listening.

Feeling "good" at The Meadows just isn't good enough. You have to define your terms, describe them, expand on them. They try to get you to think why and how you're feeling good, or bad, or whatever. The idea is to get you to dig a little under the glib words. And gradually, you find yourself digging deeper and deeper.

Some of the patients in that first session were like me, really hard-core. The group really jumped on them. One guy said, "I drink because my old lady's always giving me trouble. Never shuts up. If I didn't drink, I'd kill her."

"What are you blaming it on her for?" somebody countered. "You're the turkey, turkey!"

"Yeah," somebody else chimed in, "you're the one who drank the stuff. Nobody held the bottle to your lips, did they? If you want to know who's fault it is, a——, just look in a mirror!"

Stuff like that. They really socked it to them.

At first I thought the reason the other patients didn't come down on me was that I was new. But they never did get really tough. I'm sure it was because I was in baseball. They tended not to contest my version of things. Of course, Lois did her best to counteract this kid-glove treatment I got. She always went at me with gloves off, never letting up for a minute.

She really ticked me off. I couldn't see at first that she was just trying to get me to look inside and stop with all the lies and rationalizations.

I began to hear a phrase in group therapy: "tough love." It's a relatively new concept. Parental groups use it in dealing with troubled teen-agers. They also used it on us. The idea is that you're tough on someone you care about, not coddling them in their anti-social behavior, because that only encourages them to keep playing games. It's being tough even when it hurts you to do it, because you know that being soft will actually help destroy that person. That's why Lois was hard on me.

I found at The Meadows they don't *tell* you anything. It was aggravating, because I wanted quick answers, and they were supposed to be the experts. Instead they expected *me* to think about things I'd done and come up with my own answers. I didn't want that, because for one thing, I was lazy. And I was afraid—afraid to disturb the mounds of garbage inside.

"Darrell," one of the other patients told me after a particularly tough session, "if Lois gives you the answers, they won't be *your* answers. Don't you see? They'll be somebody else's answers just laid on you. They won't mean much."

Many times during the first two weeks, I wanted to pack up and leave, it was so hard, so painful. But the fact that Joe Burke had told me I couldn't play again for the Royals until I got a clean bill of health kept me there. They were always picking at my defenses, trying to crack the shell I'd built up over the years out of half-truths, lies, and just plain bull.

The day was structured at The Meadows, though there were periodic "free time" breaks. We were up by seven and in bed by ten. The first group therapy session of the day was at 8:00 A.M. There was very little individual therapy, because one-on-one the addict can con anybody, even a doctor. It's harder to fool other addicts, especially a whole group of them. They've been there themselves; they've used all the lies. It's like looking into a mirror.

When I was there just a few days, they called me in to the director's office. The director showed me a copy of *The Sporting News*. There across the front page, a banner headline screamed: PORTER FACES ALCOHOL PROBLEM.

It was Dad! He had talked to the press!

I couldn't believe it! This was the last straw! I had asked him *not* to, and he had broken his word! I nearly blew a gasket reading that story. In it, Dad talked about me as though he was a doctor or some kind of expert.

"Ray Porter," the article went, "blamed his son's problem, in part, on pressures and the environment professional athletes are in all the time. 'There are a lot of lonesome times. Darrell is no exception.' "

"What the h—— does *he* know about *my* loneliness!" I shouted, throwing the paper on the director's desk. "How dare he! How f—— dare he!"

That night, without my knowledge, the director called Dad in Oklahoma City.

"Mr. Porter," he began, "do you want to be responsible for your son's death?"

"Of course not! What do you mean?" Dad replied, all indignant.

"Then, why did you talk to the papers when your son specifically asked you not to? This has had a devastating effect on him. It may have even destroyed the little progress he's made since being here."

"I . . . I didn't want to tell that nosy reporter a thing," Dad protested, "but he kept after me and kept after me. Said he'd find out some other way if I didn't tell him. And I *am* Darrell's father, after all."

"Mr. Porter, what you are is a big mouth. And you broke a promise. Mr. Porter, you are playing with your son's life!"

"I didn't mean to harm him. I only did what I thought was right!" Dad cried.

"We would appreciate it . . . Darrell would . . . if you would not hold any more press conferences. Now, you'll be getting a letter from us shortly. We would like the entire family to come out here. Plan to spend a week. You're all an important element in Darrell's therapy."

"Well, I'll have to take some vacation time," Dad hedged.

"Mr. Porter, this is extremely important to your son's well-being. You *will* be here."

One night after I had been at The Meadows about a week, I stepped out onto the patio for a breath of air. The desert was hushed and still. Overhead, the sky was ablaze with ten thousand stars.

Standing there in the soft darkness, beneath that glittering canopy, I began to think about Teri. My love for her had begun to subside. I still felt a lot of hatred. *Then why did I miss her now?* Was it just the beauty of the night, the heart-breaking glory of the stars? I couldn't shake the thought of her. For the first time a thought crossed my mind: *Could I have been at fault? Could I?* But the stars and the desert gave back no answer.

The next morning at breakfast, Lois came up to our table. "Darrell," she said, with her typical directness, "would you like to see your wife? She's here." Just like that.

"Oh, no!" I said, almost dropping my spoon. Teri at The Meadows? I hadn't seen her in almost three years, since the night she went storming out of her friend's house. I was petrified.

"Darrell . . . Darrell, are you all right?" Lois was asking.

"Yeah, sure. Okay, I'll see her."

Teri was in Lois's office. She was just the way I had always remembered her.

"Hi, Darrell," she said in a small voice.

I don't remember what we talked about. It's all a blur. I do know it was an awkward, forced meeting. We were like two strangers. She asked me how I was doing, I think. I suppose we made small talk. I do remember one thing she told me: "Darrell, I pray for you every day."

Before she left she said she would be back for "Family Week," with Mom and Dad. Then she was gone.

Seeing her again after all this time, and so suddenly, left me dazed and confused. It was really strange that I had been thinking about her like that the night before, probably about the time she was arriving in Wickenburg. Kind of spooky in a way. The whole experience had an air of unreality about it, like a dream.

I was fitting more and more into the routine. Life at The Meadows had its (unplanned) lighter side. Something funny happened one night when we were playing Ping-Pong. Ping-Pong was our sport. I would beat everybody, and nobody could get me off the table. But this particular night something did.

I was really going great guns; my paddle was *hot*. Suddenly the nurse was standing in the door yelling, "Darrell, you didn't take your vitamin! Do it right now."

"Be right back!" I said, putting my paddle down. I dashed to the table where they kept the vitamins, grabbed one of about five little paper cups standing in a row, and washed down the contents with water.

I returned to the table. After about ten minutes, I was seeing five Ping-Pong balls. Then things started spinning. I lost the game—my first in days.

The nurse was in the door again, hands on hips. "Who took Mr. Clauson's Librium capsule? Now, confess! Who did it?"

I kept my mouth shut and held tightly onto my chair, so I wouldn't go floating off into space. I never mentioned it in group therapy. I was still paranoid. And besides, they would have torn me apart for being irresponsible, even though it was an honest mistake.

There was a new woman patient whom I'll call Clare. Clare was in her midforties though she looked about sixty. It was clear that old Clare had done a lot of living in her day.

She had a flippant attitude when she arrived, much like mine had been. I had a feeling she wasn't going to last.

One night, about two days after Clare arrived, there was a commotion at the nurses station. They were holding up a clear plastic bag filled with every kind of pill I'd ever seen and then some, hundreds of them all mixed together in a rainbow of pretty colors. Old Clare had smuggled those pills in, via very private means. I'm not sure whether they instituted body searches of women patients after that. A few days later Clare left, which a patient could do at any time.

28

I Find God—Again

I was making some progress in group therapy. I was beginning to feel my feelings again. I was trying to think hard about my life, my motives, my relationships. It wasn't easy; everything was so tangled up and blocked. Would I ever get it all straightened out?

We were asked to keep a journal. Putting things down on paper was supposed to make us think. It did. It helped me clarify and organize my thoughts, get a handle on things. It helped me to "open up." And did I ever! In five weeks I filled five notebooks. Some of the stuff was from lectures we had on behavior and human sexuality and things like that, but most of it was personal, dealing with my relationships and my religious beliefs.

Here is a typical entry:

My name is Darrell Porter. I'm an alcoholic and a drug addict. I've lived in a world that I can only hope you'll never find. It's a cold, lonely, miserable world, filled with insecurity, hatred, and low self-esteem....

I lost sight of reality. I was sad when I should have been happy, I cried when I should have been happy. I was surrounded by wonderful people, yet I was lonely. I could no longer see the beauty in the world. I couldn't accept victory; all I knew was defeat....I lost God. Drugs had become my God. They never gave me a chance to lay back and relax for one little minute. They made life become one monstrous hurdle, so high I couldn't jump it, so broad I couldn't go around, so strong I couldn't break through. I had nowhere to go....

My journal entries were jotted down in pencil. I wrote a great deal about Teri, most of it angry, angry stuff. I wrote some harsh things about Dad—fragmented, tortured stuff:

He wants me to do things that are always good for other people!

He gets drunk and makes my mom cry....

It made me mad and afraid when he made me fight when I was young.

He used to beat my sister.

I was angry when he told me that I owed it to the high school and to the community to get to bed early one Thursday night, before a Friday-night game.

I was angry when he decided to invest my money in a swimming pool & trailer park. I was angry when we ended up selling it and losing money.

He made me mad by releasing that story to the papers on me....

My journal entries weren't all angry and negative, though. About the middle of my stay at The Meadows, for example, I began to write poetry. (And *I* was the guy who got D's in English!) They weren't Longfellow or Rod McKuen by a long shot. But they showed I was beginning to feel better about myself. I was more accepting of the fact that life isn't perfect, that I'm not perfect. And that was okay. And, if sincerity counts for anything, those poems were written from the heart. Here is my favorite:

Baseball is a fickle game,
The glory you can see.
But every time you get right there,
It always seems to flee.

So what I want is just to be,
The best that I can be.
And if by chance that's not enough,
It's good enough for me.

My brother Eddie, who is a country-western singer and writes songs, liked that poem so much he set it to music!

At The Meadows, they believe that the spiritual side of life is important. They talk about a Higher Power, as they do at Alcoholics Anonymous. That's fine for some people, but my Higher Power had to be Jesus Christ. I've said it before in this book, that I always knew if I was ever going to get straight, if I was ever going to be happy again, it was going to be through Christ. I knew that by myself I was just too weak.

I had been praying a lot and reading my Bible every day. I needed the Lord so badly in my life. But I could feel nothing. They talk about the "grace" of God—His love, His concern, His salvation—freely given as a gift. And most people feel that grace operating in their hearts, and it gives them great happiness; it encourages them to continue in their spiritual quest. I had no such feelings.

But, having been a Christian once, I had one thing to hang on to: I *knew* that Christ was real. I knew that only He could save me. I had experienced His great, saving love once, a long time before, in the Wilmont Baptist Church on a hot summer evening. And even though I couldn't feel it, I remembered it, so I knew it was real.

The saving love of Christ was a fact. And it occurred to me that it didn't really matter if I couldn't *feel* inspired when I read the Bible. It didn't really matter that I couldn't *feel* God's presence when I prayed. It was not a question of feelings at all. My feelings had betrayed me, and drugs had deadened them. But I *knew*, I *believed* that God was there, and the only way I would ever reach Him would be to continue to press forward through the desert of my dried-up feelings.

So it was by sheer will power that I daily continued to seek Him. I went on, not with comfort, but with faith. And I think that's what faith is really all about: going on when you can't feel anything, when you can't see one little ray of light. You go on because in spite of everything, you believe God's promises are true.

During this tough time, I found a verse in the Bible that became very precious to me: "And ye shall seek me, and find me, when ye shall search for me with all your heart" (Jer. 29:13).

And that's what I was doing.

Gradually, my faith in God, the faith that had remained dormant in me for so long began to stir once more like a tree that puts forth blossoms after a harsh winter.

I wrote a prayer in the form of a letter. It made Him seem so real:

Dear God,

I need Your help. I feel so sad, because I won't treat others with the respect they deserve. I need people to like me, dear Lord. I need You to help me with this.

I love You,
Darrell

P.S. Dear Lord, I know how You feel about that kind of thing. Release me from those bad thoughts. Make me whole, dear God. I only want to be a loving, caring person, to raise a family and love them....

I wrote some poems about Jesus and my love for Him, about how much I needed Him. Here is one:

Jesus You're the One for me,
The only One who knows,
What's on my mind in these hard times,
What's in my heart and soul.

You know I only want to love,
You know I really care;
My life has just come all apart,
My world just seems so bare.

But when I think of You, my Lord,
These hard times seem so few,
You bring me peace and joy again,
You make my life brand new.

In other poems I tried writing about my feelings:

Oh, why can't I just open up,
So others they might see,
What makes me real, what makes me tick,

I Find God—Again

What's there that makes me, me.
I guess it's just a hidden fear,
  The things that they will see,
And in the end I guess it is,
  That some, they won't like me.

Why can't I only like myself?
  I'm really not that bad.
It's mental pain, it's punishment,
  It only makes me sad.
So give me strength to find out why,
  I treat myself this way,
To know that I'm just human, Lord,
  That I need You every day.

Yes, things were happening inside. At least I was able to feel anger, joy, sorrow, and the beginnings of faith. I had a long way to go. I had spent years ignoring all the junk inside, and it was so hard to pick through that scrap heap of my life. But I was making a beginning. With God's help I would do it.

Week three. Family Week. Mom, Dad, Pat, Eddie, and Denny showed up. (Jimmy wasn't able to make it.) Teri came. Even John Schuerholz came, representing the Royals.

While the patients had their usual group sessions in the morning, the families had their own group sessions in which individual members took turns confronting the others. They put Dad through the wringer, I'm told, and hung him out to dry. They just knocked him off his throne. Pat, for one, confronted him about the beatings he had given her as a girl.

"I hated you for that, Dad!" she screamed in his face. "You never loved me. And I hated the drinking and the tension in the house all the time. I was glad when you were away. Do you know that? I *hated* to see you come home! Sometimes I just hated you so much!"

When it was Dad's turn, he tried to defend himself: "It isn't true, Pat. I did love you. I *did*! And I know the hitting was wrong. I know it now. Maybe I needed help myself then. Pat, I'm so sorry for that. I'm asking you to forgive me. All my life I'll be sorry about those times I hit you."

They wound up crying on each other's shoulders.

In the afternoon I got together with the family. I'd confront them, and they'd confront me. There was no fooling around. I'd put my chair in front of each one, and we'd have it out—nose to nose, toe to toe.

I don't remember most of it—except Pat yelling in my face that I was a selfish pig, saying I loved the family so much, then flying in to Oklahoma City, and sneaking back out without so much as a phone call.

I do remember what I said to Dad: I accused him of betraying me by talking to the papers. "You swore you wouldn't and then you did! You just wanted to be the big shot, is all! Get your name in the papers! You've always been living off my glory, 'cause you never made it!

"You never cared a flip for me—it was always Jimmy this and Jimmy that! You never paid attention until I began to make it in sports! All you ever did was criticize me! Never one word of praise, not ever. Even last Christmas. I had just had my best season ever. I got 20 home runs for crying out loud! And all you did was put me down in front of company, asking me about the passed balls. Always making me feel like a piece of s——!

"Truth is you never loved me! You never gave a d—— about me!"

When it was Dad's turn, he sat there, nervously twisting his fingers. He had been through hell with Pat, and now he was going through it again with me.

"Darrell, I didn't praise you 'cause I wanted you to work hard, and I knew you wouldn't have done it. You'd have wasted your abilities. I could see that." He stopped and blew his nose.

"I know now I was too harsh. Maybe it's too late now to be sorry. Maybe I have no right to ask you to forgive me. I know, Darrell, I hurt you real bad . . . and your sister . . . all of you. But I did love you . . . *do* love you!"

I had waited all my life to hear him say it. He looked at me, his eyes all tears and pain. Something seemed to give way in me. Grabbing his shoulders, I pressed my forehead against his and wept. We both wept. "Oh, Dad . . . Dad," I whispered. "I . . . I love you!"

It's strange, in a good way, but I went to The Meadows to

straighten out *my* messed-up life. But in the process, our entire family began to be healed.

Pat, Eddie, Denny, Mom . . . they all went home stronger, freer people. Now they were people who could better express their love for one another—and their irritation, too. All of us had been forced to be honest with one another, to dredge up the unspoken resentments that had been festering inside all our lives. In getting it all out in those shocking, terrible sessions, we finally were in a position to forgive one another. And in that there was the start of cleansing and healing.

The family's problems did not all disappear in one session or even in one week. Tensions that have built up over years are not so easily disposed of. But we had needed those dramatic confrontations if we were ever going to learn to live together in true peace and harmony.

As for Dad, he is no longer "king" in his home. "I don't have to be king any more," he says. "I don't have to be telling everybody what to do, running everybody's life, trying to run the whole show, my way. That's wrong! And you know what, now that I just worry about my own self—telling me what's wrong with me—I'm a lot happier. I'm at peace within myself."

You know, there are many families out there, hurting just like the Porter family was. Some families, even Christian families, live together for years in a state of cold war, crippled by all sorts of misunderstandings, unspoken resentments, unexplored love-hate feelings toward the people they care about most. Many Christians mistakenly believe it's a sin to feel resentment toward family members, so they repress their honest feelings instead of dealing with them. God will not magically make the misunderstandings and hurts between people go away, but He gives us the strength and the wisdom and the courage to struggle through them in a spirit of love, if we will ask Him.

I think the beginning of the solution to this kind of thing lies in our spiritual lives. If we could really be honest in confessing our faults, our sins against others, including our families, and if we could ask God to help us really be honest in looking at our inner lives (our hopes, our fears, our motives) and to give us the grace and the courage to change, then maybe a lot of hurting families would begin to stop hurting.

Of course, I think it would be ideal if every family could go through the kind of experience we Porters lived through, not once, but say every five years. It would get all the accumulated junk out and would free us to love one another as we should.

After the family left, I felt a change in me for the better. I was calmer. I felt almost as if a dam had broken and all the water had rushed out. I was more "together," able to relate to the other patients and to the counselors in a more open, positive way. I did so well that I was made a group leader—a "peer group" captain.

I was in my last week and was looking forward to "graduating" and getting my pin.

After my sessions with the family, I had to face my problems with Teri. Actually, I might have left a week earlier had it not been for that. I couldn't handle her being there. It knocked me out of kilter.

The morning after Teri's arrival, I was late for our group therapy session . . . the one I was to lead. I was late the next morning, too.

"Darrell," Lois said, "as a peer group leader, you're acting irresponsibly. We think you have problems you haven't begun to deal with yet. We feel you need another week."

"What?" I shouted. "Hey, I want to get out of here! I've earned it! And now you're telling me I'm not ready?"

"I'm sorry you feel that way," she replied, "but we wish you'd give it another week."

I was all set to quit. But I knew that if I left, they wouldn't give me my graduation pin, which meant the Royals wouldn't take me back.

The fact was that the staff saw belatedly how big a thing my relationship with Teri had been. Not to minimize the importance of the family sessions but, in a sense, what happened there was small potatoes to me compared to what was wrong between Teri and me. I believe I would have made progress more quickly had I been able to confront Teri first. Then I would have been a lot freer to deal with my family.

Now, a special group session was arranged for Teri and me, with our respective groups acting as commentators and interpreters.

The others in our groups sat in a semicircle, while Teri and I sat facing one another, knee to knee in the middle of the floor. At the start of the session I had such a dreadful free-floating fear that I thought I might be sick. Teri seemed nervous, too.

It was my turn first. "Teri," I began, my voice trembling with emotion, "I loved you more than anything in life . . . anything! But when you loused up, you destroyed it. And I hate you for that! *I hate you!* You took all that love I had for you and trampled on it, like it was garbage! Why did you do that? How could you?

"You'll never know how that hurt me . . . hearing you fooled around with Al. And how many others were there? How many other guys did you sleep with?"

Teri wasn't allowed to say anything in her defense. She just sat there quietly weeping. Her tears only made me more angry.

"Yeah, go on and cry! I cried, too! D—— you! D—— you!"

I held a rubber baseball bat with a foam rubber bulb at the end. I was supposed to hit a chair beside the person I was confronting if I felt the need to physically strike out. Now, while I screamed at Teri, I beat the chair beside her, venting years of pent-up hurt and rage against her imagined infidelities. I beat that chair so hard that the foam bulb tore apart, the pieces flying in every direction.

Then it was Teri's turn. With a tear-stained face she said, "Darrell, I loved you, too. I still do, in a way. And I was never unfaithful to you, though you can't believe it. But loving you wasn't enough. You never understood me. And you didn't even try. I thought you had no consideration for me, no respect.

"I think the only time you gave me anything . . . attention, respect, love . . . was when you felt like it, when it pleased *you* to do it. You were the 'star' in the family. My feelings, my plans, they didn't count. I tried to tell you, but you never took me seriously.

"I wound up not liking you very much."

"Face it, Darrell, you were a real pig!" the woman from Teri's group sneered. "You're just a male chauvinist pig!"

"Hey, Porter," somebody else yelled. "Tell 'er you're sorry!"

I looked at Teri. She returned my gaze, an expectant look in her eyes that were still red from weeping.

That night on the patio shortly after I had arrived, I had wondered if I was partly to blame. Now it was clear. I was.

"Teri . . . I never realized. . . . Will you forgive me?" I said, almost in a whisper.

"Louder!" someone shouted.

"TERI, WILL YOU FORGIVE ME?" I yelled.

She smiled, nodding her head. Then she asked my forgiveness. We hugged one another.

It was amazing, the cleansing power of forgiveness. Within a few hours I began to feel remorse over the way I had treated Teri. I went over things in my mind, all the terrible fights we had. For the first time I saw how badly I had acted in each instance. I recalled insensitive, selfish things I had done to her. It was as if I was looking at our life together from an entirely different angle. I didn't like what I was seeing.

Later, on the patio, we met again. I was feeling so bad, I asked her to forgive me all over again. "Teri, I'm so sorry. I just never knew. . . ."

"Darrell," she said in her soft voice, "we were both so young. We were foolish and stubborn. We were both wrong. Thank God, we've grown up a little."

I knew in that moment that it was all over between us. Hate was gone, but so was romantic love. In the place of that grand, consuming, tormenting passion that had dominated my life for so long was a gentle, quiet caring.

The death of that love in which I had invested so much of my strength, my passion, and my tears was sad. But then, it was strangely fitting. Teri, who had been the living embodiment of the little sister of my boyhood dreams, my sister-wife-mother figure, was that no more. Now she was something less romantic, but far more real: a true sister and a good friend.

29

Back in Baseball

I had graduated from The Meadows. I had returned to Kansas City and baseball after an absence of six weeks. I had faced my teammates and the media in that tense locker-room press conference, and I had survived.

From the dozens of yellow ribbons I had seen tied around every tree on our block, when my brother Eddie drove me home that first night, it appeared as though the Royals fans might be in a forgiving mood. But that remained to be seen.

"Bill Katzbeck call at all in the last day or two?" I asked, sorting through a stack of mail. I wondered why he hadn't met me at the airport or come to the press conference. I mean the guy broke down and cried when he learned I had gone into the rehab center.

"Haven't heard a thing from him, D.P., or from Frank either."

I dialed Bill in Pittsburgh. After the amenities, I asked him, "How come you weren't here for the press conference today, Bill?" I was kind of hurt, and I think my voice showed it.

"D.P., we tried calling you at The Meadows, but they wouldn't put us through! It's policy at those hospitals. Then I tried getting through to you this afternoon at the stadium, and it was a madhouse. Anyway, we knew you'd be under pressure right now, everybody crowding around, asking questions. I didn't want to add to it. I figured you'd appreciate a little breathing space for a few days."

"Bill, I wish you could have been here. You know you mean a lot to me as a friend. I need my friends now."

"Gee, D.P.," he replied, "if I had thought you needed me there ...I meant well. So did Frank."

"Thanks, buddy. And I appreciate all you've given me...so much support. You've been a good friend. The best."

I felt better after our talk.

Eddie and I had a quiet dinner and talked. He said that Dad was really trying to change. We talked about the press conference, what the papers would make of it all. We agreed they would have a field day. I'd just have to grin and bear it. As they say, if you want to make an omelet, you have to break eggs.

I turned in early. It had been a tough day, but it was finally over. I mumbled a quick prayer of thanks for having gotten through it.

PORTER RETURNS TO KANSAS CITY, SEES ROYALS WIN! the headline in the *Kansas City Star* read the next morning. There were pictures of us at the airport and another of Pete LaCock hugging me. It was a nice, fairly accurate story, not all negative as I feared it would be.

The phone rang off the hook all day. Eddie screened my calls.

That afternoon I drove out to Royals Stadium. Management wanted me to work out for a while before reactivating me. I had tried working out at The Meadows, but I was too preoccupied there. I had only practiced throwing for a few days before leaving.

I had had trouble with my arm in spring training, so even though I wouldn't be playing right away, I was worried about it.

When I got to the stadium, I found I was late. The game was about to begin. Management had neglected to tell me that the game with Baltimore had been moved up an hour because it was going to be nationally televised. There would be no time for batting practice.

I quickly changed into my uniform, feeling harried and embarrassed about the mix-up—and on my first day back. I felt guilty somehow...just like in the old days.

I had a few minutes to practice throwing near the dugout. It was a clear, cool day. It felt good to be back in uniform, to see and hear the sights and sounds of the game.

The fans crowded around. There were so many people on the steps near the dugout that the ushers had to hold them back. Everyone was wearing a yellow arm band. They shouted encouragement.

Inevitably, the reporters were there, asking questions. Without stopping, I said, "I'd appreciate it if you'd limit your questions to baseball, at least for the time being."

"Sure, Darrell. O.K. Uh . . . how's the arm?"

"I don't feel a bit of pain. Maybe in a week or so I'll be ready."

"How does it feel to be in uniform again? Comfortable?"

"Sometimes comfortable . . . sometimes not. I can deal with it," I replied. "It's a whole new game for me. A whole new life."

The Royals lost that day, 4–0. Sitting there on the sidelines, I fretted. *I should be in there playing, I thought, but no use thinking about what ought to be.* I determined I'd be back playing in a week.

I took batting practice after the game. As the grounds crew rolled the batting cage into place and I walked out of the dugout to loosen up, the crowd was on its feet, giving me a standing ovation. I looked up. There must have been two thousand people there, waving yellow ribbons and scarves! Tears sprang into my eyes.

The reporters and photographers were back, surrounding the batting cage. Out of nowhere a TV crew appeared. The mood was festive. I hit a long fly.

"Way to go, Darrell!" a fan yelled from behind the third-base dugout. I swung again and connected solidly—a line drive. Applause rose from the stands.

Between pitches I turned to look. Our manager, Jim Frey, was still on the field. So was General Manager Joe Burke. In the right-field bleachers a woman held up a big sign: WELCOME BACK, DARRELL! I waved.

A rhythmic clapping arose from the stands. A thousand yellow ribbons fluttered in the afternoon breeze. I had to stop for a few seconds. I was so filled up—glad, sad, humble, happy, proud. How a man can feel so many contradictory emotions at the same time I don't know, but I did. I could feel waves of support, of love, coming from those fans. Oh, I had hoped they would be understanding, maybe kind. But I had no idea they would react like this! I knew the days and weeks ahead would be difficult, but I could do it with all that wonderful support from the Kansas City fans. I'd be doing it for them, as well as for myself!

I didn't know it then, but high above the crowd, in one of the executive suites, a girl was watching me. It was her birthday, and her friends had invited her to the game.

"Who is that down there?" she asked a girlfriend.

"Deanne, where have you been? That's Darrell Porter. He's been to a drug rehabilitation center in Arizona. Gosh, the papers have been full of it for weeks!"

"Oh, I don't follow baseball much. But I do remember reading about it. They love him, don't they?"

"Well, it's his first day back," the friend replied.

"Hey, come on, Deanne! We've lit the candles!" someone called.

"Just a minute," the girl replied, studying the figure down in the batting cage. "I think he must be a brave guy," she said to her friend. Then she blew out the candles on her cake. There were twenty of them.

Down on the field I was just warming up. When I hit a drive off the right-field wall, the crowd cheered wildly. I took a final swing, then walked away from the batting cage with a smile. I stopped and raised my cap. That wonderful crowd of loyal fans was on its feet, giving me a standing ovation! How I loved Kansas City! How I loved those fans! It was so good to be back!

The next day, Sunday, was another story. I left with the team for Canada, for a series of games with Toronto.

I was uneasy. It was one thing to be warmly welcomed back by the home-town fans, but what would they do in a strange city in an unfriendly stadium? Everybody was saying I was in for it, but good.

I needn't have worried. I never had to face the Toronto fans. At The Meadows my counselor had told me: "Don't worry about the future; eight out of ten things you're worried sick over never happen." Well, the weather in Canada was bad. The first game on Monday was postponed. Then it rained again on Tuesday, so we had no batting practice. It was pure frustration. The Royals' management, almost as anxious as I was to see me work myself back into shape, sent me back to Kansas City and the sunshine, along with outfielder Amos Otis, who had suffered a tendon injury to his right hand.

But I escaped the fans who had me so worried. *So that's what they were talking about at The Meadows when they told us not to worry about tomorrow so much!* I told myself. *They were right!*

I spent the rest of the week throwing, but not strenuously. I had to build up the strength in that arm and get off some of the excess weight I had put on at The Meadows. Frey told me he wanted to gradually work me back into the line-up. Hitting was the number one priority, fielding was secondary. I was beginning to feel really confident with hitting. One day, during batting practice, Frey was walking past first base. When I hit the ball, I directed it at him. As he moved around the infield toward second, I kept directing my hits toward him. I had such control. I kept it up until he reached third base.

But catching was something else. As catcher, I can tell you that it requires a lot of strength in the legs. It places tremendous strain on the thighs and knees. Although I'd worked out a little at The Meadows, it wasn't the same as catching. (The only way to get in shape for catching is to catch.)

A series of games with the Boston Red Sox was coming up next, the weekend of May 3. Management was debating about whether I could play.

On Friday, just before the game, I was sitting on the bat rack near the tunnel leading to the clubhouse, twirling a yellow rose a fan had handed me. Inside the clubhouse Joe Burke was talking to the team—presumably about me. I was nervous again: I had been activated as one of the extra players. Of course, I had hoped to be a designated hitter. But it turned out that my debut was going to be a one-shot deal, pinch-hitting for shortstop U. L. Washington. It would be tough going to the plate and getting one chance, cold turkey. Still, I was grateful for it.

The moment came in the bottom of the sixth. As I stepped into the batter's box, the fans—almost 26,000 of them—were on their feet, roaring, waving yellow ribbons, scarves, and shirts. I was happy, thrilled. I had forgotten baseball could be such fun! I felt like a kid all over again.

The score was tied 3–3. Mike Torrez of Boston was pitching. I wish I could say I belted one out of the park, but after three pitches I popped out to Boston center-fielder Fred Lynn. But I had gotten my feet wet. I was really back with the Royals. And we won the game.

Later, I told reporters that I was comfortable. My timing was good; I was seeing the ball well. I was feeling good—inside myself—for the first time in ten years. I was grateful to the press and fans for making my comeback relatively easy.

But I was getting really tired of the constant questions, of being followed around. Dressing quickly, I decided to slip out of the stadium by another exit, to avoid the crush of fans and reporters. I took the elevator to the clubhouse level.

Just as I stepped off the elevator, along comes a friend, Gerry. His son Chris is a ball boy for the Royals. Well, Gerry had this really beautiful blonde with him. I mean, she was unbelievable—blue eyes, peaches-and-cream complexion, and a small, heart-shaped face. Dresden china, but with a golden tan. This girl had a regal quality about her, quiet and refined. She had to be an angel come to earth.

Gerry was talking to me about a golf date, but I hardly heard a word he was saying; I kept sneaking glances at this vision. She wasn't paying a bit of attention to us; she was looking off the balcony.

Gerry must have seen my slightly dazed expression, because he said, "Deanne, come here. I want you to meet someone."

As the girl came toward us he said, "Darrell, this is Deanne Gaulter, a friend."

"Hi," she said with a small smile.

"Hi," I replied, my mouth going dry.

"Deanne, this is Darrell Porter."

"Oh," she said, surprised. "I didn't recognize you in your street clothes!" We laughed.

Gerry continued talking about golf. I still didn't hear a word. I just couldn't believe how beautiful she was.

"Deanne was here to see the game today," Gerry said.

"Great," I replied. "Uh, excuse me for saying so, but you're *very* beautiful. What kind of beauty contest did you just win?" I wasn't being fresh; I was just trying to be clever, but it came out sounding awful. I mean, how does a mortal talk to an angel? I could have bitten my tongue off, but it was too late. She blushed, a delicate pink suffusing her cheeks and making her even more beautiful—if such a thing was possible. Then she smiled again, and I knew she had taken it as a compliment. The smile was dazzling. My heart did a tiny flip-flop.

We walked to the parking lot, Gerry still talking a mile a minute, Deanne and I in our own private worlds. I wanted to say something else, but nothing would come out. I felt big and foolish. The truth was I had never in my life felt I was smart enough or cool enough to converse with pretty girls, even as a kid in school. The years had taught me nothing of sophistication in the romance department or made me any less shy. So here I was again—mute.

"Uh, do you play golf?" I finally managed. Not bright or witty, just clumsy and flat-footed.

"No," she replied. Her voice had a slightly nasal quality, very pleasant. Oh, this girl Deanne was just perfect!

When we got to the parking lot, a date was waiting for me in her car. It was awkward; I had forgotten all about her the minute I set eyes on this new girl. I didn't want to hurt her, but I couldn't let this girl Deanne leave without my saying something else. I might not ever see her again! As I started to cut out to go to the car, I reached out and grabbed her hand. "See you sometime," I said.

Deanne blushed again and looked at my date sitting in the car and doing a slow burn. Deanne gave her a helpless look as if to say, "Sorry, I don't even *know* the guy!"

"Who's *that!*" my date fairly hissed when I slid in beside her.

"Oh, just a friend of Gerry's," I mumbled, looking off into space. "Say, where are we going to eat, darlin'? I'm starved!"

The evening was a disaster. I tried to be polite, to pay attention to her, but I kept seeing Deanne's face in my mind's eye. I was remembering how beautiful she was.

"Darrell, am I boring you?" my date finally asked.

"Oh, no!" I protested. "I'm just feeling a little tired after the game. Maybe we'd better call it an early evening. O.K.? Sorry I'm not better company."

I spent the next couple of days wondering how I could meet Deanne again. Should I just go up to the suite? Truth was, I was scared to death of her . . . scared of being rejected. I wouldn't have been able to take that. I was shaky enough as it was.

30

My Comeback Continues

In the meantime I had other things to worry about. Things like playing ball. On Sunday, May 4, two days after I met Deanne, they had put me back into the starting line-up as designated hitter in another game against the Red Sox. The first news I had of it was from the Sunday morning papers. It was just as well. My arm still wasn't ready; it wasn't sore, just weak. As long as I couldn't throw full strength, I didn't want to think about catching. And I *was* confident about my hitting.

When I got to the ballpark, I saw my name in the line-up. It was definite. Then I went to Baseball Chapel with my teammates. I prayed for strength and guidance.

Though it was only my second at-bat since returning to the Royals, I had an overriding feeling of confidence, almost relaxation, as I strode to the plate my first time up. There were two outs. Hal McRae was on first. Boston pitcher Bob Stanley was on the mound.

The first pitch was a ball. So was the second. Then I fouled one off. Then . . . ball three. On the next pitch I hit a high-arcing ball toward the left-field fence. The crowd was on its feet with a roar. As I neared first I was thinking: *Oh . . . I popped up; it's an out.* Then I thought: *Hey . . . it's going to go out of the park!* I amended that quickly to: *Well,* maybe *it's not a homer.* When it hit the wall at the 400-foot mark, I thought: *Shoot! Oh, what the heck! That's good*

nough for me! There was no sense in being greedy. I had a double
l drove in a run.

I was feeling my oats. In the third inning, with runners on second and third, I lined a single to left-center, making the score 3–0.

In the seventh, we got another run, and then with bases loaded, I lined to deep right field. In spite of the fact that Jim Dwyer caught it, making it the final out of the inning, the crowd cheered me. I could do no wrong. I'm not sure who drove in the last run, but we won 5–3.

Afterwards the reporters were all over me again. I was almost dizzy with joy over the way my comeback was going. I talked excitedly, answering a steady barrage of questions. Then I lapsed into a happy, confused silence. Everything was going so fast! I was high on victory!

The reporters asked me if it was my best day ever. "It's hard for me to compare it to anything in the past, because I don't remember the past!" Although I said it lightly, it wasn't quite funny: the truth was I couldn't remember so many things in my past life—drugs had robbed me of those precious memories.

What about the future? they asked. "I wish I didn't have to think about it," I confessed, "but I have to, a little."

I didn't even want to think about the next few days because of the upcoming road trip and the prospect of confronting hostile fans. That had been my problem in the past—worrying over what was going to happen tomorrow, instead of living today. I was determined not to fall into that trap again.

I told them, "All I'm trying to do now is to take one day at a time. There'll be good days and bad days. I'll have to learn to cope with both."

Easier said than done. I had been spared the derision of the Toronto fans, thanks to the bad weather. But we had this road trip coming up to Chicago, New York, and Boston. The fans, particularly in the Windy City and the Big Apple, are notoriously rough on unpopular players. The consensus was: They're going to eat you alive, Darrell!

I laughed it off, but inside I was scared.

On a Tuesday in mid-May I made my first appearance in a game away from friendly Royals Stadium—at Chicago's Comisky Park.

Every time I came to the plate as the designated hitter, there was a rumble from the White Sox fans, laced with catcalls and raucous laughter. "Hey, Darrell, want a beer? Come on, Porter! Just a sip!"

At one point a drunk came weaving down and leaned over the railing, a can of beer in one hand. "Hey, I'm wish you ... all the way, buddy! I went through the same treatment you did!" With that he nearly fell on his face. There were guffaws.

Most of the ribbing was good natured; I had to expect it. Still, it must have gotten to me, because I was 0 for 4 that night. But I put it down to the fact that I was hitting off a lefty pitcher. The Sox won 2–0.

The next night we bounced back, trouncing them 12–5. I got a hit and drove in a run. I felt a little better about things.

But the Royals weren't doing well at all. After twenty-five games we were playing what one analyst described as "borderline .500 baseball." He compared us to the painting of a mule in an Independence, Missouri, bar with a caption reading: "I'm not doing as good as I expected, but I never expected I would."

We had reasons. Amos Otis was still out with a torn finger tendon. Third baseman George Brett was having troubles with an injury to his right heel. We just couldn't (in the words of Jim Frey) "consistently put together a string of winning games." Jim was frantically moving guys around the outfield to fill the void created by Otis. I was trying not to feel the pressure; I couldn't go back to catching before I was really ready.

We dropped the final game with Chicago 8–2, then flew to Boston. There things began to turn around. We won the first two games 6–5 and 13–8. I did well in the second game with two hits and three RBIs, though U. L. Washington eclipsed everybody with *four* RBIs and a single and a double. In three games we established a season high in hits and runs.

We were full of confidence as we flew to New York. But I was worried—not about the Yankees, but about the Yankee fans. The dire predictions everyone had been making about Chicago and Boston hadn't come to pass, except for an incident or two. But New York had me scared.

"He never should have admitted it was a drug problem," Hal McRae told a reporter—who duly reported it on the sports pages.

"That was a big mistake. People can take that and say real mean things, personal things. I mean ... people can accept a drunk. Go medians make jokes about them. But nobody makes jokes about drug addicts. Wait till Darrell is in a slump ... what do you think people are going to blame it on?

"Darrell's always taken a lot of crap from the fans anyway. Now it's going to be a thousand times worse!"

Somebody else told me. "They ain't going to have a shred of mercy on you in New York. They're going to chew you up and spit you out all over home plate! Wait and see if they don't."

"Don't listen to them, Darrell," my roommate Jerry Terrell said. I was glad Jerry had asked me if we could room together.

"I won't listen, Jerry," I said. "I'm glad I told the truth. It was the only way. No more lies. No more dishonesty. That was my trouble in the first place!

And it was true: I didn't regret baring my soul, not for one minute. But as we packed to leave for New York I was apprehensive. I tried praying, but the fear would not go away easily.

Maybe I was just paying the price of my mistakes. Be that as it may, I was still unsure of myself inside ... shaky. The doctors at The Meadows had told the Royals' management it would be eighteen months before I was fully recovered from the effects of my addiction to alcohol and drugs. I didn't need hostility and hatred. I needed support.

We boarded the plane at Logan Airport for the quick hop down to Kennedy. I was depressed. Would people ever forget what I had done? Would they ever really forgive the way I had betrayed them? Betrayed baseball?

Dad had warned me. The day I called him to tell him I was at The Meadows, he told me he was afraid what the papers would do to me, what the fans would think. "Dad, I don't care!" I had shouted into the phone. "I'm not going to live like this anymore! Even if I never play another day of baseball, at least I'll be at peace with myself!"

Fine words then. But now where was the peace I thought I would have? The truth was I was still much too concerned about what other people thought of me. Hadn't I somehow earned a certain measure of peace by being honest? Wasn't the truth supposed to make you free?

Drugs! How I hated them now! Drugs had gotten me into this mess . . . had nearly destroyed my career, my sanity, my life! It had all been so much *fun* when it began. It was a social thing; it made me feel in, a part of the crowd. Popular. I always wanted to please the people I was with.

Now, as the plane winged southward I sat wondering how something that started out being so much fun could end up leaving me alone and scared, could earn me the contempt of thousands of people, strangers I didn't even know.

An hour later I was saying a quick prayer as the jet taxied to the terminal at JFK International Airport. The Royals were in New York to play a three-game series against the Yankees. It was what I had been dreading.

"You all right, Darrell?" Jerry Terrell asked me, leaning over and grabbing my arm reassuringly.

"Yeah, just fine, Jer," I replied, giving him a quick smile.

But I was scared by those Yankee fans. I don't think I was being paranoid, either. One sports writer has observed that Yankee Stadium "is the cruelest arena since they shut down the Colosseum in ancient Rome."

Jerry could tell how apprehensive I was. During the ride from JFK into Manhattan, he said, "Darrell, do you remember Philippians 4:13?"

I'm not too hot on Bible verses, but I made a stab: "Isn't that the verse that goes, 'I can do all things through Christ which strengtheneth me'? "

"You've got it. Now, just hang onto it. Keep saying that verse to yourself, and you'll get through this. I promise you."

"I can do all things through Christ," I repeated slowly, letting the words sink in. That meant ALL things—even facing fifty thousand jeering Yankee fans. Christ would be by my side, enabling me to take it.

And He was. The sports pages of the newspapers on Tuesday May 14 tell the tale: "Gura, Porter Spark 12–3 Victory" read one. But my favorite was the story clipped by my brother Eddie from (would you believe?) the *Saudi Gazette*, Saudi Arabia's English-lan-

guage daily: PORTER HITS FIVE AS ROYALS SMASH YAN-
KEES.

The story read in part: "Porter, who rejoined the Royals on April
26, after recovering from drug and alcohol addiction, pushed his
RBI total to 15 in his ninth game of the season. He delivered a run
in the first inning on a groundout, drove in two more with a bases-
loaded single . . . and added another two-run single in a six-run
ninth."

"He's worn our butts out!" Yankees' Manager Dick Howser was
quoted as saying in another story.

During that first game, a few fans started in on me. There were
two guys behind home plate who kept saying, "Hey, Pohtah, you
wanna beah?" And they'd wave their bottles at me. I just ignored
them.

Surprisingly, there was a smattering of applause every time I
drove in a run. That was encouraging, let me tell you. I began to
relax a little.

After the game, I was surrounded by reporters in the visitors'
clubhouse. Jerry tried coming to my rescue: "Hey, Darrell, need
anything? How about an oxygen mask?"

The reporters ignored him and kept firing away. They wanted to
know all about the drug thing, how my life was going.

"I still have days when I don't think I can make it," I told them,
"days when a beer looks mighty good to me. Sometimes I wish the
Lord would snap me perfect in an instant, but I'm learning patience. I know I can only do it with God; there's no other way for
me."

There was a momentary lull in the questions. Talking about
God in the locker room embarrasses reporters. I don't think they
really understand what serious Christianity is all about. They sort
of ignore the "religious stuff"; drinking and drugs make better
copy.

In another five minutes Jerry was back. "Gentlemen, Darrell has
a bus to catch in a couple of minutes. Come on, Darrell, we'd better get going." And he led me through the crush.

The fans were just as nice the next night, when I got a couple
more hits. Those supposedly-mean New Yorkers were actually accepting me—even when we won the game.

In the final game of the series, we were being trounced 12–1. About five minutes before my final time at bat, I went into the runway leading to the visitors' locker room. I bowed my head.

"Dear Lord," I prayed, "if it be Your will, please let me hit a home run for the people of New York City. Let me do something to show them how much I appreciate the support they've shown me."

Then I went to the plate, full of peace and a quiet confidence. There was a nice spot, between the right-field bleachers and the stands. I thought, *It sure would be great, Lord, to hit one right there in that spot . . . right in the bleachers.*

Yankees' pitching ace Ron Guidry eyed me for a moment, then wound up and threw a fastball. I swung—and connected. The ball arced up and into the right-field bleachers, sending chills down my spine!

"Thanks, Lord!" I said, as I headed toward first. As I trotted around the bases a roar rose from the stands, like hail beating on a tin roof. I looked up as I rounded third. The Yankee fans were giving me a standing ovation!

Oh, the feeling of gratitude that rose within me! It was one of the finest moments of my life. When I reached home plate, I looked up again and tipped my cap to those wonderful people. They roared back their approval, their acceptance of me!

31

Deanne

We returned to Kansas City. The reporters never let up, especially after that home run. They were in the clubhouse every day. I began to experience chest pains. I had it checked out. "Nerves," the doctor told me, "just nerves." I was determined not to let those people rattle me. I began saying no to requests for interviews.

I was still thinking about that beautiful blonde Gerry Winship had introduced me to when I first got back. How could I meet her again?

Sometimes—rarely—you meet someone and right away you know it's going to be something special. There can be many women, some of them beautiful and smart and fun to be with. But then a girl like Deanne comes along and it's magic. You don't plan it; it just happens . . . something precious and rare and wonderful.

Funny I should meet Deanne at this critical point in my life. Maybe I was just dreaming. What would a beautiful young girl like that want with a guy like me . . . a divorced man, a recovering alcoholic and drug addict?

Did she know all that awful stuff about me? She must. Heck, she had to read the papers. My life made real spicy reading. What did she think? Did she think I was a creep? When we talked for those few minutes, she seemed to think I was all right. Was she just being kind?

I kept torturing myself with thoughts like these, all the while hoping I would see her again.

Well, God helps them that help themselves, so I began plotting. "How's Deanne?" I'd ask Chris the ball boy. "Was she at the game tonight?" I guess he was wondering why I was getting so friendly all of a sudden. I was hoping he would tell Gerry and Gerry would get word to Deanne that I was interested. Whenever we played a home game, I'd find myself looking up toward the suite over the first-base line. Once or twice I thought I caught a glimpse of blonde hair, and my heart would do that funny little flip-flop number again. There had to be some way.

I got my chance inadvertently. During a home game the umpire said something to me. Jokingly I shot back, "Oh, you turkey!" Well, the guy took me seriously and tossed me out of the game. (I guess I still had a bad reputation with umpires, from the "old days.")

There was nothing to do but shower and change and watch the rest of the game. But after I got dressed I went up to the club level, on the off-chance that Deanne might be in Gerry's suite. She was.

Everybody in the suite began ribbing me about getting thrown out of the game. Except Deanne. She had a gentle smile on her lips. Gosh, she was even more beautiful than I had remembered.

She said hello. We talked a few minutes. "I'm kinda glad I got thrown out," I confessed.

"Why?" she said with a twinkle in her blue eyes.

"'Cause I got to see you again, that's why!" I felt foolish, but I *had* to let her know.

Before I left I invited her to a barbecue at teammate Larry Gura's place the following week. When she said she'd come, I felt as if I had just hit a grand slam!

The next day I was supposed to go fishing with a good friend, Larry Seaman. I had told him about Deanne and about how much I liked her, even though I didn't know much about her.

Well, darned if Larry and his wife hadn't met Deanne and didn't have her in the car after the game, the night they were going to have me sleep over. I was all flustered when I saw her sitting there when I came down.

Only problem was I had a date waiting for me, just three cars away!

I stared daggers at Larry for getting me messed up with two girls that way, then I went over and explained to my date that "something's come up" and I couldn't go out with her after all. She took off in a huff. It was unfair, but it was no contest.

Meanwhile Deanne was trying to get out of Larry's car, because she saw me talking to the other girl and she got the picture. "Relax," Larry told her. "Darrell wants to see you, believe me." So we got in her car and followed the Seamans to their house.

We wound up spending a pleasant two hours together, sipping Cokes and talking. I asked Deanne if she knew much about me. "A little," she replied. Then I asked if she knew about my drug addiction. She said she had read a little about it in the papers.

"Does that bother you?" I asked.

"No," she replied, flicking an imaginary bit of lint off her sweater. Then looking me directly in the eye, she added, "Everybody makes mistakes. We're all human."

"I don't think you are," I said. "You're so beautiful, you look just like a princess in one of those fairy stories."

"And you're a nice person, even though you stood that poor girl up tonight. Now, I'd better be going, because I've got to get up early in the morning."

We went out to her car. Just before she got in, I leaned over and kissed her on the mouth. It wasn't a friendly peck, but a long, serious kiss. Her lips were full and soft. She had a delightful fragrance about her. She returned my kiss. Then she gently drew back, her face flushed, making her more beautiful.

It was strange; we hardly knew each other, but that kiss seemed appropriate . . . somehow right. Already there seemed to be something special between us. I sensed it. I asked her for her phone number and she gave it to me.

As her car pulled away, I felt a small twinge—a love pang? I vowed I would stop seeing that other girl.

I called Deanne the next day and asked her to the game. We saw each other that night and talked together every night the team was in town.

The following week we went to the barbecue and had a wonderful time. As soon as we got there I asked her if she wanted a beer. "Sure," she replied.

I got her one. It's funny, but once I stopped taking drugs, I was never tempted to go back to them again. They had wrecked my life, and toward the end, I didn't even like the way they made me feel. But beer . . . oh, how I missed the taste of a good cold beer on a hot summer's day! Even more than that, I still sometimes got desperate for a way to escape all the pressure.

I handed the bottle to her, and she stood there with it in her hand, making small talk. She didn't even take a swallow. She saw me eyeing it and said, "I guess I didn't really want this after all. I don't even like to drink."

"Hey, Deanne. Do you know how to fish?" I asked, changing the subject.

"Well, if you include cane-pole fishing with a bobber in my dad's farm pond with my six brothers and sisters."

"They've got the neatest little pond here, with some great bass in it. I'll borrow a couple of rods and reels. How about it?"

"Fine," she replied.

So we slipped away from the party and did some fishing. Standing close to her, showing her how to tie the lure on the line, I felt weak in the knees. "This lure is called a chuggar spook," I explained. "I'll tie it on for you the first time."

"Just toss your line in over there," I said, pointing.

"There?" she asked, casting the line a little awkwardly. She looked so pretty standing there, with the sun shining on her blonde hair. All of a sudden there was an explosion around her lure.

"Oh, I've got a fish!" she cried.

"Already?" Darned if she didn't catch a three-pound bass! (I caught nothing.) I'll tell you, when Deanne hooked that old bass, I think she hooked my heart, too!

I had done really well in my month as designated hitter. Then the Royals put me back to work catching. I was out of shape, and I began to get tired quickly, what with all the squatting and jumping up and down that catching requires. My game began to suffer. By July, my .300 batting average had shrunk to .274 and continued to fall.

In spite of the stats, I was named as reserve catcher in the All-Star game by AL manager Earl Weaver, along with three other Royals—Larry Gura, George Brett, and Jim Frey (as coach). It was to be my fourth All-Star game, the third straight.

I did get to catch part of the game because starting catcher Carlton Fisk of the Red Sox was nursing a sore elbow. But I had trouble handling pitcher Dave Stieb. Two wild pitches and a passed ball in the seventh didn't help the AL cause any. The National League won again 4–2. I was embarrassed. How nice it would have been to drink away the situation. I wanted to, but I knew I couldn't.

After that poor performance, I vowed I would do everything in my power to improve my playing in the second half of the season. In the twenty-two games I had started as catcher I was batting .272 with no homers and only three RBIs. I hoped that now that every reporter in the United States and Canada had interviewed me, maybe they would let me get back to business. Their constant questions about my health were getting to me.

Instead I went into a batting slump. I guess I was too tired. Another reason was that I was still struggling to find emotional balance. There was so much going on in my life besides baseball. Fighting the temptation to escape the real world by going back into beer and drugs was a constant struggle. My contract was up at the end of the season, and I was concerned about my future with the Royals. And there was Deanne.

At the beginning of August, Mom and Dad came up to visit, and I introduced them to Deanne. They took to her right away. So the folks invited her to come to Oklahoma City with me at Christmas.

Things were getting really serious between us. When I was home, we saw each other after the games, and when I was on road trips, we called each other every day.

She talked to her parents about me. Her dad expressed reservations about her dating a professional baseball player—especially a man with a history of alcoholism and drug addiction. He told her professional athletes live very different lives from the one she had known growing up. Deanne had lived a quiet, orderly life compared to mine. She had gone steady with one boy for several years and a year earlier had broken up with him. After finishing high school, she had worked for an attorney. She had just taken a job with the telephone company.

She was mature and level-headed, and she argued with her fa-

225

ther about me. She was sure all that negative stuff was behind me. After her folks met me and got to know me better, and her dad saw I was really trying, he seemed more agreeable to our relationship.

With my contract up in December, Bill Katzbeck and Frank Knisley approached the Royals about a new contract. But management was evasive, though they kept insisting in the newspapers that they were anxious to sign me again. I wanted to believe them. I loved the Royals and Kansas City. I didn't want to be anywhere else. But I wished they'd get busy and negotiate. Even though I was having my ups and downs since coming back, everybody thought I was an asset to the team. Sports writers were saying that with my salary of slightly less than $150,000, I was not a bargain but a steal.

The Royals' management was cautious, though, and evidently unconvinced. They were thinking that The Meadows had told them it would take up to eighteen months, and maybe more, before I would be fully recovered from the effects of my double addiction.

Though I didn't know it at the time—refused to see it actually— the Royals' brass didn't think I was worth taking a chance on. In baseball there is such a thing as loyalty. The Royals had stuck by me throughout my crisis, even going so far as to send John Schuerholz to The Meadows for family week. But when it comes down to cases, baseball is a business like any other. And if I was a risk and a liability to the team, I was expendable. But as I say, I knew nothing of this at the time.

In late August, we went on a long road trip to the West Coast to play the A's, the Angels, and the Seattle Mariners. I missed Deanne terribly, even though we talked almost every day.

Finally, one day I called her at work. "Why are you calling so early?" she asked, concerned.

"Deanne . . . ", I replied, feeling all flustered. "Shoot! I just can't stand being away from you like this anymore."

"It won't be long now, Darrell. I miss you too."

"Well, when I get home I don't want us ever to be apart again. What I mean to say is, I want you to be with me all the time, night and day. Oh, shoot!"

"Darrell, are you asking me what I think you're asking?"

"Yeah, I'm . . . askin' what you think I'm askin'. Well, will you?"

"We'll talk about it when you get home." Later, Deanne told me that when she got off the phone, she was on cloud twenty-nine all day.

When I left The Meadows, they had advised me not to make any major changes in my life for at least a year. Well, my contract was about to be up, and I'd be a free agent. That could mean one big change. I hadn't counted on Deanne coming along either.

I really felt I needed her. All my life I had refused to accept responsibility. Now I needed someone to be responsible for, someone to help me maintain structure and stability in my life. And I honestly believed (and so did she) that our meeting so soon after my release from The Meadows was no accident. God had sent her to me, because He understood my deep needs, my loneliness.

When I got back to Kansas City after that road trip, Deanne met me at the airport in a driving rainstorm. I got into the car and looked at her lovely face, a few drops of rain glistening on her cheeks. Seeing her again was food and drink. We kissed while the rain beat a steady tattoo against the roof and windshield. I was home safe . . . with her in my arms.

We drove to my house and had coffee. Then we talked. I told her that though we had known each other only a short time, I was truly in love with her. I asked her to marry me.

Before she gave me an answer, we talked about the problems of baseball life—the road trips, the separations, the fans, all the uncertainties and pressures of the supposedly glamorous life of a major league ballplayer. She said she had thought about all that and she was sure she could deal with it. She accepted my proposal of marriage. I gave her an engagement ring.

We set the date for November 29, 1980.

32

Losing Out

In late August and early September I went on a nine-game hitting streak. I felt I was up to 90 percent of my old form.

Jim Schaffer, a Royals' coach, said my catching had improved since my return. "When he first came back," he told reporters, "his throws were erratic. His releases were still quick, but he was leaning and maybe throwing the ball a little sidearm, which caused a tail on the ball. But he's got great velocity on his throws now."

But it was too little, too late. At the end of the regular season my batting average was .249. I had hit just seven home runs and driven in fifty-one runs. I'm sure the stats weren't lost on management.

The team had had a terrific season. Since June the Royals had been playing with championship form. On September 17, we defeated the Angels in the first game of a double-header, 5–0, clinching the American League West title once more. It was our fourth division title in five years.

There was a celebration in the clubhouse after the game. For once I didn't drink any of the champagne that was flowing— though I did get doused with it!

Again we were to meet the Yankees, winners of the American League East title, for the American League championship. I would be starting catcher, and I didn't feel ready. In fact, during the season I had often gotten mad at God for not restoring me to full physical and emotional health immediately. Now, still feeling shaky from the tremendous pressure I was under, still agonizing over every out and every poor fielding play I made, I would have to perform in front of the whole world.

On Wednesday, October 8, before a crowd of over 42,000, we played the first of the best-of-five series. Larry Gura (a former Yankee) pitched our entire game, allowing his former teammates only two back-to-back home runs in the second inning.

In contrast, the Royals pounded Yankees' starting pitcher Ron Guidry for four runs, before he was relieved after the third inning. I was 1 for 4. We won by a score of 7–2.

In game two, we put together four straight hits in the third inning. Frank White and I singled. Then Willie Wilson tripled, sending us home. Finally, Wilson scored on U. L. Washington's double. We edged the Yanks 3–2.

Game three moved to New York. Thanks to George Brett's three-run homer in the seventh inning, we had a 4–2 victory.

That three-game sweep of the Yankees gave us the AL championship. That night I got doused again at another champagne bash. Now it was on to the World Series, my first!

But who were we going to play? The Philadelphia Phillies and the Houston Astros were battling it out for the National League championship. I'll tell you, after having lost the AL championship so many times to the Yankees, settling their hash was so sweet that the World Series was going to seem like something of an anticlimax. After our celebration, there was a letdown. We had to rev ourselves up all over again to meet the NL winner in the Series—which turned out to be the Phillies.

The first game of the seventy-seventh World Series was played in Philadelphia on October 14, 1980. We had the distinct advantage in that first game, having rested several days while the Phils were still chasing balls around the Astrodome.

A capacity crowd of almost sixty-six thousand jammed Veterans Stadium in Philadelphia. The Phillies' pitching staff was so exhausted after their tough battle with the Astros that their starting pitcher was rookie Bob Walk. We figured it would be like taking candy from a baby. By the third inning he had allowed two, two-run homers giving us a 4–0 lead.

Early in the game I had committed a terrible blunder: When

Phils Manager Dallas Green went to the mound to talk to Walk after we got two men on in the third, it looked as though he was getting ready to take him out of the game. But something happened: When Clint Hurdle singled to left, I tried to score from second. As I rounded third base, I realized my stride was off. I came lumbering down toward home plate, totally out of sync. Now sliding is an art that requires almost as much rhythm and footwork as dancing. It's the hardest thing to do when everything is out of kilter. So I was obliged to come into home plate standing up—and I got tagged out.

It was an awful mistake, especially since I was the third out. Not only did I kill the our chances for a big inning, but by the time we were at bat again in the fourth, Walk had found the groove, and he pitched four innings of shutout ball!

When Tug McGraw finally replaced him, he held us in check with his fastballs. The Phils rallied for a 7–6 victory.

A photographer snapped my picture after the game as I sat in the locker room, chin in hand, pondering the "if-onlys." It was my first game in a World Series, and I had failed. All those old guilt feelings that I had thought I was getting under control were suddenly crowding me. *I had let my team down. What would Deanne think . . . and Dad?*

Reporters asked me if my playing that night had been affected by the death of my buddy Jerry Pemberton, who had just passed away a few days before from injuries sustained during an auto crash. I told them no—but Jerry's death had been weighing heavily on me. He had been such a loyal friend. Who can say for sure if it affected my playing? The other pressures and inadequacy I had been feeling had been bad enough.

In game two of the Series I was benched, though Jim Frey denied it was because of that play. But the big news in the second game was that George Brett had to come out of the game in the sixth inning. His . . . er . . . hemorrhoids were acting up. Poor George. I sympathized with him. But his problem provided some comic relief for an otherwise dismal situation, when the Phillies took the game 6–4. Their big inning was the eighth, when they got four runs off our ace reliever, Dan Quisenberry. Cracked one sports writer: "So the Royals went home with a 2–0 deficit, and the world's most celebrated case of hemorrhoids." Somebody suggested to George that this was his chance to make a bundle doing TV commercials for Preparation H.

When we moved to Royals Stadium for game three, the Royals found relief. So, evidently, had George Brett, who slammed a first inning homer, though he was only hours out of minor surgery on his bum. Said George, "All my problems are behind me."

The game seesawed back and forth and finally went into extra innings. In the tenth, with two men out and two men on base, Willie Aikens drove in Willie Wilson for a 4–3 Royals win. I had contributed nothing to our offense and felt miserable.

Aikens was again the hero in game four. He had hit two homers in game one of the Series, and now he turned around and did it again! He blasted George Brett home in the first, giving the Royals a four-run inning. Then, in the second, he slammed another homer, putting us ahead 5–1. After that, the Phillies couldn't see us for the dust. The final score was 5–3. The Kansas City fans were ecstatic!

In the fifth game, my first time up I singled to right field, finally breaking my 0 for 10 World Series—I broke the darned bat, too! We lost the game 4–3 and found ourselves just one defeat away from blowing the Series.

For the crucial sixth game we were back in Philadelphia. Security was tight, in case of a rousing Phillies victory. After two scoreless innings, there was some excitement in the third; Phillies power-hitter Mike Schmidt got a two-run single to right field, giving the Phils the 2–0 lead.

By the ninth inning the Phillies were leading 4–1. But although we had two outs, the bases were loaded after Tug McGraw gave up a walk and two hits. Then Willie Wilson came to bat. It would take a grand slam to give us the desperately needed winning run. Could Willie do it?

Maybe. McGraw later admitted his arm was growing numb at that point.

McGraw delivered one of his fine screwballs. It was a called strike.

Next pitch was a slider, but Wilson fouled it into the stands. Next . . . a ball.

Phillies catcher Bob Boone signaled for another screwball, but McGraw shook him off. Instead he slipped a high fastball past Willie's futile swing.

It was all over. The final score was 4–1.

Only the presence of that army of helmeted riot police restrained the jubilant Philadelphia fans from tearing the stadium down.

In my first World Series I had fourteen at-bats and had hit safely only twice. My lack of success climaxed what was probably my most difficult year in baseball. I had felt tremendous pressure all season from the fans and the ever curious reporters all across the country. I had struggled with myself and wrestled with God.

In the wake of our loss of the Series, stories flew thick and fast that as many as ten Royals players, including me, might be wearing the uniforms of other teams in the spring of 1981.

A vicious rumor began circulating that I had fallen off the wagon and was back on alcohol and drugs. I was really upset. I had worked so hard to keep clean since my release from The Meadows. It was a low blow.

I agreed to a complete physical—I had no intention of living with an ugly shadow over me. The results laid that lie to rest: I received a clean bill of health. There was not one iota of evidence to substantiate that incredible story.

In spite of published statements that the Royals "are interested in retaining Porter," management continued to hedge on making a firm offer to re-sign me, though Joe Burke had told Frank Knisley as early as August that the Royals would be making a formal offer. Now, Burke, who had a conservative streak in him, was saying he had no intention of getting into a bidding war over my services.

By late October I had become a free agent. Eight teams, including Oakland, Toronto, California, Milwaukee, Pittsburgh, Houston, and St. Louis, picked me in the free-agent draft.

The Royals, still playing their cards close to the vest, retained their negotiating rights to my contract, still insisting they were interested. By the time Deanne and I were married at the end of November and were preparing for our honeymoon, Joe Burke had not yet made an offer, or even set up a meeting with my agents.

Deanne and I were on a cruise ship in the middle of the Caribbean when Frank Knisley called to tell me that Whitey Herzog, who was now managing the St. Louis Cardinals, had made us a handsome offer—a whopping $3.5 million for five years (roughly $700,000 a year). Before I could fully digest that bit of news, Frank said, "If you don't accept Whitey's offer right now, he's going to take it back."

Whitey, aware that the Royals were pussyfooting, was trying to force a deal. As much as I loved the guy and could picture myself working under him again, I was angry over the strategy and the fact that they thought none of this could possibly wait until I returned from my honeymoon.

"Frank," I said, "there is no way I am going to make that decision this minute. Furthermore, I won't make any decision at all until you call the Royals and give them the opportunity to make a counteroffer. If they can come close, then I'd like to stay in Kansas City. Money isn't the most important consideration."

Although my faith in the Royals was beginning to waver, I was hoping against hope that they would come up with a decent offer that would show they still wanted me and believed in my potential—as Whitey Herzog obviously did.

Well, they didn't even come close. Re-signing with Kansas City would have cost me $1.5 million. And that was just too much of a sacrifice, considering everything that had happened.

The following week I flew to St. Louis and put my signature on a contract with the Cardinals.

Whitey seemed very pleased to have me on board with him once more. And so was I. He insisted he wasn't concerned about the falloff in my playing in the 1980 season. "I'm not worried about last year," he told reporters. "Darrell's hard-nosed; he'll play good. People say Darrell had a bad year, but he carried the Royals in May, and it was good he even came back at all, the way he did."

It was good to have Whitey in my corner again, to be working with a manager who believed in me! I knew I was still not fully recovered from the effects of the alcohol and drugs. I needed more time. The Royals hadn't seen fit to give me that. Whitey had—and at some cost to himself.

In hiring me, Whitey traded his star catcher, Ted Simmons. As soon as the change was announced, the St. Louis fans began crying the blues. Simmons was a very popular player, and rightly so. He had given the Cardinals some great seasons.

Though I didn't know it then, the sullen attitude of the Cardinals fans over the loss of Simmons was going to have a direct effect on my career with the Cardinals come 1981.

33

On to the Cardinals

Deanne and I had a busy fall and winter. She moved into my home in Kansas City and did some redecorating. There were tons of thank-you notes to write for our wedding presents, and then, before we knew it, the busy Christmas season was upon us. We spent the holidays with the folks in Oklahoma City.

As soon as New Year's was over, I was busy organizing the annual fishing tournament I run at Lake Taneycomo in the Missouri Ozarks. In that off-season Deanne and I got in a lot of trout fishing. She was really working at becoming a fisherperson. She picked up plastic-worm fishing right away, and that's one of the hardest, slowest ways to fish, because you have to have a sensitive touch.

Once we'd catch the fish we had a nice division of labor worked out—I'd fillet them and Deanne would cook them. So it worked out nicely.

Sometimes in those early days of our marriage, I'd be afraid that I wasn't sensitive enough to Deanne. Not only was I haunted by the mistakes I had made with Teri, but I was still struggling with my drug-damaged emotions. My fear of hurting Deanne caused me anguish. I prayed about it all the time.

"Darrell," Deanne would say to me in those dark moments, "please don't be so hard on yourself. You're a very loving, giving man. Try to believe that. You make me very happy."

While she was reorganizing our home in Kansas City, from time to time she would come across scraps of things I had written during those dark years of my drug addiction . . . confused, disjointed jottings of a tormented mind. It gave her insights into the pathetic person I had been before I met her. Those ramblings—scrawled on hotel stationery, the backs of envelopes, anything—aroused in Deanne a deep sorrow for the lost man I had been and left her wondering sadly if she could have helped had she known me in those days.

One night she came to me with a prayer she had found, one I had written just after I returned from The Meadows. In it, I had poured out my confusion and anguish to God, asking Him for grace and wisdom to sort out the tangled skein of my life.

"Oh, Darrell," she said, her eyes full, "tell me. What can I do to help you?"

Taking her in my arms I whispered, "Just keep loving me. Don't ever stop!"

In February 1981, we reported to spring training at the Cardinals' complex in St. Petersburg, Florida. Almost immediately I began to have problems throwing; my shoulder was sore. Oh, it was a *really* good start with the new ballclub! We tried everything— whirlpool, massage, heat, rest—nothing helped. I struggled along with it.

When the baseball season began, Deanne and I rented a house in Kirkwood, a suburb of St. Louis, for the season, but we kept our home in Kansas City. While Deanne had her hands full organizing things at the new house and trying to adjust to life as a baseball wife, I found to my chagrin that I had more to contend with at Busch Stadium than sore shoulder muscles.

From day one, a few of the Cardinals fans (it seemed like the whole stadium) took an instant dislike to me. And they showed it every chance they got. Though I was struggling with my aches and pains and poor playing, it wasn't just those things. They were also bitter over Ted Simmons's being traded away to the Brewers. And since I was Simmons's replacement, I was the target of their anger.

Having people like me has always been important to me—probably too important, as I've indicated many times in these pages. Consequently, this vendetta by the St. Louis fans really hurt me.

Things got worse and worse, and gradually it affected my game to the point that I hated coming to the stadium.

As we got into the season, I began to look forward to the road trips—I actually got less abuse from opposing fans than I did from the home-town crowd. And my playing was much better on the road.

At home, it seemed, the harder I tried the more the boo-birds were on my back. On top of all that, my shoulder was getting worse. In May, they finally diagnosed it as a slightly torn rotator-cuff. The specialist who examined me suggested that I not play for a month. I was actually relieved at the news—that's how much the fans were getting to me.

Then, on June 12, 1981, just as I was getting ready to don my uniform again (and dreading it) we were hit by the baseball strike. At issue in the strike (which was to drag on and on) were not only salaries, but the touchy issue of free agentry.

As bad as the strike was for baseball and the lower salaried players, I felt as if I had been sprung from jail, and frankly, it felt good. Deanne and I returned to Kansas City to wait it out. Our house is right on a lake, so we did a lot of swimming, boating, and fishing. We practically lived on the water.

While negotiations stalled and broke down repeatedly, we whiled away our days. Actually, a summer in which I was free to do as I pleased was totally strange to me. All my adult life I had been obligated to one baseball team or another during the summer months. Now, just being able to relax and enjoy myself was a wonderful thing. But, this relaxation was an indirect benefit; on another level we all wanted the strike to be over, because a lot of people were hurting, both fans and players. Many players who didn't have fat contracts had to work at other jobs to make ends meet, and I sympathized with them. But there were others like myself who couldn't help but savor the bit of summer freedom dropped into their laps.

During the strike, one really negative thing happened, and it was my fault. One day I went fishing, and on the way home I stopped and bought a beer. Just one little bottle of beer. And I drank it.

To this day I don't know why I did that. Maybe I just wanted to taste it again. Or maybe I was tempting God.

At any rate, after I finished it, I put the bottle under the seat of my car. Why I did that instead of tossing it, makes me think I had a death wish, because I knew Deanne would murder me if she even suspected I had a beer.

As you may know, an alcoholic (and a drug addict for that matter) is never cured in the sense that, say, someone suffering from measles or pneumonia is cured. All his life, he is only a recovering alcoholic/addict. One taste of beer, one snort of coke (or whatever), can put him back in the gutter. Knowing that keeps you humble, believe me.

And if Deanne had one reservation in marrying me, I suppose it was the possibility, however remote, that one day I might revert to my old ways. It had happened to better men.

Knowing all this, why did I drink that beer? And why did I put the bottle under the seat? I think I wanted Deanne to find it.

She did.

The next day, when she was looking for something in the car, she just happened to put her hand under the seat.

I was sitting in the living room when she came strolling in acting casual—too casual. "Who drinks Coors?" she asked, holding the bottle in front of my face.

I was stunned, petrified.

I was scrambling for words. There was no use lying at this point. "It's . . . it's mine."

"I can't believe it!" she screamed. "I just can't believe it! What is wrong with you? Are you crazy? Are things going too smoothly for us? Are we too happy? DO YOU WANT TO SMASH OUR LIVES?"

I thought she might hit me with the bottle. Instead, she turned and ran from the house, down the hill, and out onto the dock. I watched her from the window, my heart thumping wildly. Running to the very edge of the dock, she hurled that bottle far out into the lake. Then she sat down and cried.

I left her alone for a few minutes. (Shoot, I was scared she might kill me yet!) And I had to give her space. After a while, I called from the door, "Deanne, please come up here for a minute."

"No, just leave me alone!"

"Please ... I have to talk to you."

Slowly she got up and walked toward the house, without raising her head, like a sullen child.

"I want you to know I'm sorry," I said. "Maybe you can't forgive me. And I know what I did was a terrible, terrible thing. A foolish thing! But I'm so sorry it ever happened."

She began weeping softly.

"Deanne, I don't want to hurt you. I'd never....Why, I don't even know why I bought the thing! It was crazy! Do you think I'd really want to jeopardize what we have? I promise you, it will never, ever happen again! Please say you'll forgive me!"

Then she was in my arms, crying as if her heart would break.

"Oh, Darrell, Darrell, I'm just so scared!"

We both tried to forget the incident. But six months later, at a church conference Deanne attended with Jerry Terrell's wife, the memory came back and she couldn't forget it. She broke down and cried. That's how upset she was. Then she prayed about it.

"Please, dear Lord, watch over Darrell. Keep him safe from all harm and danger and from any evil thing. Keep him clean, Lord."

Neither of us ever mentioned that incident to anyone until now. I tell it at this point because too many people tend to make professional athletes into superior beings. Since I had gone on record as totally rejecting any further use of alcohol and drugs, people wanted to believe I was above stumbling. It makes things neater, with no messy loose ends. It makes a better story. It's sad that life refuses to conform to our fantasies of perfection.

When I returned to the Royals from The Meadows, I told my teammates and the world: "With God's help and your understanding I will be a better man." So I'm not proud of having "gone off the wagon" that one time.

But folks, Darrell Porter is not perfect. In fact, he is a weak, fallible human being, just like everyone else.

I asked God to forgive me that lapse. And I believe He has, because in the Bible Christ told us He will forgive us. And I have been able to forgive myself and get on with my life.

As I told those reporters that time, I don't like being tempted, and I don't like failing. I'm impatient. I really would like God to "snap me perfect" in an instant, so I wouldn't have to keep falling on my face and picking myself up again (with His help). You can't snap into perfection, however, because it is a process of becoming, and becoming always takes time and effort and involves the risk of failure.

The strike dragged on. On Monday, July 13, baseball-hungry fans gathered in downtown Cleveland to boo the cancellation of the All-Star game, which had been scheduled for their city.

Finally, after two months, the longest strike in baseball history was over. When we went back for what was left of the season, my arm had healed, but the hearts of those St. Louis fans hadn't. They seemed worse than ever.

In one sense baseball is a mirror of life. Nowhere can you see the passing glory of the world more accurately reflected; nowhere can you see the fickleness of the crowd more clearly and dramatically revealed—its joyous approval of success and its cruel jeers at failure. Today's hero is tomorrow's candidate for tar and feathers.

Sometimes I felt Deanne was my only friend in the stands at Busch Stadium. I know it was tough for her, too, because she had to sit in the middle of all those hecklers. Once, when a guy behind her kept yelling, "Hey, Porter, why don't you have a beer; it'll improve your game!" Deanne turned around and snapped, "Why don't you just drink *your* beer, buddy, and leave him alone!"

That fan evidently figured out who the blonde with the fire in her eyes was because he stopped heckling me.

Enduring the spite—the hatred—of that handful of St. Louis fans was one of the hardest things I have ever done. It was almost harder than kicking the beer and drugs. I was still plagued, too, by the struggle to face the pressures of life and my fear of failure without resorting to the temporary escape offered by drugs. Only God's grace, given in part through Deanne, got me through.

Toward the end of that bad, bad first year at St. Louis, we had one wonderful bit of news—Deanne was expecting! The baby was due to be born the following spring. We were so happy! At first I thought I might want a boy, but then I thought maybe a little girl would be nice. Somebody once told me, "Boys go down to the corner, but girls stay at home with their daddies." I was determined that I was going to really show our child love—with lots of hug-

ging and kissing. I would open to our child all the doors of opportunity—let him or her explore many avenues, to help him or her
reach full potential. Oh, it was going to be grand!

I finished that dismal first season with the Cards with a low, low
.224 batting average earned in sixty-one games. Even taking into
consideration time lost during the strike, I was hardly earning my
hefty salary.

After the season, Deanne and I went on another Caribbean
cruise. And I needed that cruise to unwind. It had been one of the
worst seasons of my career.

Once more we returned to Oklahoma City for the Christmas
holidays. Then, back home in Kansas City in January, we busied
ourselves getting the nursery ready for the baby, which the doctor
was now saying would arrive in early April.

Our excitement over the baby helped ease the nagging fear I had
about the arrival of something else—the 1982 baseball season.
Deanne went with me to St. Petersburg for spring training, but she
returned to KC in early March to await the birth of the baby.

We talked often, and I told her to be sure to call me as soon as
the pains started, so I could hop on a plane and be there to coach. I
had gone to the natural childbirth classes with Deanne, and I
looked forward to being with her to "help" with the delivery, to see
the birth of our child.

Well, the baby decided to come a week early—on March 31,
1982. Deanne called me to say I'd better hurry, or the stork would
beat the plane to Kansas City.

Plenty of time . . . don't be nervous, I told myself as I dashed to
the airport. The flight seemed endless. When I arrived at KC, I
thought I might stop off at the house first to pick up our camera,
but at the last minute I decided I'd better get right over to the hospital. I was trying to remember all the techniques we learned . . .
about how Deanne was supposed to breathe and all that stuff, and
what I could do to help comfort or relax her. Shoot! I'd never get it
all straight!

When I arrived at the hospital, a nurse handed me a surgical suit
and mask and said, "Quick! Go in there and change!"

Just as I was coming out of the dressing room I heard a baby crying! I figured it might be ours. It was! I was disappointed (but a lit-

tle relieved) I didn't have a chance to take part in the birth.

They let me go in. Deanne lay there, all spent and pale, but smiling. I kissed her damp cheek tenderly. Then I went to the little crib where they had the baby . . . our baby. It was a little girl. I picked her up.

"Oh, she's a keeper!" I crowed. "I'd say she's a seven-pounder!" (A keeper is a fishing term for a fish that's big enough to save.) As it turned out, I was only off by an ounce. Little Lindsey (that was to be our little beauty's name) weighed in at seven pounds, one ounce.

34

Triumph

The Cardinals began the 1982 season on the road. I started off with a bang—hitting a home run. But as soon as we returned to St. Louis, I went downhill again. I had prayed often over the winter, asking the Lord to give me the ability to handle the fans and the tremendous pressures I felt myself under, in addition to my ever present fear of failing and humiliating myself in front of the world.

Finally, about mid-season, the answer came, not by some miracle, but by that "still small voice" speaking in the quietness of my heart. I came to realize as I spoke to the Lord in prayer that the jeering fans didn't even know me and forgot about me as soon as they left the stadium after a game. So why should I suffer so much over their lack of support?

I also came to the conclusion that all I can do is the best that I can do. In other words, I developed the attitude that if I concentrate on doing my very best each day, that's all I or anyone else can ask of me. If I know I've given everything I have to give in a game, there is no reason to tear myself apart afterward because I wasn't perfect.

As I grew in this attitude, I was more and more able to deal with the critical fans and the pressures of the game. Not that the jeers didn't hurt or the pressures went away, but I was able to take them in my stride. Gradually, I started to relax and play better. My batting average snuck upward, and I was performing better behind the plate.

It hadn't taken eighteen months for me to feel normal again, but the experts had been close. It took just over two years. I was finally feeling really healthy and back to normal.

Yet the roller coaster pattern of playing that had been my hallmark since my rehabilitation—batting streaks and great catching, alternating with slumps and not-so-great-catching—began to reassert itself, though I continued to play well on the road. At the end of the '82 season my batting average was .231—a shade higher than that of 1981—and I had forty-eight RBIs.

The team really had a good season, however, and again I found myself in the play-offs—but this time it was for the National League title against the Atlanta Braves.

Having been in three play-offs at Kansas City, I knew the feeling; I was used to it. So I decided to approach the championship series with a relaxed attitude. I would go out and have fun. Either I would do well or I wouldn't. Whatever happened, I vowed I wouldn't get up-tight or carried away. I wouldn't demand miracles of myself.

It paid off. In the first game I managed to reach base three times, with two hits and a walk. Then, the first game was postponed after only four and a half innings because of rain.

The next day Bob Forsch was on the mound for us and pitched a three-hit shutout over the Braves. We won 7–0.

The second game was also postponed due to the rain. It was played on October 9. Atlanta had taken a 2–1 lead in the third. Then in the fifth they had scored another run. We succeeded in narrowing the gap in the sixth when Keith Hernandez scored on my double, and I scored the tying run in the eighth on Willie McGee's chopper over the mound. I was on base four times in that game and had two doubles and two walks. We won 4–3 in the bottom of the ninth when our Dave Green scored on Ken Oberkfell's hit.

In the third game of the best-of-five series, I had a single and walked twice. Hernandez scored in the second inning. He had singled, I followed with a walk, and George Hendrick's single got him home. Then our Willie McGee tripled, driving me and George Hendrick home. McGee scored on a single by Ozzie Smith. The final score was 6–2.

Triumph

We had copped the National League championship!

In that three-game sweep of the Braves, I was 5 for 9, with five walks, and I wound up being named the most valuable player in the championships!

I could hardly believe it. When I thought of the agony of the past two seasons—my own poor playing and the cruelty of the fans—it *was* a kind of miracle after all. One that I hadn't looked for or expected.

Well, all of a sudden the booing turned to cheering in St. Louis, even from those hardnosed fans. I was feeling so good about things, it was hard *not* to forgive them!

So, I was going to play in my second World Series. Ironically, we would be playing my old team, the Milwaukee Brewers. A double irony lay in the fact that the former St. Louis catcher, the beloved Ted Simmons, had been traded to Milwaukee and would be returning for the first game to Busch Stadium.

I had no animosity toward Simmons. Yet I couldn't bear the thought of the St. Louis fans cheering him at the start of the Series, when the teams would be introduced, particularly after the shabby way they had been treating me for two seasons. Just before the introductions, I retired to the clubhouse. I needn't have bothered. The fans gave Simmons only a light smattering of applause.

The first game of the seventy-ninth World Series was a disaster for us.

It started in the first inning when the Brewers' Ben Oglivie drove in a run. Then, Gorman Thomas drove in another, giving them a 2–0 lead.

The Brewers then proceeded to trounce us. Third baseman Paul Molitor became the first player in a World Series to have five hits in five trips to the plate. All of his hits were singles. His teammate Robin Yount got four hits. Then, irony of ironies, our friend Ted Simmons slammed a homer in the fifth. (I had managed a double in the second.)

Our starting pitcher, Bob Forsch, was relieved in the top of the sixth after allowing two singles and a two-run bloop double by Yount. Forsch was replaced by veteran Jim Kaat, who did the only effective pitching for us that dismal night. He in turn was relieved by two rookies, Dave LaPoint and Jeff Lahti, who allowed the final four Brewers' runs between them.

Their pitcher, Mike Caldwell, was dazzling. He threw only 52 pitches the first five innings, and by the time the game was over only 101—and 64 of those were strikes. After my double in the second, he retired twelve of us in a row and walked only one.

When the dust had settled, Whitey grumbled, "I don't like losing 10–0." Not a very quotable line. But one from the heart.

Just before the game that night, one of the famous Clydesdales had "dumped" on a coaching box. Horse manure! Maybe that horse knew something the Cardinals didn't.

In the second game, Don Sutton pitched five great innings for the Brewers, but by the bottom of the sixth he was growing tired. With two outs and a man on third, he walked George Hendrick.

Then I came to bat. After one strike and two balls, Sutton hung a slider on the outside part of the plate. I got lucky and hit a double down the left-field line (I hadn't hit a ball there in a year!). I drove in two runs, evening the score at 4–4. The St. Louis fans were cheering their lungs out. (Oh, what satisfaction there was in that!)

In the eighth, with the score still knotted at 4-4, Brewers pitchers Bob McClure and Pete ("Big Foot") Ladd allowed us to load the bases. I was one of our men on base, having singled. Then, up came our Steve Braun. Ladd promptly walked him on four straight balls, forcing home Hendrick with the go-ahead run.

Bruce Sutter protected our lead in the ninth, allowing only a bunt single by Molitor. A minute later he tried to steal second. I fired the ball, and Molitor was tagged out. We took that second game, 5–4.

After the game, Whitey talked about my performance and the fickleness of the fans. He was grinning from ear to ear. My performance in game two gave me a postseason batting average of .563—with nine hits in sixteen at-bats. I was happy that I had vindicated Whitey's unflagging faith in me.

Willie McGee was the hero of game three—driving in four runs on two homers and making two great catches, one of them spectacular—to keep the Brewers at bay.

McGee's first homer, a three-run shot against Pete Vuckovich, came in the fifth inning of a game that until then was scoreless.

Then, in the top of the seventh, with us leading by four runs, McGee hit another homer into the stands on a change-up, giving us a 5–0 lead.

Left-fielder Lonnie Smith shone in that game, too. After going three for nineteen in postseason play, he doubled in the fifth and tripled in the seventh.

When the Brewers came to bat in the ninth inning, our first baseman Keith Hernandez made an error, allowing Oglivie to reach first. It looked for a while as if the Brewers might be catching fire when Gorman Thomas nearly put one over the wall—should have, actually—except for Willie McGee's really spectacular leap and catch.

Sutter then struck out the next two batters to end the game. The score was 6–2.

Game four, which like game three was played at Milwaukee's County Stadium, seemed like another easy win for us. In the seventh we were leading the Brewers 5–1, with one out. Ben Oglivie hit one toward Hernandez, who snagged it after it bounced and then fired it to pitcher Dave LaPoint—who dropped it!

Right then, things began to unravel for us: Don Money singled to right, Charlie Moore popped out, then Jim Gantner connected for a double, bringing Oglivie home.

Next, Paul Molitor walked, loading the bases. Robin Yount then drove in two runs with a bloop single to right, cutting our lead to a narrow 5–4.

Crisis time: Whitey sent lefty Jim Kaat to pitch to left-handed-hitting Cecil Cooper and switch-hitter Ted Simmons. Cooper got a single to tie the game, and when Kaat began pitching erratically to Simmons, Whitey relieved him with Jeff Lahti—who promptly walked the dangerous Simmons, loading the bases again.

Gorman Thomas next connected with Lahti's slider, driving it into left field, giving the Brewers the go-ahead runs. The final score was 7–5.

The hero's mantle passed to Milwaukee in the fifth game—to shortstop Robin Yount, who led the Brewers to another victory—6–4, and giving them a 3–2 Series lead. In that game he became the only player ever to rap four hits twice in a World Series. (He had also done it in the opening game.) His performance was so impressive that even Whitey dubbed him one of baseball's top players, admitting at the same time that our pitchers couldn't handle him.

We didn't do well in that game. In every inning we left a player stranded on base. Also, our pitching was off, while the Brewers' fielding was excellent. For instance, Lonnie Smith was robbed of a hit by Yount in the third inning and then again in the fifth by Charlie Moore (who caught a line drive) and still *again* by Molitor, who caught his chopper and threw him out in the ninth.

In the seventh there was fancy fielding by Cecil Cooper, who made a dive and snagged my right field smash.

My feelings at that point were a good indication of just how far I had come in my recovery from my addictions and in my ability to live one day at a time. We were now down three games to two, just one game from losing the Series. As bad as things looked for us, however, I had a quiet confidence that we would still come back and win the whole thing—that *I* could perform well and do what needed to be done in crucial situations.

The Brewers had made what *Sports Illustrated* described as "at least six defensive gems." There was no arguing that. We didn't stand a chance against such playing. The experts thought the Brewers were now going to carry the Series on their powerful hitting. But, one never knows in baseball . . . does one?

In the sixth game, the Brewers suddenly developed butterfingers, making what seemed like one error after another. Even Robin Yount, who was to be the American League's MVP that year, had *two*.

In the first inning, a chopper by Willie McGee went through Yount's legs, giving us our first run. Then in the second inning, McGee scored on Tom Herr's double off the right-field wall, when catcher Ted Simmons missed Charlie Moore's throw home.

In the fourth inning, I drove a homer over the right-field wall, driving in Hendrick and giving us a 4–0 lead.

In the same inning, Don Sutton gave up a triple to Dane Iorg, who then scored on Tom Herr's single. We now led 5–0.

In the fifth, Keith Hernandez rose to the occasion with a two-run homer, which resulted in Don Sutton's being replaced by Jim Slaton. Then, in the bottom of the sixth, Slaton was in turn replaced by George (Doc) Medich.

Medich proceeded to give up a double to Iorg, singles to Herr and McGee, a two-run single to Hernandez, and on and on. We got a total of six runs in the inning, which took about two and a half hours to finish because of a rain delay in the middle.

One of our young pitchers, John Stuper, shone in that game. The kid's fastball jumped like a bass on a tight line. In a nearly perfect pitching performance, he allowed only two hits and a walk in eight innings—and no runs. His shutout was ended in the ninth inning on a single by Paul Molitor and a double by Jim Gantner. (Dave Nightingale of *The Sporting News* described Stuper's performance as "maybe stupefying.") It was Stuper who led us to that 13–1 rout of the Brewers.

Now came the final, crucial seventh game in St. Louis.

It was cold, forty-four degrees, but the crowd of almost sixty thousand was oblivious to the temperature.

We lost an early 1–0 lead when Ben Oglivie's home run into the right-field seats in the fifth inning tied things up briefly.

In the sixth, a throwing error gave the Brewers an unearned run, and a sacrifice fly by Cecil Cooper put Milwaukee ahead 3–1.

Then, in the bottom of the sixth, there was a hint of a turnaround: Our Ozzie Smith made it to first base, then Lonnie Smith doubled. At that point, the Brewers took out their starting pitcher Pete Vuckovich, and brought in left-hander Bob McClure. McClure promptly walked Gene Tenace, loading the bases.

When Keith Hernandez came to bat, you could have sliced the tension in the air with a butter knife. The 3–1 pitch was an inside fastball. Hernandez connected—a single to center field, bringing home both Smiths and tying the game once more.

The roar from the stands sounded like Niagara Falls.

Next, George Hendrick, one of our most fearsome right-handed hitters, singled, bringing home Mike Ramsey (pinch-running for Tenace). We were now ahead 4–3. The fans were in a frenzy of joy.

In the top of the eighth inning, Whitey brought out his big gun in the person of a well-rested Bruce Sutter, who relieved Joaquin Andujar. (Andujar had pitched seven innings of great ball.)

Sutter earned his keep by retiring three Brewers in quick succession.

When we came to bat, Lonnie Smith hit his second double of the game off Moose Haas, who had replaced McClure. Then Mike Ramsey struck out, Keith Hernandez walked, and George Hendrick was out on a fly to center field.

Then I came to bat and singled off lefty Mike Caldwell (who had relieved Haas), bringing Lonnie Smith home. Left-handed-hitting Steve Braun singled too, scoring Hernandez.

We were now ahead 6–3!

The ninth inning. The crucial inning.

It looked as though we might have it sewed up, but in baseball the game is never over until the last pitch . . . the last out.

Now, the huge crowd was on its collective feet, shouting, stomping, clapping, whistling. Those Cardinals fans were willing us to victory!

Bruce Sutter was on the mound. Ironically, the first batter was former Cards catcher Ted Simmons. The pitch was a called strike. The crowd roared its approval.

Then, a ball. On the next pitch, Simmons bounced the ball toward the mound. Sutter scooped it up and tossed it to Hernandez for an easy out.

The fans were delirious; you could feel the ground vibrating from the shouting. One down; two to go.

Ben Oglivie came to bat. The first pitch was again a called strike. Then a ball. Next pitch, Oglivie swung—and missed. Then, like Simmons, he connected, but the ball bounced, this time to Tom Herr at second. Herr fired to first for the *second* out.

Two down; one to go.

Now the noise from the stands was a steady and unrelenting roar, like a dozen jet planes.

Our teammates mounted the steps of the dugout, watching . . . waiting. Gorman Thomas came to bat. Sutter threw a called strike. The next pitch was a ball. On the third pitch Thomas swung . . . and missed. Strike *two*! But then, two balls. Full count.

Next, Thomas fouled off a pitch. Then he fouled again. (Sutter was giving him his split-fingered fastball.)

Both teams and the crowd were in an agony of suspense.

Sutter breathed on his freezing hands, then threw two more split-fingers. Thomas fouled both into the stands!

It was time for a change in tactics. Sutter looked at me, and I signaled a regular fastball. Sutter fired it over the plate.

Thomas swung with all his might—and missed!

He struck out!

It was all over!

We had won the World Series!

Pandemonium! As Bruce raised his arms in a victory gesture, I threw off my catcher's mask and ran toward him, as many of those nearly sixty thousand fans, ignoring pleas for order, erupted from the stands onto the field, sweeping aside the security police. Bruce and I grabbed one another and did a victory polka of sorts around the infield, while all around us fans danced, shouting their delight into the cold night air while fireworks burst over Busch Stadium. It was one of the greatest, zaniest moments of my entire life!

Later in the clubhouse, I was drinking champagne (nonalcoholic!) and shouting, "Oh, my goodness! Lordy! Lordy! I ain't *never* had so much fun playin' ball!"

Even though there were many outstanding players in the 1982 World Series—Bruce Sutter, Joaquin Andujar, Robin Yount, Keith Hernandez, Dane Iorg—I was awarded the coveted World Series Most Valuable Player Award.

It was incredible—unbelievable, really. I was only the second player in baseball history to win MVP honors in both the league championships and the World Series! (Willie Stargell of the Pirates was the first, in 1979.)

But why me? Sports writer Robert L. Burnes said it nicely in the *St. Louis Globe Democrat*. After conceding that though I had earned the MVP Award, he insisted every member of the Cardinals deserved one! Then he wrote: " . . . the one name [the judges] kept coming back to was Darrell Porter, much maligned Cardinals catcher during his first two regular seasons here.

"Porter, it seemed, didn't have a friend in town . . . except one: Whitey Herzog: 'He was a leader for me in Kansas City, he is a leader for me here. He is a sensitive man and I know criticism has hurt him. But he has kept his chin up.' "

There was one touching moment following the game. I ran into my former boss on the Brewers, owner Bud Selig. I gave Bud a big bear hug. It wasn't his fault I had loused up at Milwaukee and got traded. Selig had wanted to help me, had tried, only I wasn't ready. It was ironic that after all he had put up with from me, now that I had gotten myself straight, someone else's team was profiting from it—at Selig's expense!

But nothing could dampen our victory. President Reagan called Whitey to congratulate us. It was fantastic! Hugging Deanne and little Lindsey to me, in that joyous triumphant, crazy moment in the Cardinals' clubhouse, I told the crowd: "I've got me a beautiful wife, a little baby six-and-a-half months old, who's gonna be a looker; I haven't had a drink in two years and no pills or pot . . . or whatever!

"I'm a *happy* man!"

But later, when I was proudly showing reporters my "little punkin'," Lindsey, I said, "She is the neatest thing that ever happened to me. Baseball is just an ole fun game and win or lose . . . I'm having a blast. Oh, it was neat to be named MVP and I'm glad I've contributed to the Series. But lookee here!" And I held our baby up for all to see.

"You know," I added, "happiness is *not* going to come from playing ball. Sooner or later, the game will humble you, no matter how big a shot you are. You better get your forever kind of happiness somewhere else." And I meant it.

The next week was a blur—a triumphant ticker-tape parade through downtown St. Louis the next day, then a flight to New York to receive the MVP Award at a fancy bash, then out to California to do a Johnny Carson Show (hosted by Steve Allen). Everybody wanted to interview me, to see me, to touch me.

Of course, Frank Knisley saw in the exposure an open door to lucrative endorsements. "We've got to strike while the iron is hot, Darrell!" he kept telling me as he booked more and more appearances.

He was only doing his job . . . looking to feather my nest. But I was tired, so tired I was hurting. Finally I put my foot down: "Frank," I said, "the extra money means very little to me. I don't need millions and millions of dollars. I've got a perfectly nice contract. And I'm not on an ego trip, where I need the fame and the adulation. I'm just a normal—tired—guy who needs to go home to his wife and baby. So let's cool it."

Of course Frank and Bill keep trying. But I'm a committed

Christian (or I try to be one), and I have to be careful about things like greed (it can sneak up on you) and with what and whom I'm associated. For example, a chewing tobacco firm wanted me to represent them. (Chewing tobacco is my one vice.) In the wake of the NL championship and the World Series triumphs, they offered me a lucrative contract.

The offer was very tempting, especially since it included the opportunity to host a fishing show on television, something I've always dreamed of doing. But I had known for a long time that tobacco isn't good for your health, and I was also concerned about what kind of example I would be setting for young people, as well as what the endorsement would do to my Christian witness. In the end, Deanne and I concluded that it was something the Lord just didn't want me to do, and I couldn't have felt right about going ahead with it.

Lest you think I'm bragging or tooting my own horn, let me be honest. It was very difficult to turn down that offer. Frankly, there's a side of me that is as lazy and greedy as the next guy. I don't enjoy being tried and tested. There are still times when I get tired of having to grow, to stretch emotionally, spiritually. There's that perverse streak in me that wants to lie back, that says, "Snap me perfect, Lord, in an instant."

But His way, the slow, steady way of daily struggle and growth, is the best way after all, and I'm learning to accept it. There's a beautiful verse in the Bible that puts it nicely: "Trust in the LORD with all thine heart; and lean not unto thine own understanding. In all thy ways acknowledge him, and he shall direct thy paths" (Prov. 3:5–6).

Hey, I believe it, because I *had* to trust Him. I had nowhere else to turn. And He brought me back from the brink of hell, one slow, painful step at a time. He carried me all the way, and He has crowned my life with love and goodness. And I know that He will continue to carry me through all the days of my life.

Epilogue

Some people write books for fame and prestige. Others write for money. I have written this book for neither of those reasons. I am not an ego-maniac, and as I've told Frank Knisley, I don't need millions of dollars to be happy.

I have written my story in the hope that I can keep a few young people away from drugs. If there is a theme in my story besides baseball, it is the torment, the hell, of drug addiction. Drugs nearly killed me—it is only by the grace of God that they didn't.

Why do people deliberately put chemicals in their bodies that will eventually destroy the mind, health, and life itself? The Bible teaches us that there is something flawed in our makeup, and I believe it. We will do stupid, dangerous things if "everybody else" is doing them, too.

It's done so gradually; nobody deliberately sets out to destroy his mind, body, and soul, and it isn't done in a day. We do it by degrees, over a period of months, or years, with small choices and little compromises. I know I didn't become a drug addict by smoking one joint or even ten. But it always starts with that first joint or pill (or whatever), the one you take "just this once" and "just to go along with the crowd." Everybody wants to be liked. It's natural. I know that desire to be accepted, to be "in," got me started on beer and drugs.

It's interesting to me that when I was in high school I had the backbone to say no when the gang wanted me to drink a beer. But as soon as I got away from home in minor-league ball, I caved in. Maybe it was being away from the support of my family and friends that did it; being lonely and under pressure to succeed. I needed friends, and, hey, if they drank and smoked pot, then I would, too.

It takes a lot of courage to stand up against the crowd, to know your own mind, to have your own set of standards and stick to them. But in the long run, the only way to gain the respect of other people and to have any self-respect is to do what *you* know to be right. I wish I had had that kind of courage; I could have saved myself a lot of misery.

I'm not saying it's easy. It's tough. The teen years especially are an age when young people are learning to adapt socially outside the family. Because they are groping toward independence from their parents, teens tend to value the opinions of their friends more than those of Mom and Dad. So what does a guy or girl do when half the gang at school are drinking and doing drugs? Where does a young person turn for guidance? There *has* to be a better standard by which to live one's life, besides the fickle opinions and the questionable standards of the gang.

Some of you might be saying, "But, Darrell, I know lots of guys and girls who smoke pot and pop a few pills. They say it makes you feel good. So what's so bad about feeling good?"

I have to admit there is some truth in their claims. Drugs and drinking *do* make you feel good; they make you feel *real* good. The "high" you get from a snort of cocaine is pure ecstasy—*when you first start it.*

That's the catch. (And it's a great big catch!) That's the seduction, the curse of drugs. They make you feel good at first. Then, when they get you suckered in, when you've been led down the garden path a while—WHAM! The whole thing caves in on you. The good feeling deserts you, and you find yourself doing more and more of whatever you're doing to maintain the "high" you felt at the beginning, when it was all new and "fun." And if you continue to do drugs, after a while, no amount of money and no amount of junk snorted up your nose, popped into your mouth, or shot into your veins can make you feel good. You'll be just miserable and messed up all the time. Ask somebody who's been there— me.

I remember when my sister Pat used to chew us out for smoking pot. I'd say, "Oh, Pat, it's not so *bad!*" I wasn't listening to her. I had to find out the hard way just how bad it is.

The fact is, people who do drugs are weak. They can't face reality, so they escape into a chemically induced world of fantasy. *I was weak.* Oh, I was a big, strapping guy, a power-hitter with the Kansas City Royals, and I could punch people out when I was drunk or flying on drugs. But *inside,* where it really counts, I was a weak person who couldn't take being lonely or disappointed or less than perfect.

Instead of being tough on me, many people indirectly and unintentionally encouraged my headlong rush toward destruction by indulging my terrible behavior.

Aside from the fact that many professional athletes behave like kids let loose in a candy store, the attitude of the public doesn't help. Adoring fans, the press, and even authorities tend to wink at the moral and legal lapses of sports stars. This only encourages destructive behavior.

You'll recall the incident in the winter of 1976 when I was arrested with some friends for being drunk and disorderly. As soon as I let the police know who I was, they let us go. Maybe it would have helped straighten me out if I had cooled my heels in jail for awhile. But in those days, I acted like a privileged character and was treated like one.

Professional athletes must be made to be responsible for their behavior, like the rest of the adult world. As you have seen in my case, it does a spoiled-rotten jock no good in the long run to be let off the hook time after time. It also does teen-age drug and alcohol abusers no good to have their parents constantly making excuses for them and bailing them out of trouble. Such indulgence on the part of family members and the public, including law-enforcement officers, only postpones and possibly worsens the shock of the inevitable rude awakening.

Drugs are a lie and a cheat, because they tell you there is a quick, chemical shortcut to happiness and fulfillment. It just isn't true. I tried them and I know. There are no instant solutions, no easy answers to life's dilemmas—at least none that being zonked out on drugs can help you with.

A friend once overheard the owner of a posh restaurant telling a young man that he had to "open the cells of the brain" to experience the "liberating" thrills of cocaine. (As I've indicated in this book, every cocaine freak thinks he's on top of the world; he *feels* he's dazzling and brilliant; he's got a handle on everything, knows all the answers. The truth is that he's just a fool on drugs.)

Two years after my friend overheard that conversation, the restaurateur had sold his successful business—he imagined people were "after" him. And he was carrying around thousands of dollars on his person—he no longer trusted banks. He was suffering from a mental aberration common to heavy cocaine users—rampant paranoia. (So much for "opening the cells of the brain.")

One of the verses of Scripture goes like this: "There is a way which seemeth right unto a man, but the end thereof are the ways of death" (Proverbs 14:12). That might have been written about people who do drugs.

Have you ever noticed that people who smoke, drink or do drugs, are always trying to get other people to join them? Why is that? I suspect that deep down they know they're weak—that what they're doing is wrong. They want plenty of company to help them feel less helpless and alone in their vice.

For whatever reason, it seems folks have a positive itch to get others to try what they're into. I didn't mention it earlier, but I introduced my own brothers to pot! It's something I'll regret all my life (although I know God has forgiven me for that great sin, along with all my other sins). Fortunately, they no longer use the stuff.

Aside from the damage drugs do to the body and brain, there are other sound reasons why they're evil. For one thing, drugs are expensive. People impoverish themselves and their families through buying them. I was very well-paid and so managed to spend thousands of dollars to support my cocaine habit without going broke. But many people who are not so well-off end up having to sell everything they own, maybe even themselves, to support their addictions. Many of them then resort to stealing. And even wealthy addicts often impoverish themselves in the effort to stay high. That might well have happened to me if I hadn't gotten into and out of cocaine relatively quickly.

Then, too, drugs are illegal. You can be sent to jail for possession. Although the law has relaxed somewhat in certain parts of the country regarding the possession of small amounts of pot for personal use, the possession of a drug like cocaine is a felony offense. If you're caught with it, even if you don't go to jail (which you may well do), you could wind up with a permanent police record that could haunt you all your life.

And would you want to help support a business that Satan masterminds and the Mob runs? Last year a guy got his eyes shot out on a Brooklyn sidewalk over a drug deal. If you take drugs, you become a part of an evil, satanic system of law-breaking, greed, violence, and murder. Maybe that connection seems very indirect to you, but the bottom line is that you support the whole dirty, evil business when you buy drugs.

Drug abuse wrecks thousands of young lives every year. It nearly wrecked mine—*did* wreck it for a long time. I'm only sorry that, having accepted Jesus Christ as my personal Savior at seventeen, I turned my back on Him and began to drink and do drugs. Maybe that wouldn't have happened if I had had someone to help me develop as a Christian by getting into a regular program of prayer, Bible study and church attendance. For whatever reason, I didn't take Christ and my commitment to Him seriously enough, and I turned and walked away from Him. When I think of the misery—the hell on earth—I lived through because of that betrayal, I could cry. It was such a tragic waste of precious time, money, effort, and potential. You know, I sometimes wonder if I could have been a better baseball player if I had kept my nose clean and had truly honored my commitment to Jesus Christ. How sad it must have made Him when I turned my back on Him, because He knew what I was letting myself in for. But He waited long and patiently for my return.

I hope and pray that other young men and women won't make the same mistakes I did, particularly those of you who are reading this. You have one advantage in your fight against the seduction of drugs that I didn't have: you have just read the story of a baseball player who had it all and then nearly threw it away because of drugs; a baseball player who had to pay the bitter price of his mistake—almost with his life.

You don't have to shoot yourself in the head to know that a bullet in the brain will kill you. Having read this book, you now know that you don't have to *try* drugs to know their effects—to know they'll kill you just as sure as that bullet in the brain, only slower. In a sense, *I* did all that for you, and I'm telling you they're evil, and they'll destroy you and those around you.

My standard of living now comes from Jesus Christ. He is the One to whom I turn for the answers to the tough problems life throws at us all the time. And I know that Jesus Christ is opposed to drugs, or anything else that will mess up my mind and body. The Bible tells me that Christ loves me and died for me (see Ephesians 5:2). He didn't die for me on the cross so that I could louse myself up on drugs the way I did, nearly flush myself down the toilet. I'm too valuable for that. He thinks *you* are too valuable for that.